THE ESSENTIAL RETIREMENT TOOLKIT

3-in-1 Complete Guides to Social Security, Estate, and Retirement Planning

RETIREWISE

© Copyright 2024 - All rights reserved.

The content contained within this book may not be reproduced, duplicated or transmitted without direct written permission from the author or the publisher.

Under no circumstances will any blame or legal responsibility be held against the publisher, or author, for any damages, reparation, or monetary loss due to the information contained within this book, either directly or indirectly.

Legal Notice:

This book is copyright protected. It is only for personal use. You cannot amend, distribute, sell, use, quote or paraphrase any part, or the content within this book, without the consent of the author or publisher.

Disclaimer Notice:

Please note the information contained within this document is for educational and entertainment purposes only. All effort has been executed to present accurate, up to date, reliable, complete information. No warranties of any kind are declared or implied. Readers acknowledge that the author is not engaged in the rendering of legal, financial, medical or professional advice. The content within this book has been derived from various sources. Please consult a licensed professional before attempting any techniques outlined in this book.

By reading this document, the reader agrees that under no circumstances is the author responsible for any losses, direct or indirect, that are incurred as a result of the use of the information contained within this document, including, but not limited to, errors, omissions, or inaccuracies.

Other Considerations	45
Check Your Understanding	45
Summary	46

3. REAPING REWARDS - HOW TO OPTIMIZE YOUR SOCIAL SECURITY BENEFITS — 49

Timing Is Everything: What to Consider When Claiming Retirement Benefits	50
How to Decide What's Right For You	52
Reasons People Don't Wait to File	53
Doing A Benefit-Cost Ratio to Help You Decide	55
Considering When to Retire	56
Considerations if You Are Married	59
How Your Spouse Claiming Benefits May Impact Your Decision	61
Benefits for Divorced Spouses	62
Survivor Benefits and Strategies for Widows	63
The Earnings Test for SSA Benefits	65
Quiz Yourself!	66
Summary	67

4. BEYOND THE BASICS - SPECIAL CASES IN SOCIAL SECURITY — 69

Benefits for Disabled Adult Children	70
Benefits for Disabled Minors	71
The Pickle Amendment	72
Deceased Parent Benefits	72
Unique Circumstances for Disabled Workers	73
How Disability Benefits Are Calculated	75
Additional Special Circumstances to Consider	76
Quiz Yourself	78
Summary	80

5. THE ABCDS OF MEDICARE - NAVIGATING YOUR WAY TO BETTER HEALTH — 83

Medicare Basics	83
Today's Medicare Has Four Parts	84
Medicare vs. Medicare Advantage	87
How Medicare Works With Other Insurance	89
Your Medicare Checklist	90
Summary	91

Table of Contents

Social Security Simplified
A Comprehensive Guide to Maximize Your Benefits, Understand Your Options, and Secure Your Retirement for Financial Independence
RETIREWISE

Introduction	15
1. SOCIAL SECURITY DECIPHERED - YOUR STARTING POINT FOR RETIREMENT PLANNING	**21**
The Basics: How, When, and Why to Use Social Security	21
What Exactly is Social Security?	25
Purposes of Social Security	25
What Programs Exist Under Social Security?	26
The Structure of the Social Security Administration	28
How to Apply for Social Security Benefits	29
It's Important to Keep Up With Your Benefits	29
Are Government Employees Covered?	30
How Social Security Has Evolved Over the Years	30
The Role of Social Security in Retirement Planning	32
Meet The First Social Security Recipient	33
Quiz Yourself!	35
Summary	35
2. CLAIM WHAT'S YOURS - UNDERSTANDING ELIGIBILITY FOR SOCIAL SECURITY BENEFITS	**37**
Earning Credits for Retirement Pay	38
Types of Benefits	39
Taxes and Social Security	40
How Much Do Widows Get?	41
Social Security Benefits Are Recalculated Yearly	41
How Retirement Benefits Are Calculated	41
Working While on Disability	42

6. CHOOSE WISELY - YOUR GUIDE TO THE RIGHT MEDICARE PLAN	93
Reviewing The Different Options	94
Part A: What Exactly Is Covered if I Have to Be Hospitalized?	94
Part B: Outpatient Treatment Coverage	95
What Does Medicare Advantage Cover?	96
Are All Prescriptions Covered?	96
Medigap Coverage	97
Should I Enroll in Medicare Advantage?	98
How to Choose the Plan That Is Right for You	100
Summary	101
7. SECURING YOUR HEALTH - CONTROLLING COSTS IN RETIREMENT	105
Rising Healthcare Costs Among Seniors	106
Variables Influencing Healthcare Spending	108
Strategies to Cope With Unexpected Medical Expenses	109
Should You Consider Long-Term Care Insurance?	110
Using Medigap or Medicare Advantage to Lower HealthCare Costs	111
Create Your Healthcare Cost Worksheet	112
Summary	114
8. THE GOLDEN YEARS - UNDERSTANDING YOUR GOVERNMENT PENSIONS	117
What are Government Pensions?	117
Managing Your Pension Among Other Income Sources	120
Meet George	122
Pension Checklist	123
Summary	124
9. SECURING YOUR RETIREMENT - BUILDING A FINANCIAL FORTRESS	127
What Is Retirement Planning?	128
Steps to Consider	129
Estate Planning Is Also Important	131
Key Factors in Retirement Planning	132
Top Ways to Prepare	133
Balancing Various Sources of Retirement Income	135

Retirement Bucket Strategy	138
Staying Informed About Policy Changes	139
Make Your Budget	142
Summary	143

10. FROM PLANNING TO ACTION - PUTTING YOUR RETIREMENT PLAN INTO MOTION — 145

Seeking Professional Advice	148
Tips for Keeping Track of Your Pension	149
What if My Plan Is Terminated?	150
Action Plan Worksheet	150
Summary	151
Conclusion	153
References	155

Estate Planning SIMPLIFIED
Safeguard Your Legacy with Wills, Trusts, and Inheritance for Effective Asset Management
RETIREWISE

Introduction	163

1. ESTATE PLANNING: THE WHAT, WHY, AND HOW — 165

Defining Estate Planning	166
The Importance of Estate Planning	168
The Process of Estate Planning	170

2. DECODING THE LEGAL LEXICON OF ESTATE PLANNING — 175

Understanding Legal Language	178
The Role of Legal Terms in Your Estate Plan	181

3. THE KEYSTONE OF ESTATE PLANNING: WILLS EXPLAINED — 185

What Exactly is a Will?	186
The Role of a Will in Estate Planning	188
How to Create a Will	190
What Happens If You Die Without a Will?	193

4. FORTIFYING YOUR LEGACY WITH TRUSTS	197
The Concept of Trusts	198
Different Types of Trusts	202
Setting Up a Trust	204
Trusts and Tax Implications	207
5. ESTATE STRATEGIES FOR EVERY STAGE OF ADULT LIFE	211
Planning for Single Adults	211
Estate Planning for Married Couples	214
Addressing Needs of Blended Families	217
Estate Planning for Unmarried Partners	219
6. SAFEGUARDING YOUR DIGITAL LEGACY	223
Defining Digital Assets	224
The Importance of Including Digital Assets in Your Estate Plan	226
How to Inventory Your Digital Assets	228
Steps to Include Digital Assets in Your Estate Plan	230
7. NAVIGATING THE WATERS OF ESTATE TAXES	235
Understanding Estate Taxes	235
How to Minimize Estate Taxes	238
Estate Planning and Income Taxes	242
State-Specific Estate Tax Laws	245
8. NAVIGATING THE WATERS OF HEALTHCARE DIRECTIVES	249
The Importance of Having a Healthcare Directive	252
Understanding Power of Attorney	254
How to Set Up a Healthcare Directive and Power of Attorney	257
9. GUARDIANS OF LEGACY: EXECUTORS AND TRUSTEES EXPLAINED	261
The Role of an Executor or Trustee	262
Factors to Consider When Choosing Your Executor or Trustee	264
The Pros and Cons of Choosing a Professional Executor or Trustee	267
How to Appoint an Executor or Trustee	270

10. CLEAR HORIZONS: THE ESSENTIALS OF COMMUNICATING YOUR ESTATE PLAN	275
The Importance of Communicating Your Estate Plan	276
Strategies for Effective Communication	278
How to Handle Difficult Conversations	280
Planning a Family Meeting	283
11. KEEPING YOUR ESTATE PLAN CURRENT AND RELEVANT	287
When and Why to Update Your Estate Plan	288
Common Life Events That Require an Update	291
Reviewing and Updating Your Will and Trusts	294
Updating Your Healthcare Directive and Power of Attorney	296
12. ADAPTING TO THE DIGITAL FRONTIER IN ESTATE PLANNING	301
Online Tools for Estate Planning	305
The Role of Digital Advisors and Online Legal Services	308
Staying Updated with Law Changes in the Digital Age	311
Conclusion	315
References	317

Retirement Planning Simplified
The Complete Toolkit for 401K, IRA, and Smart Tax Strategies to Maximize Your Wealth
RETIREWISE

Introduction	325
1. CHAPTER 1	327
1.1 The Importance of a Retirement Vision	328
1.2 Crafting Your Retirement Vision	330
1.3 Aligning Your Financial Goals with Your Vision	332

2. DEMYSTIFYING RETIREMENT ACCOUNTS: 401K
   AND IRA DECODED 337
   2.1 Demystifying 401K and IRA: What You Need
   to Know 337
   2.2 Roth vs. Traditional: Making Sense of Your
   Choices 340
   2.3 Understanding Asset Allocation and
   Diversification 343

3. LAYING THE FINANCIAL FOUNDATION FOR
   RETIREMENT 347
   3.1 Tools and Resources to Assist Your Audit 350
   3.2 Calculating Your Net Worth for Retirement
   Planning 351
   3.3 Setting Up Your Emergency Fund: A Pre-
   Retirement Must 354

4. MAXIMIZING YOUR RETIREMENT POTENTIAL 359
   4.1 The Power of Compounding in Your Retirement
   Accounts 359
   4.2 Catch-Up Contributions: It's Never Too Late to
   Start 362
   4.3 Employer Match: Maximizing Free Money 365

5. SMART INVESTMENT CHOICES FOR RETIREMENT 367
   5.1 Building a Diversified Portfolio: A Beginner's
   Guide 367
   5.2 Understanding Risk Tolerance and Time Horizon 370
   5.3 Index Funds and ETFs: Investing Made Simple 373

6. TAX-SAVVY STRATEGIES FOR RETIREMENT
   SAVINGS 377
   6.1 Roth Conversions: Timing and Strategy 380
   6.2 Harvesting Tax Losses to Optimize Retirement
   Income 383

7. NAVIGATING HEALTHCARE COSTS IN
   RETIREMENT 387
   7.1 Navigating Medicare: What You Need to Know 391
   7.2 Long-Term Care Insurance: Is It Right for You? 394

8. MAXIMIZING YOUR SOCIAL SECURITY	399
8.1 Understanding Your Social Security Benefits	399
8.2 The Best Time to Start Taking Social Security	403
8.3 Strategies for Married Couples to Maximize Benefits	406
9. ESTATE PLANNING MADE CLEAR	409
9.1 Estate Planning Tools Everyone Should Consider	412
9.2 Beneficiary Designations: Avoiding Common Mistakes	415
10. CRAFTING A FULFILLING RETIREMENT	419
10.1 Finding Purpose After Retirement	419
10.2 Staying Active and Connected in Retirement	422
10.3 Budgeting for Hobbies and Travel in Retirement	424
11. NAVIGATING NEW WATERS: IDENTITY AND FINANCE IN RETIREMENT	429
11.1 Coping with the Identity Shift in Retirement	429
11.2 Protecting Your Retirement Savings from Inflation	432
11.3 Adjusting Your Investment Strategy in Volatile Markets	434
12. EMBRACING TECHNOLOGY FOR A RICHER RETIREMENT	439
12.1 Automating Your Savings and Investments	442
12.2 Staying Informed: Financial News and Resources for Retirees	446
13. THE ANNUAL RETIREMENT PLAN HEALTH CHECK	451
13.1 How to Conduct an Annual Retirement Plan Review	451
13.2 When Life Changes: Adapting Your Retirement Plan	455
13.3 Staying Flexible: The Key to a Successful Retirement	458
14. THE EARLY EXIT: ASSESSING YOUR READINESS FOR EARLY RETIREMENT	461
14.1 Understanding the FIRE Movement	465
14.2 Healthcare and Insurance Before Medicare	468

15. LEGACY BEYOND WEALTH: MAKING A
DIFFERENCE IN RETIREMENT   473
15.1 Philanthropy and Charitable Giving in
Retirement   473
15.2 Teaching Financial Literacy to Future
Generations   476
15.3 Documenting Your Life and Values for Posterity   478

Conclusion   483
References   487

Social Security Simplified

A COMPREHENSIVE GUIDE TO MAXIMIZE YOUR BENEFITS, UNDERSTAND YOUR OPTIONS, AND SECURE YOUR RETIREMENT FOR FINANCIAL INDEPENDENCE

RETIREWISE

Introduction

Is the idea of applying for Social Security confusing or overwhelming for you? If you're like most people, you might not know much about it and may be afraid that you'll make a mistake that'll ultimately cost you a LOT of money.

It can be easy to leave money on the table if you're unsure what you're doing, especially if you have a less-than-straightforward situation. Many people get confused about the rules when it comes to what ex-spouses are entitled to, when the best time to apply for retirement benefits is, or what program you should be applying to.

Just imagine what you could do with that money! You could pay off your mortgage (if you haven't already), buy a new car, or just be generous with your gifts to your children or grandchildren.

Most people miss out because they can't navigate the complex Social Security system and assume they are getting what they're supposed to get. But that's not you! You picked up this book because trying to get your Social Security benefits was like walking through a hedge maze blindfolded, and you wanted to ensure you understood the system.

That's what we're going to explore together in the pages of this book. By the time you finish reading this guide, you'll have a far better handle on what Social Security is, all of its benefits, and how to claim every last penny you are *rightly* entitled to.

Shortcuts to Success

It would take years to learn each and every detail of Social Security. Fortunately, with this guide in your pocket, you won't need to.

Instead, in the coming chapters, you'll learn exactly what you need to know:

- **How to maximize your benefits:** You'll learn about all the factors that can impact your benefit amount and how to get the most possible money from Social Security.
- **How to make an informed choice about Medicare:** Medicare plans can be confusing. You'll learn how to choose a plan that fits your healthcare needs better, and can save you the most money on needed services each year.
- **How to budget for extra health care costs:** Some healthcare costs may not be covered by Medicare, but there are still ways to save money. You'll learn how to plan ahead and save for these costs.
- **Insights into government pensions:** Social Security may not be the only government pension you're entitled to. You'll learn about all available pension plans and how to take advantage of them.
- **Comprehensive retirement planning:** You won't be stuck working, when you're more than ready to retire, if you

learn how to plan for your golden years. Social Security is an important, but not the only, aspect of this plan.
- **How to avoid common traps:** You'll learn about the more common mistakes people make that lose them money, and how to sidestep these traps.
- **Stress reduction:** You'll learn how to plan your finances so that you're not stressed out as you approach retirement, or after you've already stopped working.
- **Save time and energy:** Theoretically, you could read a ton of books about Social Security or retirement planning, but that'll sap your energy and take a long time to complete. Instead, you can learn everything you need to know in one fell swoop with just this book.

The Most Important Step You Can Take

If you want a successful retirement, the most important thing to do for yourself is plan for it. Retirement is both an exciting and a scary time for many people. If you've planned properly, you'll have a solid foundation: a nest egg you can draw upon to support yourself and your family and live the life of your dreams. However, poor planning makes this impossible; you could run out of money or be unable to afford to retire at all!

Retirement planning doesn't just involve how much money you'll need to achieve your goals. While you are still working, you'll need to put some money away for retirement. It's helpful to understand the different types of retirement plans. In addition, you'll need to know the basics so that you don't risk money unnecessarily or make any bad investments that waste your hard-earned cash before you're ready to retire.

As you can see, retirement planning is complicated. But it's worth it for several reasons (Foneville, n.d.):

- **You don't know what you don't know:** Sure, you could learn through trial and error, but mistakes you make with retirement planning could get extremely costly. It's better to learn about retirement plans and set something up for the future NOW than waking up later to realize you had an expensive blind spot.
- **Reducing stress is good for your health:** Many people live 25 or more years past retirement, but extra stress can shorten your post-retirement lifespan considerably. Stress can cause heart disease and has been implicated in the development of cancer. By planning ahead, you'll have less financial stress, and in turn, enjoy better health during your golden years.
- **Proper planning saves you on taxes:** The less you pay in taxes, the more money you have to enjoy! But to fully take advantage of tax savings, you need to know what the rules are and how to plan your finances to take advantage of them.
- **Make better career and financial decisions:** It's hard to consider your long-term interests if you don't have a plan. Rather than planning day by day or paycheck-by-paycheck, use a retirement plan to help you identify and prepare for the next step in your career and your eventual retirement.
- **Provide for your children:** Nobody wants to think that they will be a burden to their children during their old age or that their kids will be stuck under a mountain of debt after they die. Retirement planning ensures that won't happen.
- **Be the grandparent you've always wanted to be:** Spoiling grandchildren and taking them on special outings is half the fun of being a grandparent! You'll need good money to do these things, so plan for your retirement so that you can be that "ultra-cool" grandma or grandpa!

- **Continue (or begin) giving to charity:** Many people want to leave behind a legacy that includes charitable giving. If you have a cause you're passionate about, you'll want to plan your retirement accordingly so that you can give both time and money to it.

Why and How RetireWise Can Help

This book is one way we can help people like you to live the life of their dreams after retirement. We've gathered all the information you need to get started on your retirement planning in one place, offering you facts and ideas that you won't find anywhere else.

The reason that people fail to plan adequately for retirement is that they don't know how to go about it. Websites and Google searches can get you basic information about Social Security or retirement plans, but they only go so far. In these pages, we share secrets that most people don't know—information that will allow you to maximize your savings and live far more comfortably than you might have thought possible. And that's what we want for every reader: a life well lived... both before and after retirement.

Let's Get Started!

Retirement planning can make the *real* difference between living a full, happy life and being miserable. For example, before reading this book, some people had to consider taking a part-time job after retirement or delaying retirement, and are now being able to live fully and freely, giving donations to their favorite charities and spending more quality time with their children and grandchildren.

That could be you, too.

Social Security and other aspects of retirement planning can be confusing, but reading this book will change that for you. Retire-Wise has helped hundreds of people like you to set and achieve financial goals so that you can live a post-retirement life that exceeds your wildest dreams.

Retirement can, and should be, an exciting adventure. Turn the page and let's get started!

1

Social Security Deciphered - Your Starting Point for Retirement Planning

Are you using Social Security for at least some of your bills? If so, you're not alone. Social Security makes up 49% of income for people over the age of 65, and for about a quarter of people your age, it makes up a whopping 90% of your income (SSA, 2017). Although this program is an extremely important part of financial planning for most older Americans, most people have limited understanding of how it works.

Let's change that in this chapter. We'll start by discussing the principles this program is based on, including its purposes and how it's paid for. Once you understand this, we can discuss how Social Security benefits can help you create the retirement of your dreams.

The Basics: How, When, and Why to Use Social Security

As you may know, the original Social Security program was instituted in 1935—at the height of the Great Depression. It's considered one of President Franklin D. Roosevelt's (FDR) flagship accomplishments; we'll discuss the history later on, but first let's look at the program's purposes, how it is funded, and what it doesn't do.

FDR envisioned a society where the government helped take care of its senior citizens. After the widespread economic troubles of the Great Depression, he became aware that family support or help from charity wasn't a given; he wanted to ensure that everyone could afford to retire once they reached the appropriate age to do so (today, the retirement age is 67, although you can begin taking Social Security benefits as early as 62).

Social Security also protects two other classes of people:

- Those who cannot work because of a disabling condition.
- Those who lose significant income because of the death of a spouse.

Although today, many politicians call Social Security a type of welfare program, that's not accurate—working people fund the program via payroll taxes, so the benefits you get revolve partially around how much you paid into it. These taxes are mandatory; employers deduct them before you get your paycheck, and if you have your own business. you pay double (your taxes and those of your employees').

The program is based on several principles:

Principle 1: Protection is Universal

In order to reduce poverty, Social Security tries to distribute resources equitably (Ball, 1998). Relatedly, Social Security is a universal program. If you are a US citizen or permanent resident, you have the right to claim Social Security benefits.

In contrast, programs like SNAP benefits are "means-tested," which means you have to be low-income to qualify for them. Social Security does not have this rule. The only requirement is that you are at the right age to begin claiming benefits. And like all government programs, discrimination against members of protected classes, in terms of race and age, is strictly prohibited.

Principle 2: Everyone Pays Into the System

Your benefits are based on your earnings over a 35-year period (We discuss this in detail later in the book). Thus, Social Security is not the type of program where everyone's tax dollars go to a few people; your taxes fund your Social Security benefits. Think of Social Security as a type of government pension. You get what you pay into it.

Principle 3: Benefits are Adjusted to Create Equity

In general, as mentioned above, higher wages lead to higher benefits. However, there is a built-in equity factor. If wages were the only consideration, low-income workers might not get enough benefits to live off of. Thus, their benefits are adjusted to ensure they receive enough after retirement to support themselves.

Principle 4: Social Security Is Not Paid for by Deficit Spending

Politicians who are looking to cut social programs to save money sometimes suggest that Social Security costs too much. However, Social Security is not financed by income taxes; each worker pays into it. These employee contributions means that the program doesn't contribute to federal deficits, and cutting it won't help reduce the national debt. In addition, since workers pay for the program, it's unfair not to give it to them. Workers generally are against excessive cuts to Social Security for this reason, but may not want large increases in benefits either—this would mean contributing a larger percentage of their paychecks to Social Security taxes.

Principle 5: Social Security Benefits Follow You if You Change Jobs

Social Security benefits don't disappear if you change jobs—this would otherwise defeat the purpose of the program. Instead, the Social Security Administration keeps track of all of your earnings and payments into the system so that you receive benefits based on your top 35 years of earnings, regardless of how often you've changed jobs.

Principle 6: Social Security Takes Current Economic Conditions Into Account

35 years is a long time, and in many cases, your wages—when you began—aren't worth much now because of inflation. Social Security takes this into account; wages are adjusted for inflation before benefits are calculated to ensure you're getting enough money to support yourself in the current economy. In addition, the SSA occasionally raises benefit amounts to reflect higher costs of living. That way, you won't fall short of what you need if groceries, gas, and other necessities become more expensive because of inflation.

Principle 7: You Can't Opt Out of Paying for Social Security

One of the reasons the SSA uses payroll taxes to fund its activities is to ensure that everyone pays their fair share. Neither bosses nor employees have a choice; they have to pay payroll taxes. This ensures that Social Security will never run out of money and that people who object on principle can't refuse to contribute.

What Exactly is Social Security?

If you're still a bit confused about exactly what Social Security is, don't panic! The principles we outlined above will make more sense once we've discussed more fully what the program is and isn't.

Most people know Social Security as a program for senior citizens. But, in actuality, Social Security comprises several different programs:

- Retirement benefits for those aged 62 or older
- Survivors' benefits for those who have lost their spouse
- Disability benefits for those who are unable to work because of permanent disability.

If you have a disabled child, you may also be eligible for benefits on their behalf until they turn 18.

All three programs are run by the Social Security Administration; the full name of the Social Security program is "Old Age, Survivors, and Disability Insurance Program," or OASDI. Approximately, 67 million people will receive benefits from one or more of these programs in 2023 (Connett, 2023).

Purposes of Social Security

Social Security was created with several purposes in mind:

- **To provide for families:** During the Great Depression, it became clear that people might need government assistance to provide for themselves, often because of events that were beyond their control. Thus, Social Security was created to provide a safety net for families that might experience hardship because of death or disability. In addition, Social Security created a retirement pension program to ensure that senior citizens could live comfortably in their golden years, regardless of economic conditions.

- **To help offset the cost of health care for vulnerable populations:** Both older people and those who are disabled may have medical conditions that require frequent doctor visits or expensive treatments. Thus, the Social Security Administration offers Medicare to ensure that those who are eligible have their healthcare needs duly covered.
- **To keep families together:** If it weren't for Social Security, some people might not be able to provide adequately for their children or might need to go out of state for work, leaving their children and families behind. In addition, families with a disabled member may need some extra-help caring for that member at home rather than placing them in a facility. Thus, Social Security benefits can help keep families together.
- **To give children equal opportunity to grow up in healthy, secure situations:** Survivor and disability benefits help ensure that children, who live in a home where a parent has passed away or someone is disabled, exercise the same opportunity to live healthy lives like children from more affluent homes.

What Programs Exist Under Social Security?

The Social Security Administration (SSA) oversees many programs. In addition to the three main programs (Retirement, Disability, and Survivor benefits), the SSA offers a wide range of government-funded programs to help people:

- Help with health care needs, such as Medicare and Prescription Drug Coverage programs for eligible people
- Veterans' Benefits
- Supplemental Security Income for those with disabilities or who have extremely low income
- Unemployment Insurance
- Temporary aid for those in need, including:

  - Temporary assistance for families
  - Medical assistance
  - Maternal and child health services
  - Child support services
  - Parent and child welfare services
  - Food stamps
  - Energy assistance

In most cases, self-employed individuals are also covered by Social Security—in fact, 9 out of 10 workers, whether they work at a job or own their own business, are covered. Self-employed people pay their own Social Security taxes based on their yearly earnings as well as the taxes for any employees they hire and pay during the year.

Throughout this book, we will concentrate mainly on the "big three" programs (Retirement, Survivors, and Disability) as well as Medicare and other healthcare benefits. But, as you can see, Social Security offers many benefits to those in need! If you or your family are ever in dire straits, keep in mind that there is help available.

The Structure of the Social Security Administration

The Social Security Administration has both a central office and a number of local offices. The central office is located in Baltimore, Maryland.

While not every town has a local office, many towns and cities do. If you don't have a local office in your immediate vicinity, you may have one a few towns over. Hopefully, your local office is only a few minutes away by car or bus! It's important to find out where your local office is because this is where you will do most of your business. Local Social Security offices offer most of these services:

- Applications for new Social Security numbers or replacement Social Security cards
- Applications for any benefits you need, such as retirement or survivor benefits, healthcare coverage, or disability benefits
- Enrolling in Medicare or other healthcare coverage programs
- Assistance with applying for food stamps or other welfare programs
- Information about how much you've paid into the program and what your benefits should be
- Information about your rights and those of your family to Social Security benefits

These services are all free of charge; you will never have to pay to receive information, assistance, or benefits at a local Social Security office.

The Social Security Administration also has 10 regional offices that oversee all the local areas in a given region. Finally, there are tele-service offices in major cities throughout the United States. These offices field telephone calls and refer people to the correct local or regional office to take care of their needs.

How to Apply for Social Security Benefits

You can fill out your application online, though you may have to mail some supporting documents. You can also apply over the phone or in person at your local SSA office.

If you aren't sure where your local office is, there are two ways to find out: (1) You can use the online [SSA Office Locator] (https://secure.ssa.gov/apps6z/FOLO/fo001.jsp) or (2) call the SSA at 1-800-772-1213 between the hours of 7 a.m. and 7 p.m. EST. This number is toll-free, so you won't be charged for your call.

In some cases, the nearest Social Security office may be too far away for you to get to easily. If you're in this situation, the Social Security Administration offers visits to specified locations called "contact stations." You can get this information from the phone number listed above. If you can't find a convenient location, you can also arrange for a representative to visit your home.

Finally, you can apply for benefits via telephone using the 800 number.

It's Important to Keep Up With Your Benefits

Social Security coverage is extremely important. Not only can it be a vital part of your retirement plan, but it can also offer support to you and your family in dire and unforeseen circumstances.

About three months before your birthday each year, you should receive a statement in the mail listing your Social Security benefits. If you do not receive this statement, or you have any questions about benefit amounts, contact your local office. You should also contact your relevant employer if you don't see your job listed on your statement.

Are Government Employees Covered?

Federal civilian employees hired before 1984 may not be covered. If you are this type of employee, but later switched to the "Federal Employee Retirement System," you will still be covered. In addition, even those federal employees who are not entitled to Social Security retirement benefits are still covered by the hospital insurance program.

Similarly, not all state and local government employees are covered. Originally, these employees were not part of Social Security coverage; however, the law has changed—if you are a government employee whose employer has entered a Section 218 agreement, you are covered. Check with your employer to find out whether this is the case.

Even if your employer does not have a Section 218 agreement with the Social Security Administration, you may still be covered. In July 1991, Congress passed a law extending coverage to state and local government employees, who are not otherwise covered, either by a Section 218 agreement or a public pension system.

All workers hired after 1986 have Medicare coverage even if they do not qualify for retirement benefits.

How Social Security Has Evolved Over the Years

Social Security was originally signed into law by Franklin D. Roosevelt (FDR) in 1935, a little over a year after creating a committee on Economic Security to try to find out what factors most influenced economic problems for ordinary people, and how the government could help them. FDR intended for this program to be "a cornerstone in a structure that is being built but is by no means complete" (SSA, 1984).

Initially, the program was meant to do two things:

- Assist current senior citizens by using government funds to pay pensions for the next 30 years.
- Allow younger people to provide for their own retirement pensions by requiring them to pay into the system (Miron & Weil, 1998).

During this initial period, all workers paid into the system via payroll taxes; however, people were not eligible for benefits unless they retired. No benefits were paid to anyone who made over $15 that month, regardless of their age. This requirement changed gradually, and, in 2000, Congress finally eliminated it altogether; today, anyone who meets the age threshold and has earned wages is eligible for Social Security retirement benefits.

In 1939, the Social Security Act was amended to include survivor and disability benefits. Farm workers and self-employed individuals didn't begin to receive benefits until 1950, a full 15 years after the program was first implemented, and it wasn't until 1972 that the Act was again amended to account for inflation and ensure that benefits would keep up with increases in the cost of living.

These changes to Social Security don't negate FDR's original vision for the program, which was based on European models. FDR understood that it was important for the government to provide assistance to seniors and that the program must be self-supporting. He also knew that the program he proposed was only the beginning of creating financial security for senior citizens and that the program would evolve over the years.

The Role of Social Security in Retirement Planning

Social Security can—and should—play a role in your retirement planning. Despite the political back-and-forth about the program's solvency and longevity, it's mostly funded by taxes and won't run out of money any time soon. Thus, you should continue to track your Social Security earnings and consider how much you can expect to get per month.

Social Security carries benefits that other retirement plans don't, and that includes:

- You are guaranteed income; it doesn't matter what the economy is like or how the stock market is doing.
- Once you begin collecting Social Security, you will continue to receive payments for the rest of your life.
- Payments are adjusted to take inflation into account.
- Only 85% of your Social Security benefits are taxed, meaning you get to keep more of your money than you would with other retirement plans.

When creating your retirement plan, consider Social Security payments as a source of income. You can also calculate how much you will get based on which year you begin accepting benefits; although the minimum age is 62, you will receive a higher percentage of your earnings if you wait till 67 or 70 to begin collecting.

Before making any decisions, create a retirement budget. Consider the things you want to do after and during retirement, such as travel or spending on gifts for your grandchildren. How much will these things cost? What are your living expenses going to be? If you have a mortgage, will it be fully paid off before you retire, or do you need to ensure you have the money to pay it?

Take all these factors into account and list all your expenses. Then consider how much income you will need each month to not only meet your needs, but also live the way you want to. You can then check this against your Social Security estimated benefits (if you begin collecting at 62 or later). That will help you make a decision about when to start collecting as well as when to retire.

Your plan should include maximizing your Social Security benefits. Only 23% of people consider this factor (Vanguard, n.d.); be among them, so that you can get as much money as you're entitled to. After all, the more you can get from Social Security, the more income you'll have each month to pursue the things you dream of doing during your retirement.

It's important to be flexible, too. You may have dreamed of retiring at 65, but realize after doing your budget that you need to wait until the age of 70 to hit your financial goals. Similarly, you may have to change your mind about when you are planning to begin collecting Social Security benefits to maximize your earnings.

Meet The First Social Security Recipient

The first person to ever collect Social Security was named Ida May Fuller. She received her first retirement check only three years after the program was implemented in 1935, but she enjoyed her benefits for many years to come; she passed away at the age of 100 in 1975!

Ida May, whom friends affectionately dubbed "Aunt Ida," was born on September 6, 1874, on a small farm outside Ludlow, Vermont. She was a classmate of Calvin Coolidge, the 30th President of the United States! That wasn't the only brush she had with fame prior to becoming the first Social Security recipient; she also began working as a legal secretary in 1905, and her boss was none other than John C. Sargent, who later became Attorney General under Coolidge.

Like most Americans in 1939, Ida May wasn't sure what Social Security was all about or if it would really benefit her at all. She had gone into her local Social Security office to ask what this new program was all about, and the workers encouraged her to apply; nobody knew she'd be the first person to get a check from the new program. Ida May became a minor celebrity, and the Social Security Administration made a short film about her in 1950 in honor of the program's tenth anniversary (Whitelocks, 2015).

When she filled out her application, Ida May didn't expect to get anything back. Instead, she got $22.74 for her first month's payment, which is equivalent to about $500 in 2023 (CPI Calculator, 2023). She received almost $23,000 in payments over the course of her lifetime (Ring, 2015).

Ironically, Ida May was a staunch Republican from one of the only two states that didn't vote for FDR. While she admitted that Social Security helped pay all her expenses, shortly before her death in the 1970s, she stated that she believed it was wrong to increase benefit amounts and that doing so would hurt workers.

Nevertheless, the program clearly helped her enjoy her lengthy retirement; back in 1939, when it began, few people lived to be anywhere close to 100, but thanks to the lifetime payment provision of the program, she continued to enjoy a reasonable standard of living for the last 35 years of her life.

Quiz Yourself!

Answer these "true or false" questions to see how much you've learned about Social Security.

- Social Security is paid for by the federal government.
- Social Security is only for retired people.
- My benefits are based on how much I've paid into the system.
- Social Security is intended to eliminate poverty among those who can't work, such as senior citizens and disabled people.
- Low-income workers receive very few Social Security benefits.
- FDR intended Social Security to be temporary, to help people during the Great Depression.
- Social Security does not adjust benefits to account for inflation.
- It's always best to claim your Social Security benefits as soon as you are eligible.
- The first recipient of Social Security was surprised that she received benefits.
- Social Security and Medicare are the same program.

Summary

Social Security is an important part of retirement planning that is often misunderstood. Although originally conceived of as a pension program for senior citizens, nowadays it offers three programs: retirement benefits, survivor benefits, and disability benefits. Parents of disabled children may also receive benefits on their behalf. There are nine principles that govern Social Security;

most importantly, it is a self-supporting program that is paid for by payroll taxes, and benefits are protected against inflation.

The purpose of this program is to protect against poverty by helping those who have retired or who cannot earn money to live more comfortably. The program was created in 1935, during the height of the Great Depression, as a new program to protect retirees, but has evolved into a larger program that now includes senior citizens who are still working, disabled people, and those who have been widowed.

It's important to understand how Social Security works and how to maximize your benefits so that you can plan appropriately for your retirement. Specifically, you should understand your benefit amounts and how they might change based on when you first begin collecting Social Security. You should also make a budget for retirement and figure out how Social Security payments fit into it.

Now that you know some of the history and purpose behind Social Security, and have a basic idea of how it works, you can begin learning how to maximize your benefits. The first step is to gain a solid understanding of who is eligible for benefits and what the exact criteria are for eligibility. We'll discuss that in the next chapter; turn the page when you're ready!

2

Claim What's Yours - Understanding Eligibility for Social Security Benefits

Did you know that your benefits will be different depending on what program you apply for? Figuring out what you are eligible for, and how much you are entitled to, can be really confusing, but by the end of this chapter, you'll have a solid understanding of eligibility for retirement, disability, and survivor benefits.

As we discussed in the previous chapter, Social Security offers three separate programs:

- Retirement benefits for those over the age of 62
- Disability benefits for those who are unable to work due to a permanent health condition
- Survivor benefits for those who have lost a spouse

In some cases, children of beneficiaries may also be entitled to benefits. For example, often, parents of disabled children are able to collect benefits on their behalf until they turn 18, and in some cases, even after they reach adulthood.

Earning Credits for Retirement Pay

Although it's true that most people qualify for Social Security when they turn 62, age is not the only requirement for this benefit. Workers must be US citizens or legal permanent residents, and they must have earned 40 credits with the Social Security Administration.

Credits are determined using a formula; in general, workers can earn up to four credits per year and earn one credit for each $1,640 of covered income (AARP, 2022). In other words, if you earn, at least, $1,640 per quarter, you will earn a credit for that quarter toward your eligibility for Social Security.

To earn your four credits for the year, you must earn $6,560 per year ($1,640 x 4).

Don't let these numbers throw you off; if you're earning wages from a job, or receiving revenue from a business, you are likely getting your credits each year. Basically, you need to work for, at least, 10 years and make, at least, $6,560 each year to qualify for Social Security.

The exact amount you need to make to earn credits varies from year to year based on economic factors such as inflation. So, don't worry about the specific number; just remember that you need to have worked for, at least, 10 years to be eligible.

The number of credits you earn has no bearing on how much your monthly Social Security check will be. Your benefits are determined via a separate formula; we'll discuss how benefits are calculated later in this chapter. Credits are used solely to determine whether a worker is eligible for Social Security.

You can check your Social Security record online (at https://www.ssa.gov/myaccount/) to find out whether you have earned the appropriate number of credits to be eligible for retirement benefits and what your estimated benefits are likely to be, depending on when you start collecting.

Types of Benefits

As we mentioned at the beginning of the chapter, there are different types of benefits, each with its own set of requirements.

- **Retirement benefits** are paid monthly to senior citizens. Seniors can begin to collect these benefits at any age past 62. The longer you wait to collect, the larger the benefit amount will be. Retirement benefits are not meant to be the retiree's only source of income, but many people depend on them to cover the costs of basic necessities. Benefit amounts are calculated based on your salary while you were working; benefits may also be available to spouses or ex-spouses even if they were homemakers and did not earn income.
- **Disability benefits** are available to those who can no longer work because of a disability or chronic health condition. Like retirement benefits, these are calculated based on your pre-disability salary. The amount of time you need to have worked to qualify for these benefits also varies. In some cases, spouses and divorced spouses are entitled to these benefits.
- **Supplemental security income** is available to disabled people who have never been able to work because of their disability, as well as some people who worked in the past but cannot work now due to some reason. The benefit

amount depends on what other sources of income the person has and where they live.
- **Survivor benefits** are available to the spouse and children of someone who has passed away. The couple has to have been married at one point; divorced spouses may get benefits in some cases, but those who were never married are not eligible. Survivors who were married to a same-sex partner are eligible for the benefit as well. Benefits are calculated based on the worker's age at death, their salary, the survivors' ages, and their relationship to the person who has died.

Unused Social Security benefits are used to help pay others. If you don't claim the Social Security benefits that you are entitled to, those benefits are kept in trust and used to help pay other eligible people. You cannot get a refund of unused benefits, and if the person dies before they can collect, their family may also not be entitled to their unused retirement benefits.

Taxes and Social Security

If a person earns more than $25,000 in a given year ($32,000 for married couples filing jointly), they must pay federal tax on their Social Security benefits.

In addition, 12 states currently levy taxes against Social Security benefits:

- Colorado
- Connecticut
- Kansas
- Minnesota
- Missouri

- Montana
- Nebraska
- New Mexico
- Rhode Island
- Utah
- Vermont
- West Virginia

If you do not live in one of these states, you do not have to pay state taxes on your benefits.

How Much Do Widows Get?

Survivor benefits are usually 100% of the primary benefit amount the deceased would have received if they were still alive. If a former spouse was married to the person who passed away for, at least, 10 years and has not remarried, they are also entitled to this amount.

Social Security Benefits Are Recalculated Yearly

Every year, the SSA recalculates your benefits. Benefit amounts can change based on inflation or other economic factors. In addition, if you are below full retirement age and receiving benefits, the amount can be offset by wages or earnings from self-employment. However, passive income, such as investment income, does not affect your benefit amount.

How Retirement Benefits Are Calculated

Your retirement benefits are calculated on how much you earned while you were working. Many people change jobs, start a new business, or go through periods of low income after being laid off, so your income might not have been steady over the course of your adult life. For this reason, Social Security benefits are calculated based on an average of the 35 highest-earning years of your life. This average is then adjusted to account for inflation so that you won't be penalized if your highest-earning years were a long time ago when wages and prices were both lower than they are today. After this adjustment, the SSA applies a formula to determine how much money you are entitled to receive each month.

You can begin taking Social Security at the age of 62, but if you do, you will receive 30% less each month than you would if you waited until you reached full retirement age (i.e., 66 or 67 in 2023, depending on when you were born). Conversely, if you wait until you are 70, you will receive about 132% more than you would if you took your benefits earlier! This benefit reduction is permanent; your Social Security benefits won't increase when you hit 67 if you take it at 62. However, the SSA will continue to apply cost-of-living increases to your benefit amounts each year even if you take it early. If you continue working while taking Social Security benefits before you reach the age of 67, your benefits will be reduced by $1 for every $2 you earn.

In addition, if you wait until you reach the full retirement age, you will not lose any benefits if you continue to work after you file your first claim.

Working While on Disability

The SSA encourages individuals to work while going through the process of applying for disability. This allows the SSA to see the full extent of your disability and determine how capable you are of maintaining full-time employment (SAMSHA, n.d.)

After you are approved for disability benefits, working might affect those benefits in different ways, depending on the type of disability benefit you are receiving.

Supplemental Security Income, or SSI, is meant for people who are unable to earn significant income because of a disability. The disability can be physical, mental, or both. The SSA excludes certain income from its calculation of benefits:

- The first $20 of income is excluded, whether or not that income is earned from a job.
- The first $65 of income from a job is also excluded.
- Money saved toward an educational or vocational goal, as outlined in the recipient's "Plan to Achieve Self-Support" (PASS), does not count against SSI benefits.
- Students may be allowed an exemption of a certain amount of income if they are under the age of 22 and go to school full-time.
- Impairment-related costs to get to work are subtracted from income. For example, if the person needs to hire a transportation service for people with their disability, or needs special medication to be able to perform their job, these costs would be excluded.

After calculating these amounts, the SSA then divides the remaining income amount in half and pays benefits based on this amount.

For example, suppose a person earns $750 from a part-time job. The SSA would then calculate as follows:

- Subtract $20 of generally excluded income.
- Subtract $65 of job-related income.
- Subtract $150 in savings for an educational goal.

- Subtract $100 in impairment-related costs.
- Total exclusions are $335.
- Subtract this from total income to get countable income of $365.
- Divide $365 in half to get $182.50.
- Subtract $182.50 from the maximum benefit amount to get the amount of benefits the person is entitled to.

Social Security Disability Insurance (SSDI) is calculated a bit differently. Benefits are based on past earnings, and a person who is on SSDI is allowed to work for nine months out of a rolling five-year period without penalty to see if they are capable of holding down a job. This means that if you work a full nine months, after that, you will see a reduction to your benefits; however, you can divide those nine months over five years. For example, suppose you got SSDI benefits beginning in 2023, and that summer, you tried working but quit after a month because it was too stressful. If you try again and work three months in 2024 before quitting, you still have another five months you can work any time between 2024 and 2028. After five years, your trial period starts again, so if you don't return to work until 2029, those four months of your trial no longer count.

If you complete your trial period, you still have a three-year extended eligibility period. This means that if you don't earn over a certain amount during a given month, you will still receive your full check during that month.

As with SSI, SSDI recipients can subtract impairment-related work expenses and money saved toward their educational or vocational goal on their "PASS plan" from their total income. If their countable income falls below the threshold, they can still receive their full check.

People with disability may continue to be eligible for Medicaid or Medicare benefits, depending on their income level. If they become disqualified from medical or cash benefits because of their income level, and then are again unable to work within five years, their reinstatement application will be expedited.

Other Considerations

If you are working while on Social Security and you are laid off, you can continue to get your Social Security checks while taking unemployment. Keep in mind that while you can collect both, your Social Security income might impact the amount of unemployment income you are entitled to.

However, you cannot receive both retirement and disability benefits at the same time. However, when you reach the age of 65, your disability benefits will automatically be converted to retirement benefits. The amount you receive will not change; the only difference is the program under which you will receive your money.

Keep in mind that if you make over $25,000/year, whether or not you are working, you will have to pay federal taxes on your Social Security benefits.

Check Your Understanding

Check your understanding of eligibility for Social Security with this brief "true or false" quiz.

- All three Social Security programs (Retirement, Disability, and Survivor) pay the same number of benefits.
- You need to have worked for, at least, 10 years to be eligible for Social Security.

- The more credits you have, the larger the retirement benefit you will receive.
- You do not have to be a US citizen to receive benefits.
- If you are divorced, your ex-spouse might be eligible for Social Security benefits based on your earnings.
- If you work after taking retirement benefits, you will lose part of your benefits no matter how old you are.
- There are two different disability benefit programs.
- You cannot work at all while on SSI or SSDI, or you will lose your benefits.
- Social Security income is never taxable.
- You are ineligible for unemployment benefits if you receive retirement benefits.

Summary

Understanding different Social Security programs, and whether you are eligible for them is crucial to being able to maximize your benefits. In this chapter, we discussed the various Social Security programs and how benefits are calculated for each one of them.

While many people think Social Security and retirement benefits are synonymous, this is only one of three programs that the SSA offers. In addition to retirement benefits, the SSA is responsible for both disability and survivor benefits. Disability benefits are for people who cannot work full-time due to an injury, illness, or condition, while survivor benefits are for people who have lost a spouse to death. To qualify for retirement benefits, three things must be true: you must be over the age of 62; earned, at least, 40 credits through paying payroll taxes; and be either a US citizen or a legal permanent resident.

Credits are earned automatically as you are working. Workers earn up to four credits a year by paying payroll taxes; as of 2023, they must earn $6,560/year to earn these four credits. Workers must earn 40 credits to qualify for retirement benefits, which means they have to work for, at least, 10 years. Credits are not used to calculate your benefit amount; they are only used for eligibility purposes.

Retirement benefits are calculated based on your average income, which is then corrected to account for inflation. The average is taken using the 35 years when you earned the highest income. If you did not work for 35 consecutive years, any year where you were unemployed is given a value of zero dollars.

Although you can begin getting Social Security at the age of 62, you will receive fewer benefits if you take it then. In addition, your benefits will be reduced by $1 for every $2 you earn if you continue to work while collecting benefits. Your benefit amount will not increase when you reach the age of 65 in this scenario; however, after 65, you will no longer lose any benefits if you continue working. If you delay receiving benefits until you are past retirement age, you will get an 8% increase for each year of delay, which means that if you delay until the age of 70, you will receive 132% of the benefits you are entitled to. Retirement benefits are taxable at the federal level if you make over $25,000/year (or $32,000, if you are part of a married couple that files joint tax returns).

If you are receiving disability benefits, the SSA may do a complex series of calculations to figure out your benefit amount. Benefits vary based on whether you are on SSI, SSDI, or both, and each program has rules about how "money earned from working while on disability" affects a recipient's benefits. In order to encourage people with disabilities to work, the SSA offers trial periods in which you can work without penalty for a short period of time. Currently, you can work for nine months over a five-year period without losing any of your SSDI benefits. In addition, you can continue to receive SSDI for three years after beginning a new job, if your income doesn't meet a certain threshold.

You can receive unemployment and retirement benefits at the same time, but you can't receive retirement and disability benefits simultaneously. If you receive disability benefits, they will be converted to retirement benefits when you turn 65, but the amount you receive will not change.

Now that you understand the various Social Security programs and their eligibility requirements, the next step is to learn how to maximize your benefits. Many people don't know how to do this and end up with less money than they are entitled to. But this doesn't have to be you! In the next chapter, we will begin discussing strategies for how to maximize your benefits.

Turn the page when you are ready to get started!

3

Reaping Rewards - How to Optimize Your Social Security Benefits

Getting the maximum benefit amount isn't as easy as filling out your Social Security claim forms. There are many options you have to consider if you want to get as much money as possible each month.

In addition to making sure you are applying to the best program for your needs, you'll need to think about things like whether you should claim your benefits right now or wait a few years. If you are not at full retirement age, you'll also need to decide when to retire.

These are monumental decisions, not only because retirement changes your life but also because your approach to Social Security affects your financial future. If you claim benefits just because you can, without thinking things through, you may leave money on the table that you would need to pursue the life of your dreams.

Optimizing your Social Security benefits requires strategic thinking. In the last chapter, we went over what the different programs are, and gave you a sneak preview of the decisions you may need to make if you want to get as much money as possible. Now, we'll begin talking about strategy. By the end of this chapter, you'll have a solid understanding of different strategies for optimizing your Social Security benefits and a better idea of what plan will best meet your needs.

Timing Is Everything: What to Consider When Claiming Retirement Benefits

If you want to maximize your retirement benefits, you should consider how long you can afford to wait before you file your first claim.

As of 2023, you can begin getting retirement benefits at the age of 62, but it's not always the best idea. The SSA doesn't consider you fully retired until age 67 (as of 2023), so if you take benefits earlier than that, you won't get as much money each month and your benefits won't increase once you hit 67. In addition, any wages you receive from work will count against your Social Security retirement benefit if you are between the ages of 62 and 67. Once you hit 67, that is no longer an issue, but you'll lose money each month in the meantime.

Economic research suggests that almost everyone who is currently aged 45 to 62 would benefit from waiting until they are, at least, 67 to begin receiving retirement benefits and that 90% of this age group are best off waiting until they are 70 (Altig et al, 2022). However, only 10% of people wait that long, which means that a majority of Americans are leaving money on their table. The median loss for Americans, thanks to them not following this advice, is $182,370 (Konish, 2023). This means that half the people who claim too early lose MORE than this!

There are three reasons why waiting might be the best option for you:

- **You might have the opportunity to increase your total benefits:** Social Security benefits are calculated on the 35 highest-paid years of income. So, if you work an extra few years, you might earn more money during those years and thus your benefits will be calculated based on that income.
- **You avoid reduced payments if you wait until you are at least 67:** As mentioned earlier, you will receive fewer benefits if you begin collecting retirement checks before you reach full retirement age—the SSA reduces your monthly benefits by 30% and that reduction is permanent rather than changing when you turn 67. For example, you might receive $2,000/month if you wait until the age of 67, but only $1,400/month if you begin collecting at the age of 62.
- **Delayed retirement to beyond age 67 adds to your benefits:** You will receive an 8 percent increase in benefits for each year you delay between 67 and 70. So, if you wait until you are 70 to begin collecting retirement benefits, you will get a vastly higher sum each month than if you collected earlier.

Thus, in most cases, it makes sense to delay collecting retirement benefits. Ironically, this is especially true for lower-income people, who may be more dependent on their monthly benefit check to meet their needs, and who also may be more tempted to collect earlier so that they can have an additional source of income before they fully retire.

If Social Security is not the only retirement plan you have, it's easier to delay your claim. For example, if you have a 401k or other retirement savings account, you might be able to withdraw funds from that account to help with your monthly expenses until you cross the age threshold of 67. However, you should be aware that these types of accounts make money by investing your savings in the stock market, so how much money is in store for you depends on how well the economy is doing and whether your money has been invested wisely. Conversely, your retirement benefit will be the same amount of money each month, and there is no risk that you will lose a part of your benefits if the stock market crashes.

While waiting until 67, or even 70, makes sense for the majority of people, there is one situation where you may want to collect earlier: if you have a terminal illness and don't expect to survive until the age of 70. Your retirement benefits are not transferable to anyone else, so you'll lose that money if you don't collect. However, in this case, you may want to look into how survivor benefits (discussed later in this chapter) work in addition to claiming your retirement benefits, so that you can make sure your heirs are taken care of.

How to Decide What's Right For You

If it's best for almost everyone to wait until they are 70 years old to start collecting their Social Security benefits, then why don't most people do it?

Some people may not be aware that there's any difference in benefits, but others may feel they can't afford to delay. If you are struggling financially, claiming your Social Security benefits early might seem like the best solution, especially if you don't have other sources of retirement income.

That's why it's best to have a comprehensive retirement plan in place long before you turn 62. But whether you do or not, you should do some analysis to determine what's the best time for you to begin collecting your retirement benefits.

It's helpful to calculate how much your monthly payment will change based on when you begin collecting your benefits. You can check your estimated benefit amounts online by signing into your SSA account. This will tell you what your lifetime earnings are so far, and what your estimated monthly benefit amount will be if you start collecting at various ages. You can also put your numbers into the SSA's online retirement calculator to get a rough idea of how your benefits will change, depending on when you claim them.

Reasons People Don't Wait to File

Although you can maximize your benefits by delaying your claim past the age of 70, there are several reasons people don't do it:

- **They don't expect to live that long:** If you have a terminal illness, you might only have a few months or years left. In this case, you may not see much, or any, of your money if you wait.
- **They have cash flow issues:** If you are struggling to pay your monthly bills, it can be hard, or even impossible, to wait. A guaranteed $1000 or more per month may seem like the best option for keeping the lights on and enough food on your table.
- **They don't care about maximizing their benefits:** Some people may want to live a full, active life, and it's easier to do that if you grab whatever money is available to you NOW than if you wait. Or, if you're stuck at a job that makes you miserable, and taking your retirement benefit now will allow you to escape it and have some fun during your remaining years, you might decide to take a smaller monthly check in exchange for not having to force yourself to work.

- **The math shows it won't make much of a difference:** If you live for long enough, you'll receive the same total benefits whether you start early or late. If you have an unusually long-life expectancy, you might decide to take your retirement benefits early so that you have some money coming in, with the understanding that, eventually, you will have received the same amount that you would if you wait.
- **They have a special situation:** Some people may be on disability or be entitled to survivor benefits. However, their retirement benefit might be greater than these other benefits. In this case, it makes sense to take retirement earlier.

The bottom line is that everyone's situation is different, so you should consider all the factors before deciding when to take your benefits. Although you will maximize the amount you get per month if you wait until age 70 to start collecting, it may be to your overall advantage to begin collecting earlier.

To determine what is best for you, you can do a "break-even analysis." This involves calculating how old you will be when you will receive roughly the same amount, no matter when you begin collecting (Fontinelle, 2023). For example, suppose you get $1,500/month if you start at age 62, or $2,000/month if you start at age 66. At age 78, you will have received $288,000 regardless of whether you take benefits early ($1,500/month x 12 months/one year x 16 years) or delay until age 66 ($2000/month x 12 months/one year x 12 years). Thus, the earlier you claim benefits, the longer you have to live to reach your break-even age. So, if you expect to live into your 80s, it makes sense to wait until you are 66 or older to begin collecting benefits. However, if you don't expect to live that long, you won't get much benefit from waiting and might want to claim your benefits earlier.

Doing A Benefit-Cost Ratio to Help You Decide

To determine whether it's worth it to claim your retirement benefits early versus claiming other types of benefits, you can do a "benefit-cost ratio," or BCR. This analysis tells you whether the benefits of doing so are worth the cost.

To do a BCR, divide the total cash benefits by the cost. If the result of this calculation is greater than 1.0, it means you will profit from claiming your benefits now. If it is less than 1.0, you will lose money if you do this instead of delaying your claim.

For example, suppose that if you claim your retirement benefits at the age of 62 (Option A), you will receive $700/month, while you will get $1,000/month if you wait until you are 67 (Option B). Consider your life expectancy to calculate your total benefits for each option. For this example, let's say you expect to live to about age 85. You will also want to calculate your total expenses per year so you can see how much money you will actually keep each month.

First, multiply each monthly amount by 12 to get a yearly amount. That's $8400/year under Option A and $12,000/year under Option B. However, you will also need to subtract your expenses per year. Let's say your average expenses are $8,000 per year. So, you are getting to keep $400/year under Option A and $4,000 a year under Option B.

Next, multiply that by the number of years you expect to live. Under Option A, that's 23 years (85-62), while under Option B that's 18 years (85-67). So, your total benefit amounts would be:

- Option A: $9,200
- Option B: $92,000

Now, to get your BCR, you would need to know your total costs and total benefits. Subtract your Option A amount from your Option B amount to get the costs of choosing Option A. This number is $82,800. Let's plug that into the formula:

Total. benefits / Total costs = $9,200 / 82,800 = 0.111

This number is less than 1.0, so it is not profitable to choose this option. Note, that if you forget to consider your yearly expenses and merely look at the benefit amounts, you'd be looking at:

- Option A: $193,200
- Option B: $216,000
- Cost: $22,800

CBR: $193,200 / $22,800 = 8.47, which would appear to be quite profitable despite the loss of income. Thus, it is important to consider profit, and not just income, when making this calculation.

Considering When to Retire

Deciding when to take your retirement benefits may also depend on when you choose to retire. More and more people are considering retiring before the age of 65—you may need your Social Security check at 62, if you do so.

There are several pros and cons to early retirement that you should consider before making the leap:

+ *Pros*

- It may be better for your mental and physical health if you can leave a draining job earlier.
- You'll have more time to spend with loved ones or doing activities that you enjoy.
- You may be able to travel (if you can afford it).
- You might be able to change careers or start a new business.

− *Cons*

For some people, retiring early can lead to mental and physical health problems, especially if they are already at risk.

- It can cause extra financial stress.
- You'll get fewer benefits per month if you claim Social Security early.
- Retirement savings will have to last longer.
- You may need to find health insurance.
- You might become bored, feel purposeless, or miss your old job.

One of the biggest concerns is the financial impact of retiring early. Suppose you earn $36,000/year. In that case, your job brings you a little less than $3,000/month when you factor in taxes.

If you're 62 years old, you can retire and take Social Security benefits at about $900/month—about a third of what you made before retirement. You'll likely have to supplement this with other retirement income or income from a second job (although if you take a new job, your benefits will decrease). And retirement accounts are dependent on the stock market, so if the economy crashes, you could lose money in your 401k or IRA. All of this adds up to financial stress, so it may be best to remain on the job.

On the other hand, suppose you're making over $100,000 and are bringing in $8,000/month. Here, your Social Security benefit would be even more significantly reduced—$1,685/month! But you may have more money in savings or fewer expenses because you earn more, so it may be manageable. If so, retiring early and taking less income might be a suitable trade-off for not having to work.

Of course, this decision is also dependent on other factors such as what your expenses are, who else you are supporting financially, and what kind of retirement package your company offers you. A person who is helping support small grandchildren or whose spouse doesn't work is in a different financial situation than someone who has no dependents. The existence of other pensions and how much money you have in savings will also impact your decision.

If early retirement isn't financially feasible, there are a few other options you might consider. In the post-COVID world, working remotely from home has become fairly common. If your company will allow you to do so, consider working remotely, at least, a few days a week. This will help cut out some stressors associated with work, such as dealing with traffic on your commute or having to spend time with difficult coworkers.

Another option might be to cut back on your hours. Some jobs will allow older workers to become semi-retired by adjusting schedules, so that they only work two or three days a week. This may mean a partial loss of income, but if it's significantly more than what you would get if you take retirement benefits, it may be a reasonable compromise.

Finally, if you have vacation days accrued, use them! If one of the reasons you want to retire early is so that you can travel, taking a vacation might work just as well, especially since you're getting paid for it.

Considerations if You Are Married

Married couples need to consider the impact on their spouse's benefits of various options for claiming Social Security retirement checks, which won't be a factor if you aren't married—of course, if you're widowed, or have children or grandchildren you are financially responsible for, you still have other considerations even if you don't have a partner. If you're married, you might want to consider:

- **The age of your spouse and the difference between your ages:** If your spouse is not yet retirement age and won't reach it until long after you do, any decision you make will impact their eventual spousal benefits. If your spouse is older than you, you'll want to consider your options carefully; you may want to hold off as long as possible and claim their benefit in the event that they pass away first.
- **Whether your spouse is also working:** If only one partner is working, then the other may be entitled to spousal benefits. This will impact your bottom line more than if both partners are working and entitled to their own benefits.
- **Whether there are significant differences between the amount of money each of you are entitled to:** For married couples, either spouse claiming early could impact both of their benefits. If one spouse is entitled to more benefits, that spouse may want to hold off so that they can maximize their benefit. In addition, if one spouse dies, the other is entitled to whichever benefit is bigger—their own or their partner's. So, if you have the bigger benefit you might want to refrain from claiming it right now, so that your spouse can take it in the event you die first.

- **Whether either of you is subject to special rules such as the Windfall Elimination Provision or the Government Pension Offset:** If either of you is, that'll lower your total benefit amount, so you need to know this before making any decisions.
- **Whether you need cash right now:** The biggest concern for most couples is cash flow. If you're having trouble paying your bills, saving, or affording certain things, it doesn't help you to know that you'll get a large benefit five to eight years from now.
- **What your life expectancies are:** If either of you doubts that you will not live to be 80, then you may want to consider taking your retirement benefits earlier so you can live comfortably for the remainder of your life.
- **What your work plans are:** If you plan to keep working, or your spouse does, that will put you in a different financial situation than if either one of you is dead-set on retiring in the next few years.
- **Former relationships:** If either of you is a widow, or is divorced from someone who is still alive, that will also affect your benefits. Widowed spouses may be entitled to survivor benefits, which might be bigger than what you could get if you took your retirement benefit right now. And if you are divorced, your ex-spouse might be entitled to spousal benefits if you were married for 10 years or longer.
- **Do you have any unmarried children under the age of 19?** If you are legally or morally obligated to take care of children, that is going to impact your bottom line, and you need to think carefully about whether it makes financial sense to take retirement benefits right now.

How Your Spouse Claiming Benefits May Impact Your Decision

Both current and divorced spouses can, in some cases, claim your retirement benefits based on your work history rather than their own. This is called a "spousal benefit."

If your spouse doesn't qualify for their own retirement benefits—for example, if they stayed at home with children rather than working outside the home, then they are entitled to spousal benefits. If they take this benefit before the age of 67, they will only be entitled to half of what they will get if they wait. Spouses do not get delayed retirement benefits, so there is no advantage to them waiting beyond the age of 67. However, if you are in a position to be able to work at a high-paying job until you are 70, you will increase your total benefit amount, which means that your spouse will get a bigger benefit, too, if you both wait until then to begin claiming benefits.

You have several strategies to consider, so here's how to begin to make this decision.

The best way to begin is to get both of your estimated benefits from your Social Security Administration accounts. That way, you have an idea of how much money each of you will be entitled to, if you claim benefits at various ages. Knowing these numbers can help you see what will be financially best for you. When comparing your estimates, pay special attention to which one is higher. That person has higher earnings, and the gap between your earnings and your spouse's will help you decide which strategy to use.

Many couples use a "split strategy"—the person who earns more delays claiming Social Security benefits, while the person who earns less claims them as soon as possible. This can help maximize the amount of money coming in because the higher earner will receive greater benefits when they finally make their claim, but the lower earner will have been getting retirement benefits for a while by the time that happens.

For example, suppose Mark is entitled to $700/month if he collects at age 62, $1000/month if he collects at age 67, or $1,320/month if he collects at age 70. Conversely, Mark's partner, Sally, is entitled to $1,050/month if she collects at age 62, $1,500/month if she collects at age 67, and $1,980/month if she collects at age 70. Using a split strategy, Mark takes the $700/month, while Sally waits until she's entitled to the full $1,980. By the time Sally is ready to collect eight years later, Mark has already collected $67,200 in benefits, which has greatly helped them afford the life they wanted to lead.

If one couple earns more than twice the other, both spouses may want to eventually claim benefits on the same record. To do this, the lower-earning partner would claim their own benefits early, as described above, and then file a claim for spousal benefits when their partner begins collecting benefits.

Benefits for Divorced Spouses

The basic rule for divorced spouses is that if you were married for 10 years or longer, and have not remarried, you can claim half of your ex-partner's benefits. This doesn't mean that your ex-partner gets only half of their benefit; they will still get the full amount, while you just get half that amount.

Using the same example as above, if Mark and Sally were married for 10 years before their divorce, and Mark has not remarried, he is entitled to a benefit of half of that $1,980/month that we calculated Sally was entitled to in the previous section. This comes out to $990/month. Sally would still get the full $1,980/month, and if she remarried, Mark's claim would not affect her new spouse's benefits either.

It's important to check both your own and your ex-partner's record if you're considering claiming divorced spousal benefits. That way, you can check how much you would get against what you are entitled to if you make a claim on your own record. If you have your ex's Social Security number, you can check this online. If you don't have that information, the Social Security Administration can look up the record for you; you'll need your ex's full name, date and place of birth, and the name of their parents.

You can still apply for divorced spouse benefits without your ex's Social Security number; you only need that to look up the earnings record online. Spousal benefits don't increase if you wait past full retirement age, so you can apply for them at the age of 67. You can still file a claim even if your ex-spouse hasn't begun collecting yet (if you've been divorced for two years).

Survivor Benefits and Strategies for Widows

If a post-retirement-age spouse passes away, the surviving spouse is entitled to the larger of their own benefit or their late spouse's benefit. So, if you earn more money than your partner, it might be best to delay making your claim. This way, if you pass away first, your spouse will get a larger check. It's heartbreaking to lose a spouse, so it may be difficult to think about your options if you are a new widow or widower. But there are some important financial decisions you will need to make.

Let's look at the example of Kathy, a recent widow.

Kathy's husband, Bill, passed away recently. Kathy is 66 years old and in good health, and she's considering her options. Bill was already collecting retirement benefits at the time of his death, and those benefits were $300/month (more than what Kathy is entitled to). However, Kathy would like to retire if possible, so that she can move closer to her children now that Bill is gone—but she won't reach retirement age for another year, so if she takes her retirement benefits now, they'll be reduced by 30%.

When it comes to retirement benefits, Kathy has the same options as everyone else:

- Take early retirement, which means her benefits will be reduced by 30%
- Wait a year and receive 100% of her benefit
- Wait until she's 70 and receive 132% of her benefit

As a widow, Kathy also has an additional option. She can file for survivor benefits. Survivor benefits would allow her to receive income based on Bill's earnings. However, when she later files for her own retirement benefits, that would be calculated on her own earnings, not Bill's. Thus, if she wants, she can file for survivor benefits now and full retirement benefits when she is 70. Conversely, she can take an early retirement benefit, and then apply for survivor benefits next year when she turns 67. She'll need to run the numbers to see which strategy is better for her long-term.

Let's say Kathy's delayed retirement benefit would be $2,640/month, and her early retirement benefit would be $1400/month. Her survivor benefit now would be 99% of Bill's retirement benefit, so if Bill was entitled to $1,500/month, her survivor benefit would be $1,485/month. If she waits a year, she will get the full $1,500. In this case, it makes sense for Kathy to take the survivor benefit right now and wait until she turns 70 to take her retirement benefit. This will allow her to get a little bit more now than she would if she took retirement benefits now, and a lot more once she files for retirement.

Survivor benefits are available to widows of any age who are taking care of children under the age of 16 (if your child is permanently disabled, you may be able to get these benefits even if they are adults). Widows without children can receive reduced survivor benefits starting at age 60—this benefit is 71%-99% of your late spouse's retirement benefit, while those with young or permanently disabled children receive 75% of their spouse's retirement benefit regardless of their children's age.

The Earnings Test for SSA Benefits

Whether you take survivor benefits or worker benefits, keep the "Earnings Test" in mind. The SSA has rules for how much you can earn via wages if you take early retirement benefits. In 2023, workers under the age of 67 may not earn more than $21,240. However, if you are 66, and going on 67 the year you apply, the limit changes to $56,520. These limits are set by the SSA and may be subject to changes every year depending on the economy.

If you earn more than this maximum amount while taking retirement benefits, the SSA will take $1 away from your total benefit for every $2 earned. Remember, this only applies if you are under the age of 67. For example, Kathy is turning 67 this year, so if she earns $60,000 this year, she will exceed the earnings limit by $3,480. Thus, her annual benefit will be reduced by half of that excess, or $1,740 (to be precise). For example, if she has an annual benefit of $20,000/year, and earns more than $60,000 this year, her annual benefit this year will be $18,260 ($20,000 - $1,740). Benefits are paid monthly, so that would come out to $1,521.67/month. Conversely, if she didn't earn more than $56,520 this year, she would get the full benefit of $20,000 per year, which comes out to $1,666.67 per month.

Quiz Yourself!

Read these three scenarios and list the pros and cons of taking Social Security early for each one. Then decide what the worker's best strategy is.

Scenario 1

Jennifer has just enough money coming in from her job to pay her bills, but doesn't have anything left over to save or spend. She just turned 62 and plans to keep working, but she would like to put more money in her pocket, so she's considering claiming early retirement. She also has a 401k from her job, but thanks to a recent economic crash, it has lost money. Should Jennifer take her retirement benefits now?

Our answer: It is best for Jennifer to take her benefits now. Her benefits will be reduced slightly by her wages and she will receive less of a benefit than she would if she waited, but it's the best way to reduce her financial pressure.

Scenario 2

Marilla and Matthew are both still going strong at the ages of 62 and 64, respectively, and have recently adopted their two grandchildren after the tragic death of the children's mother. Marilla makes more money than Matthew because of her side business of selling plum puffs at a local farmer's market, but now that they have two children to take care of, she's wondering if it might be a good idea for one or both of them to take their retirement benefits early to pay for extra expenses related to child care. What should be their best strategy?

Our answer: Matthew should take his retirement benefits now, while Marilla continues working and waits to take her benefit. That way, the couple has money coming in to help them with the children. Another strategy could be, if Marilla and Matthew were dependent upon their daughter, to consider whether they qualify for survivor benefits.

Scenario 3

Gary was looking forward to spending his golden years traveling and doing all the things he never got to do, but he recently learned his cancer metastasized into his lungs. He is likely going to die within the next few years. Gary is 64 this year and feels like his life has been unfairly cut short. Should he take his retirement benefits now?

Our answer: Yes, Gary may not live to see 70, so there is little point in him delaying taking his benefit., assuming he's unmarried.

Summary

In this information-packed chapter, we discussed all the factors that go into maximizing your Social Security retirement benefits.

One of the biggest questions people have pertains to what age they should start taking benefits. While you are allowed to begin collecting retirement benefits at 62, there are some disadvantages: you'll receive a permanent reduction of 30% which means getting smaller checks each month. Conversely, if you wait until you're 70, you'll get 132% of your full benefit amount. For most people, waiting makes the most sense, but if you're strapped for cash or are facing a terminal diagnosis, it might make more sense to take your benefits as early as possible.

If you are married, divorced, or widowed, the decision becomes more complex. Taking benefits early could affect any survivor or spousal benefit your partner files in the future, and if you are divorced, you may be entitled to spousal or survivor benefits if you have not remarried. Similarly, widows are entitled to survivor benefits; they may also be entitled to these if their ex-spouse passes away, but in this case, the widow must not remarry before the age of 60 to qualify for these benefits.

Finally, if you are disabled, you have to decide when to file for disability benefits, and when to file for retirement benefits, as you can't take both at once.

Now that you've learned all of this information, don't get overwhelmed! Think about what is best for your situation and start putting a plan into action. Once you have a good grip on your Social Security retirement plan, you'll need to know how to cover health care costs after you retire. In the next chapter, we'll go over some basics related to Medicare.

Turn the page when you're ready to start learning about it!

4

Beyond the Basics - Special Cases in Social Security

It's a waste of time to be angry about my disability. One has to get on with life and I haven't done badly.

Stephen Hawking

Social Security offers unique provisions for those who are dealing with disability, either their own or their child's. Having a physical or mental disability can make certain aspects of your life more challenging than they are for non-disabled people. Some of those challenges involve expensive finances—therapies, interventions, or special educational programs, and disabled adults may be limited in their ability to work, making it harder for them to earn the income needed to provide for these special services.

That's why Social Security offers disability payments for those who are taking care of themselves or disabled children. In this chapter, we will explore all the options available so that you can maximize your benefits if you are dealing with any such special circumstances.

Benefits for Disabled Adult Children

Both minors and adults with disabilities may be eligible for benefits under the Social Security disability program. If you are caring for a disabled adult child, there are certain things you should know about the benefits entitled to you on your child's behalf.

There are two different programs:

- Minors with disabilities, as well as some disabled adult children, may qualify for Social Supplemental Income (SSI), which is a program meant for people who cannot work due to a disability.
- Disabled adults, including some who have been disabled since childhood, may be eligible for Social Security Disability Insurance (SSDI). This program is considered a "child's benefit" because it is paid against the parent's Social Security earnings record; SSDI is available for adults who developed a disability prior to the age of 22.

In order to receive SSDI, the applicant must meet the Social Security Administration's criteria for disability and must be unmarried. If your child is already receiving SSI payments, don't assume that also they don't qualify for SSDI. Check the eligibility criteria and apply on their behalf if they appear to be eligible. In addition, if your child's circumstances have changed since their 18th birthday, they may be eligible for higher benefits than before. For example, if a parent has passed away or is now retired, that can also affect eligibility and benefit amounts. Thus, it's important to talk to an advocate at the Social Security Administration about your situation to find out what your child may be entitled to. Once a disabled adult child has been approved for disability payments, the payments will continue for life, as long as the adult child remains disabled.

Benefits for Disabled Minors

You may qualify for SSI benefits on behalf of your disabled minor (child under the age of 18), depending on your household income. The child must have a medical condition that makes them disabled for, at least, 12 months or is expected to result in their death. This benefit is called the "Child Disability Benefit Program."

In order to receive these benefits, you must go through a rigorous application process. The process involves sharing detailed information and documentation about your child's medical condition and how it affects their daily functioning. You will have to sign releases for therapists, doctors, and teachers to provide your child's private health information as part of the application. In some cases, the SSA will need additional information and require their own medical examination of your child. The SSA will pay for the exam and provide the doctor if this is the case.

It usually takes about three to six months for the SSA to make a decision. However, if your child has a serious physical disability such as muscular dystrophy, total blindness, or cerebral palsy, the SSA may make payments while they are processing your application. You will not have to pay this back if the SSA ultimately decides your child does not qualify for SSI.

Children do not qualify for SSDI payments until they reach the age of 18.

The Pickle Amendment

The Pickle Amendment, introduced in 1976, will help ensure that your disabled children remain eligible for Medicaid while receiving SSI or SSDI.

This amendment is named after former Representative James Pickle, who was worried that the annual cost-of-living increase in Social Security benefits would push some SSI recipients over the maximum income allowed to remain eligible for benefits. This unfair situation would cause some people to have to choose between SSI and Medicaid—and if they needed medical treatment to manage their disability, and SSI to meet their basic living expenses, this would become an impossible decision.

Thus, the Pickle Amendment changed the Medicaid eligibility rules so that cost-of-living increases are not counted toward income for the purpose of determining Medicaid eligibility. This means that if you or your child receives SSI or SSDI, the annual increase in your benefits to cover changes in cost of living will not count when Medicaid examines your eligibility.

Deceased Parent Benefits

As we discussed in Chapter 3, adults may be entitled to survivor benefits when their partner dies. In addition, children may be eligible for these benefits if a parent dies.

- Children under 18 are entitled to benefits if:
- A parent is collecting retirement benefits or disability benefits at the time of their death.

A parent passes away who has paid enough into Social Security to be entitled to benefits when they retire.

Children can receive these benefits if they are unmarried and under the age of 18, or if:

- They are between the ages of 18 and 19 and are still in high school.
- They have a disability that began before the age of 22.

As the custodial parent, you must file for benefits on your child's behalf and show proof that you have the right to do so, such as the child's birth certificate or adoption paperwork. You will also need to provide both your child's and your own Social Security number, and if you're applying for death benefits, you must provide a copy of the deceased parent's death certificate.

Unique Circumstances for Disabled Workers

It's difficult to increase SSDI benefits, but there are a few ways to do so. The SSA will automatically recalculate your benefits every year to account for cost-of-living increases. In addition, if you or your caseworker finds a clerical error or that you had additional earnings that were overlooked in your original application, the SSA will automatically increase or decrease your benefits.

You can't take disability and retirement benefits at the same time, but you can get retirement benefits if you are disabled, either by applying early or waiting until your full retirement age. If you don't claim benefits early, your disability benefits will automatically be converted to retirement benefits when you reach your full retirement age.

There are a few things you can do to increase either your retirement or your disability benefit:

Work for 35 years: Your retirement benefits are based on a 35-year work history, but if you don't work for that long, they will be calculated based on the years you did work. If you can, work for 35 years or more to increase the amount of your retirement benefit—however, if you are on SSDI or SSI, keep in mind that you cannot earn more than a certain amount without losing part or all of your disability benefits.

- **Don't apply for disability benefits until you reach the full retirement age:** At this point, your disability benefit will be equal to your full retirement benefit. The advantage of waiting this long is that you can work full-time without penalty, so you may have a higher benefit amount than you would if you'd been on disability for most of your adult life.
- **Apply for spousal retirement benefits:** have a disability. You will receive a lower benefit amount if you apply before reaching the full retirement age.
- **If you are widowed, apply for survivor benefits:** You can receive survivor and disability benefits at the same time. For that, you must have worked and paid into the system at some point to qualify for survivor benefits.
- **Hire a disability attorney:** An attorney experienced in this area of law can go over your documentation and find ways to maximize your benefits that you may not have been aware of.

If you are disabled, there are several options to maximize your benefits, but what if your income is extremely low or high?

Low-paid workers may find it challenging to delay their benefits until they reach or pass their full retirement age. If you're having trouble making ends meet, consider these options:

- **Monitor earnings carefully:** You might want to cut back on your hours so that you don't earn more than what you're allowed to while taking early retirement benefits.
- **Check for mistakes:** Read over your Social Security statements carefully. If you find mistakes in how much you earned or how much you are owed, contact the SSA immediately and report the error. You might get a recalculation in your favor!
- **Suspend your payments:** If you have been receiving benefits for less than a year, you have the right to change your mind and ask the SSA to cancel your claim. If your income increases or you decide you want to delay benefits after all, this is a viable option for you.

High-income earners have a cap on their payments. In 2023, no one can receive more than $4,555 per month even if they delay claiming retirement benefits until after age 70; those who retire when they reach the age of 67 cannot receive more than $3,627/month; and early claimants cannot receive more than $2,572/month. Keep this in mind if you have an unusually high income—it may be to your advantage to work fewer years if your early or full retirement benefits will be sufficient.

Both low and high-paid workers should speak to a tax attorney as part of their decision-making process, as adding benefits to wages can push you into a higher tax bracket, and if you bring in more than $25,000/year, your Social Security benefits become taxable.

How Disability Benefits Are Calculated

Both retirement and disability benefits are calculated based on how much money you earn while you are working. The SSA takes an average of your annual salaries. For retirement benefits, this is based on your top-earning salaries received over 35 years; for disability benefits, a slightly different formula is used that calculates your benefits based on your top-earning salaries in the years up to when you became disabled. This means that even if you don't claim disability until 10 years after you became disabled, the SSA will still calculate salaries up to the year you first became unable to work. It also drops, or declines to count, one to five years of your history, based on how long you worked before you became disabled.

The precise formula is complex, but the point is that your earnings, prior to your disability, and your age will determine your monthly benefit amount. In addition, for disability benefits, a portion of any income you still earn each month will be subtracted from your benefit amount. This is not the case with retirement benefits unless you retire early. If you take retirement benefits between the ages of 62 and 67, a portion of any income you earn will be counted against them.

If you receive survivor benefits, they are usually calculated based on your late partner's earnings. However, if your partner had already claimed early retirement benefits at the time of their death, you will receive only a partial benefit.

Additional Special Circumstances to Consider

One of the top issues that retirees face is figuring out their finances, especially given the complexity of tax laws and requirements to make mandatory withdrawals from IRAs after they reach a certain age (for 2023, that age is six months past their 70th birthday).

We will discuss financial planning in Chapter 8; you may want to jump ahead to that information so that you have the best chance of getting a handle on your finances. It also helps to hire a financial planner with expertise in tax laws, retirement accounts, and related issues.

Another issue you may face is the amount of time it takes to process a disability claim. The system is set up so that only people who meet strict guidelines receive the disability income; a side effect of this type of vetting is that the process is extremely slow, and some people who do qualify are initially turned away.

If you are homeless, at risk of homelessness, or suffer from serious illness, the SSA will expedite your claim. Those with serious diseases will be processed under the "Compassionate Allowance (CAL) program." You do not need to do anything special to apply for this program; your caseworker will automatically refer your application for expedition if you mention your illness on the forms.

As mentioned above, some types of disability qualify for a "presumptive disability (PD) determination." This means that you will get payments immediately while your claim is still being processed, and you can keep that money even if the SSA later declines your claim. Similarly, if you are facing a financial emergency, you may be able to get an advanced payment while waiting for your claim to be processed. This is a one-time payment based on federal rates and may not exceed $999. This payment will be deducted from any regular SSI payment you become entitled to in the future.

If you have a terminal illness, such as metastasized cancer with no hope of remission, your caseworker will refer it to the Terminal Illness program and expedite your claim.

Military veterans are also eligible for expedited claims:

- Those who have been rated as 100% permanently disabled by the Veterans Administration (VA).

- Those who are "wounded warriors," meaning they were seriously injured in the line of duty, but are not 100% permanently disabled.

If the VA has made this determination, you should put it on your disability application so that it may be expedited. You may also need to provide documentation from your VA doctor.

If you are in "dire need," meaning you are extremely low-income and are homeless, or about to become homeless, you can apply for an expedited hearing. You will need a letter of dire need, explaining the circumstances, and as much evidence of need as possible. For example, eviction notices from your landlord or a letter from the director of a homeless shelter where you are staying can demonstrate your lack of stable housing. If you have high medical bills because of an illness or injury, attach copies of those bills to your application as well.

Finally, if the SSA is notified that an applicant is a threat to themselves or to other people, they will notify the appropriate authorities as well as expedite the claim. The SSA is committed to the safety of applicants and people the applicant may come in contact with.

Quiz Yourself

Answer the following questions to test your knowledge of special circumstances:

- Which benefit is designed for disabled adults who have had that disability since childhood?

    a) SSDI
    b) Child's Disability Benefits

c) Survivor Benefits

d) Compassionate Allowance Program

- Children must have developed their disability before the age of __ to qualify for Child Disability Benefits.

a) 12
b) 5
c) 22
d) 18

- After you submit your application, how long will you have to wait to begin receiving disability benefits?

a) Not at all—it's immediate
b) Three to six months, but if you have special circumstances, you may receive an expedited application
c) Three to six months, unless you are in dire need or have a serious disability that allows you to get provisional payments
d) Both B and C

- What is the time you may have to wait before you receive disability benefits called?

a) Time-wasting period
b) Evaluation period
c) Delayed start of benefits
d) Waiting period

- What type of work must an individual NOT be able to do to qualify for disability?

    a) No kind of work at all is allowed
    b) Working on a computer
    c) Standing on their feet
    d) Substantial gainful work

Answers:

1) B

2) C

3) D

4) D

5) D

Summary

In this chapter, we looked at special circumstances where you may be eligible for assistance from the SSA.

Disability is a big one. The SSA offers two disability programs, depending on the extent of the disability and whether the person has ever been able to work. Severely disabled children, meaning people under the age of 18 whose abilities are limited by their condition, may qualify for the Child Disability Program, which pays a monthly stipend. Adults over the age of 18 who have had a disability since childhood may also qualify for this program. Adults may also qualify for SSDI, which pays a monthly stipend to adults who may be able to work on a limited basis.

The process for applying for disability benefits involves filling out an application, attaching supporting documentation, and waiting. If you have a medical condition, it is important to attach a doctor's note; you might also need to attach proof of dire circumstances, such as an eviction notice, and if you are applying on behalf of a child, you must also provide their birth certificate or adoption paperwork. Finally, if you are applying for survivor benefits, you must attach the appropriate death certificate. Children may be entitled to survivor benefits until they turn 18. If they are still in high school upon their 18th birthday, they can extend the benefits until they graduate.

It normally takes three to six months for a disability application to be processed, but there are special circumstances in which your application might be expedited or you may receive advance payments before your application is approved. If you have a severe disability or illness, are homeless or about to become homeless, or have sustained disabling injuries in the line of duty, your application may be expedited. You will need to note these circumstances when you apply.

We have learned a lot together about Social Security! In the next and final chapter, we will discuss how to put it all together to create a comprehensive plan for your retirement.

Turn the page when you are ready.

5

The ABCDs of Medicare - Navigating Your Way to Better Health

Medicare is known as the health care program for seniors, but did you know it's not a "one-size-fits-all" offer? Understanding the various moving parts of this program could be your key to a healthy and happy retirement. Medicare's complexity can be confusing; it's easy to overlook something extremely crucial and subsequently fail to claim all the benefits you're entitled to.

Let's simplify the program together.

Medicare Basics

As you may know, Lyndon Johnson signed Medicare into law for the first time in 1965 so that retirees could have access to appropriate health care, regardless of their medical needs. However, the seeds of this program were planted 20 years earlier by Harry Truman. Truman wanted to create a federally-funded program that would guarantee every citizen's ability to access appropriate health care, no matter their income level. And Truman wasn't the first to think of the idea either—Teddy Roosevelt envisioned a national healthcare system when he ran for President as a third-party candidate in 1912.

Truman and Roosevelt envisioned a system that paid for ALL Americans' healthcare needs, something that progressive politicians such as Bernie Sanders and Elizabeth Warren still want to enact today. While no such program exists as of 2023, Medicare does offer government-sponsored health insurance to those over the age of 65, and Truman and his wife were the first Medicare recipients.

Enacting this program was one of John F. Kennedy's priorities. He learned that 56% of people over the age of 65 did not have adequate healthcare coverage, and therefore strongly pushed for legislation to change that (Medicare, 2022). After Kennedy's death, Johnson continued the push and managed to get Medicare signed into law. It ultimately went into effect in 1966.

As of 2022, nearly 65 million people are enrolled in Medicare Part A, and Medicare accounts for 20% of the federal budget. Politicians worry that the trust fund for Medicare will be depleted by 2028. If this happens, payroll taxes may be levied to pay for Medicare, just as these taxes are used to fund Social Security.

Today's Medicare Has Four Parts

Medicare has four parts that cover different aspects of health care:

- **Part A** covers in-patient care. This is care that you receive in a hospital, such as surgery and recovery from surgery, emergency care, or severe illnesses requiring hospitalization.
- **Part B** covers all other medical treatments. It has been expanded over the years to cover things such as end-stage renal disease for people younger than 65.

- **Part C** is what's known as Medicare Advantage. This is a program that participants buy into. Like private insurance, Medicare Advantage requires premium payments as well as co-pays and deductibles.
- **Part D** is prescription drug coverage. Participants are subject to restrictions on what drugs are covered.

Medicare Part A is paid for through employment taxes; usually, enrollees do not have to pay monthly premiums. However, those who have never worked, or are otherwise ineligible, may have to pay monthly premiums of up to $506 as of 2023. If you fall into this category and do not buy in when you turn 65, you may have to pay a penalty.

As with private insurance, Medicare Part A offers coverage only for services the insurer deems medically necessary. As of 2023, these services include some home health aide services and hospice services. However, these services are only available to those who meet certain criteria, such as being homebound or being diagnosed with a terminal illness that reduces life expectancy to six months or less. Some types of care, such as in-patient hospital stays, may require deductibles to be met before any coverage kicks in.

You are eligible for Medicare Part A if you

- are over the age of 65 and receive Social Security or Railroad Board Benefits.
- are younger than 65 but receiving Railroad Board or Social Security disability benefits.
- are younger than 65 and have a diagnosis of amyotrophic lateral sclerosis.

If you are over 65 and not claiming retirement benefits, or you are under the age of 65 and have a diagnosis of ESRD (ESRD patients can get Medicare at any age), you must sign up for Medicare Part A, instead of being enrolled automatically.

If you do not qualify for premium-free Medicare, you may enroll when you turn 65 or during any enrollment periods. If you do not enroll when you first qualify, you may be subject to a 10% increase in premiums when you do enroll.

All other programs are optional and thus require premium payments. Part B is a lower-cost program than private insurance programs and works quite similarly, covering needed health care outside of hospitalization such as doctors' visits, diagnostic tests, and medications. Chemotherapy and similar treatments are covered under this plan. You only pay co-pays until you meet your deductible. As of 2023, the deductible is $226.

We will discuss Medicare Part C more thoroughly in the next section. Medicare Part C is an alternative coverage program; and Medicare enrollees choose between this and Medicare Parts A and B rather than signing up for both.

Medicare Part D offers prescription benefits. If you have Medicare Parts A and B, you will pay an additional premium for this coverage. If you have Medicare Part C, it typically covers the premium on Part D. There are limits to how much drug coverage you get through Part D; you will pay out-of-pocket once you reach this limit. However, there is a cap on the amount you will be responsible for.

Let's look at an example to make this clearer. Suppose your Part D coverage has a limit of $5,000 and a cap of $1,500—these numbers are made up; real coverage is likely much different. If you are prescribed drugs that cost more than $5,000 within a calendar year, you will have to pay out-of-pocket for any other drugs that are prescribed. However, if you spend more than $1,500 out-of-pocket, you will no longer be required to pay out-of-pocket for additional drugs. Instead, you will pay a co-pay on all additional medicines for the year.

If your Medicare plans don't cover all your medical needs, you can purchase Medigap insurance. This is a private insurance that covers services that Medicare does not.

Medicare vs. Medicare Advantage

Medicare Part C is known as Medicare Advantage. This is a program that you buy into, but how else does it differ from basic Medicare?

Medicare and Medicare Advantage cover different things. Original Medicare requires you to get three different types of coverage. Part A covers hospital stays, Part B covers other medical care, and Part D covers prescriptions. Conversely, Medicare Advantage offers coverage of all three aspects of health care. This means you only have to buy into one program. However, it's important to bear in mind that Medicare Advantage is not provided by the federal government. Instead, it is provided by private health insurance companies that have partnered with the government. Thus, the costs may be higher and you may be subject to more limits as to which doctors and services are covered.

That said, Medicare Advantage may offer coverage that basic Medicare does not, including:

- dental coverage
- vision coverage
- hearing aids and other hearing coverage
- transportation to and from the doctor's office (often through a door-to-door car or van service)

Considering whether you want or need these additional services can help make it clearer to you which plan is best for you. It's also important to consider your total costs when making this decision. When comparing costs, it's important to keep a few things in mind.

First, Original Medicare requires you to sign up for three different programs, only one of which may be premium-free. Even if your Part A coverage doesn't require premiums, you will still be required to pay premium costs for Parts B and D. You will also need to consider the deductibles for each of these programs and the co-pays and coverage limits. All of these costs can easily add up.

Conversely, Medicare Advantage requires you to pay one premium rather than two or three. You will also have to meet only one deductible before coverage kicks in, though you still may need to pay a co-pay at many doctors' offices you might visit.

The biggest difference involves coverage. Original Medicare covers all US hospitals and doctor's offices, but does not offer any coverage in foreign countries. Medicare Advantage covers only in-network providers in the United States, but may offer limited coverage in some foreign countries.

If you are somebody who does not plan to travel much or who doesn't want to go outside of the United States, it may make more sense to opt for Original Medicare. However, if your retirement plans involve a lot of travel, especially to foreign countries, opting for Medicare Advantage may make more sense.

How Medicare Works With Other Insurance

Although Medicare is designed to make health care more affordable for seniors, it may not cover all costs. Some people may have secondary insurance to cover things that Medicare doesn't, while others might be reluctant to let go of their private health insurance.

If you have both Medicare and private health insurance, various rules govern how your health care is paid for.

When you have two types of insurance, one is considered primary, and the other is considered secondary. Whichever insurance is primary kicks in first. If you've exceeded coverage limits or your primary insurance doesn't cover services for some reason, your secondary insurance will be used to cover those costs.

Whether Medicare is your primary or secondary insurance depends on your situation:

- If you have insurance through your job, in most cases, that insurance will be primary, and Medicare will be secondary. However, if you work for a very small company (fewer than 20 employees), Medicare will be your primary insurance.
- Similarly, if you are on a job-based disability insurance, that insurance is primary unless your company has less than 100 employees.
- If you are using liability coverage, Medicare is secondary for all relevant claims, though Medicare will be your primary coverage for non-related claims. For example, if you fall at work, your liability insurance will take care of injury-related care, but Medicare will be primary for your routine health care.

Some insurance programs don't work with Medicare. In this case, you have to choose between them:

- You can either use VA benefits or Medicare, not both at the same visit.
- If you are not eligible for Medicare, you must use other retiree insurance.
- If you had Consolidated Omnibus Reconciliation Act insurance (COBRA) before becoming eligible for Medicare, you must use Medicare and cannot use COBRA.

If you are on a low income and have both Medicaid and Medicare, you may only use Medicaid for services that are not covered by Medicare.

Your Medicare Checklist

Check off the following items to ensure that you understand each concept and how to maximize your Medicare benefits:

- Review the costs of Medicare vs. Medicare Advantage and decide which one to participate in.
- Enroll in Medicare Part A, B, and D or exclusively in Medicare Part C (Medicare Advantage).
- Receive your health insurance card and welcome packet. Read over all information carefully.
- Learn what your total premiums, deductibles, and co-pays are. Budget for these.

Summary

Medicare is a government-paid healthcare program that is meant to help ensure that healthcare is affordable for retirees. This is important because as you get older, you may need more doctors' visits or treatments to deal with serious health issues.

The program was created in 1965, but progressive politicians have envisioned a health care program that covered all Americans' needs since Teddy Roosevelt ran for President as a third party in 1912. Medicare falls far short of this lofty goal, instead insuring most people over the age of 65. It is important to note that this program is not free to consumers, though premiums, co-pays, and deductibles are usually more affordable than private insurance.

There are two options when it comes to Medicare. You can enroll separately in Part A, B, and D, which cover your hospital stays, outpatient treatment, and prescription costs; conversely, you may elect Medicare Part C, also called Medicare Advantage, which covers all three. Except for Medicare Part A, all Medicare programs require you to pay monthly premiums, you will also have to pay deductibles and co-pays. Medicare Advantage requires you to see only in-network doctors, while you can see any doctor you want with Original Medicare.

When evaluating these programs, it's important to consider total costs and what services you need coverage for. In addition, if you want to travel, you should be aware that Medicare Advantage offers some coverage in foreign countries, while basic Medicare does not. Additionally, Medicare can be coordinated with most private insurance companies. In some cases, Medicare will be considered your primary insurance, meaning it'll be used first, while in other cases, it will not. You cannot use Medicare at the same time as VA Benefits, and if you have both Medicare and

Medicaid, you cannot use Medicaid unless Medicare does not cover your service.

It's important to grasp these fundamentals, but equally important to ensure that you choose the optimal healthcare plan for yourself. We'll do a deep dive into different Medicare plans in the next chapter.

Turn the page to get started!

6

Choose Wisely - Your Guide to the Right Medicare Plan

Selecting the right Medicare plan is one of the most consequential choices you'll make. If you want to live the retirement of your dreams, you'll need the right coverage. Someone who wants to travel has different health care needs than a "homebody" who wants to make sure that medical expenses don't eat up all of their hard-earned retirement savings, and a person with any chronic health conditions needs different coverage than someone who only needs preventative health care.

Whatever your situation is, you deserve a retirement that is as peaceful, stress-free, and joyful as possible. Choosing the right Medicare plan can help you achieve that. This chapter will explore all the ins and outs of various Medicare plans so that you can make the best choice for yourself and your family.

Reviewing The Different Options

As we discussed in the previous chapter, there are four parts to Medicare. Parts A, B, and D work together to provide you with different types of health care coverage; conversely, Part C, or Medicare Advantage, provides comprehensive coverage.

Here's a breakdown of the various programs again:

- **Part A** covers hospital stays.
- **Part B** covers outpatient treatment, such as doctor's visits.
- **Part C** is comprehensive coverage that includes hospital visits, outpatient treatment, and prescription drug coverage.
- **Part D** covers most prescriptions.

Now let's look at each program in more depth.

Part A: What Exactly Is Covered if I Have to Be Hospitalized?

First and foremost, Part A covers hospital stays. If your doctor says you need to be hospitalized, in most cases, your hospitalization will be covered. That means that hospitalizations for severe illness, planned or unplanned surgeries and recovery, and emergency room visits are all covered.

There are also a few ancillary services that are covered by Part A:

- Temporary stays in nursing facilities or nursing homes following hospitalization, if ordered by a doctor.
- Home health care services prescribed by your doctor, such as physical or occupational therapy.
- Hospice care for those with a terminal illness who are not expected to survive for more than six months.

However, this doesn't mean that all services are free; you may have to pay out-of-pocket until you hit your deductible or pay co-pays for some services. However, these costs are usually cheaper than what private insurance requires. Your co-pays are usually about 20% of the cost of service., and if you do have to pay a premium, it will vary based on your income level.

Part B: Outpatient Treatment Coverage

Part B covers all other medical services. This includes all of your doctor's visits; whether you are having a preventative check-up with your general practitioner or seeing a specialist to help you manage a specific health condition, Medicare Part B will cover it. However, as of 2023, Medicare Part B does not cover most dental, vision, or hearing services, though it may cover some diagnostic exams, and some eye surgeries such as cataract removal procedures.

In addition to doctor's visits, Part B covers some services you might not expect:

- participation in clinical research studies (some costs related to the study may be covered)
- durable medical equipment such as walkers, canes, wheelchairs, and oxygen tanks
- mental health services
- certain prescription drugs that must be administered by a healthcare provider
- some ambulance rides

Part B coverage is optional, which means you won't be penalized if you elect not to take it when you turn 65. You will have to pay a small premium each month for this coverage.

What Does Medicare Advantage Cover?

Medicare Advantage offers comprehensive coverage, which means that hospital stays, outpatient treatment, and most prescription drugs are covered by one plan. You have to pay for the plan, and you can only see doctors that are in your network. As with private insurance, you may need referrals to see specialists or pre-authorizations for certain treatments or tests. You also have a choice of plans: Medicare Advantage consists of private insurance companies that have contracted with Medicare to provide services at reduced rates.

Unlike Original Medicare, Medicare Advantage covers vision, dental, and hearing services.

In addition, there are a few other benefits to Medicare Advantage:

- wellness services
- adult daycare services
- transportation to doctors' visits (usually a car or van service that picks you up at your door and drops you off at home after your appointment)

Medicare Advantage also offers limited coverage in foreign countries, making it a better option for you if you plan to do a lot of traveling.

Are All Prescriptions Covered?

Although Part B is optional, you can't get Part D coverage unless you are first enrolled in both Parts A and B.

Part D covers prescription drugs. Most drugs are covered, but the exact list differs depending on which Part D plan you choose. You can get a list of approved drugs from your Part D provider.

If you have diabetes, Part D will usually cover your medication and testing supplies. In 2023, a new $35 cap on insulin went into effect, meaning that Medicare recipients will not pay more than this amount for insulin under any Part D plan.

Technically, you can enroll in Part D anytime, as the coverage is optional. However, if you choose not to enroll when you turn 65, you may incur penalties for late enrollment if you sign up later. Bear in mind that you do not need Part D if you have Medicare Advantage, as prescriptions are covered under that plan.

Medigap Coverage

If you've ever seen Medicare plans with other letters of the alphabet besides A through D, those are Medigap plans. Medigap is a type of supplemental insurance you can buy to cover services that Medicare doesn't, such as hearing, vision, or dental services.

You pay monthly premiums for Medigap services, and you can choose from several providers who offer them. Each plan is slightly different than the others and covers different services, but the plan type you purchase will be the same no matter who the provider is. For example, if you purchase Medigap Plan M, it will cover the same services no matter who you buy it from, but Plan N will cover different services than Plan M.

You cannot use Medigap insurance with Medicare Advantage, which is also a private insurance program meant to cover various services.

Should I Enroll in Medicare Advantage?

There are pros and cons to Medicare Advantage; you should consider these carefully before making a final decision.

+ *Pros:*

- **Everything is covered through the same plan:** You won't have to keep track of deductibles and premiums for two or three separate plans, as you would if you signed up for Original Medicare Parts A, B, and D along with any supplemental Medigap insurance you need.
- **It may be cheaper:** Your premiums for Original Medicare Parts B and D usually take a bigger bite out of your monthly budget than Medicare Advantage.
- **There are caps on out-of-pocket costs:** You won't pay more than $8,300/year in out-of-pocket costs if you use in-network doctors.
- **More plan options that may fit your individual needs better:** Medicare Advantage has various types of plan structures. For example, you can choose a PPO if you want more options for seeing out-of-network doctors or an SNP if you need coverage for chronic health conditions
- **Vision, dental, and hearing may be covered, depending on your plan:** Original Medicare does not cover these supplementary services, which many older Americans might need help with.
- **There is coordination between different healthcare providers:** Medicare Advantage may facilitate coordination between your general practitioner and any specialists that you see, which can make it easier for you to get the comprehensive health care you need.

- **There is some coverage in foreign countries:** If you plan to travel outside of the United States, you'll need coverage in case of a medical emergency; Medicare Advantage provides this, while Original Medicare does not.

— *Cons:*

- **Restrictions on which doctors you can see:** While Original Medicare covers most doctors throughout the country, Medicare Advantage requires you to see doctors within a particular network. If you see an out-of-network doctor, you will pay more out-of-pocket and may not have any part of your service covered, depending on your plan type.
- **More red tape:** As with private insurance, you may need to get referrals or pre-authorizations before some services are covered. This can make it harder to get appropriate care, and if you have a condition in which time is precious, this could be a problem.
- **Your network may not remain stable:** Your network can change at any time. Providers can leave a practice or a practice can leave the network, which can leave you scrambling to find new providers to meet your needs.
- **Some services may not be available where you live:** If you need a highly specialized service, there may not be any in-network providers where you live and you may have to go out of state to get the care you need.
- **The choices can be overwhelming:** While having a lot of plan types leads to greater flexibility, you also may become overwhelmed and have a hard time deciding which coverage you need.

How to Choose the Plan That Is Right for You

The first decision that you must make is whether you will choose Original Medicare or Medicare Advantage. To make this decision, you should consider several factors.

First, compare the total costs for each program. Remember to factor in your estimated premiums, co-pay amounts, and deductible amounts to determine how much each plan will cost you. You also want to consider your healthcare needs and what you anticipate needing in the future. If you are in good health and not on any medications, you may be tempted to skip Medicare Part D. But enrolling later could be more expensive; does your family or personal medical history suggest you'll need extensive medications later? Or does it make more sense to get Medicare Advantage now so that your prescriptions will be covered in the future without having to purchase additional insurance?

If you currently wear glasses or hearing aids, or you have gum disease or other serious dental issues, Medicare Advantage may be a better option for you, as this plan covers all dental, vision, and hearing-related services. Original Medicare does cover some related services, such as eye exams, but does not cover materials such as glasses or contacts. However, another option may be to get Original Medicare and purchase an appropriate Medigap supplement to cover these services. In addition, you may want to talk to your dentist, eye doctor, or hearing specialist; some offices have payment plans or in-office insurance plans that may save you money. If this is the case, you could use the in-office insurance to pay for these services and Original Medicare for your medical care. Chronic health conditions are also a genuine concern. If you have prediabetes or diabetes, you'll need to be able to get specialized care to help you manage your condition.

If there's any reason that you are concerned about finding a doctor that meets your needs, you may find the in-network requirements of Medicare Advantage to be too limiting. In this case, Original Medicare may give you more options, although you should consider whether a PPO—which allows you to go out of network to an extent—might be a feasible option for you. You should also consider your lifestyle. If you plan on doing a lot of traveling, you'll want to go with Medicare Advantage, as it offers limited coverage in foreign countries. Alternatively, you may find it cheaper to purchase supplemental private insurance for your travels to use in coordination with Original Medicare.

Finally, you'll want to consider customer service. If a particular Medicare provider's office is hard to reach by telephone or email, the people staffing the phone lines are rude, or you don't think they do a good job of explaining policy decisions, these factors will cause unnecessary stress for you. If this is the first time you've used Medicare, you won't know what the customer service is like; however, you can read reviews of different providers or plan managers before you decide who to sign up with.

You may have to wait for an open enrollment period to enroll in certain parts of the program, so keep that in mind when making decisions.

Summary

Medicare is complicated, partially because there are so many plans and options to choose from. But once you understand all the options, you'll find it a lot easier to make a decision.

There are two types of Medicare most people consider: Original Medicare or Medicare Advantage. The only part of Original Medicare that is mandatory is Part A, which covers hospitalization, temporary stays in nursing or rehabilitation facilities, and hospice care for those with short life expectancies. Part A is premium-free for most retirees, but you will still have to pay co-pays and deductibles. Optionally, you can also sign up for Part B coverage, which pays for adult daycare programs and wellness programs as well as most doctor's visits; or/and Part D, which covers most drug prescriptions. Both Part B and Part D require monthly premium payments, which vary based on your income level, as well as requiring you to meet a deductible before your coverage kicks in.

Alternatively, you can sign up for Part C, or Medicare Advantage. Medicare Advantage allows you to choose an insurance plan among those offered by private companies that have partnered with Medicare. These plans work like traditional insurance; you have to get referrals from your general practitioner to see a specialist and must see an in-network doctor on most plans. This is more limiting than Original Medicare, which allows you to see almost any doctor in the United States. However, Medicare Advantage offers limited coverage in foreign countries, while Original Medicare offers none. In addition, some people prefer the convenience of having one type of insurance to cover all their needs rather than purchasing several different policies, as happens with Original Medicare. Finally, Medicare Advantage may offer dental, vision, and hearing coverage, which Original Medicare does not, and also offers additional benefits such as door-to-door transportation to medical facilities. If you have Original Medicare, you may need to purchase Medigap insurance to cover services that your Medicare does not. Medigap offers several different programs, so you must pay careful attention to ensure you're purchasing the one that most meets your needs.

In order to determine which program is right for you, compare the total costs, including premiums, co-pays, and deductibles. You'll also want to consider your current healthcare needs as well as what you anticipate you may need in the future. Finally, you'll need to consider your lifestyle. For example, coverage in foreign countries will be more important to a frequent traveler than to someone who plans to spend their retirement at home with their grandchildren. You'll also want to consider what services are available in your area, as there may be few in-network doctors in your town or city. It can be helpful to start a reflective journal while researching and enrolling in Medicare. Journaling regularly can help you organize and clarify your thoughts and make the best decision for yourself.

Healthcare can be one of the more expensive aspects of retirement. Although Medicare can help defray costs, in most cases, you'll still have to pay something toward doctor's visits, prescriptions, and hospital stays. That's why it's so important to learn how to manage your healthcare costs when you are planning your retirement.

The next chapter will help you do that.

7

Securing Your Health - Controlling Costs in Retirement

Healthcare is expensive, especially for retirees. According to the Fidelity Retiree Health Care Cost Estimate (2023), the average 65-year-old American will require almost $157,500 saved to cover their health care expenses after their retirement. The average married couple in this age bracket needs over $300,000.

Retirees often have higher healthcare costs because of chronic conditions, such as diabetes, that may begin in older adulthood. But even if you are in perfect health, preventative costs such as tests and check-ups add up, and you may also have a lot of medications that you need to purchase every month.

While some healthcare costs are unavoidable—going to the doctor is not optional if you want to maximize your health and longevity—there are some ways to save. Throughout this chapter, we will discuss how to plan and minimize healthcare costs during your retirement.

Rising Healthcare Costs Among Seniors

Healthcare costs are rising exponentially, and a big part of that burden tends to fall on older people. Between 1970 and 2009, healthcare costs rose from five to ten percent of most Western countries' GDP (Meijer et al, 2013).

Social scientists differ on why this is happening, but one thing is clear: people are living longer than ever before. That means there are more people using healthcare services than in the past, which leads to an increased need for both Medicare and private health insurance. Older people may have more health problems; in addition, they may utilize more preventative services to protect their health.

There are also several other factors that influence healthcare spending:

- New medical technology can enable people to live longer, happier lives and cure or treat diseases that were previously deemed fatal. However, this technology is often expensive, and healthcare providers must pay for it somehow.
- The way the healthcare system is organized makes a difference. In the United States, where there is no national health insurance plan (except for Medicare for people over the age of 65), healthcare costs have skyrocketed. Conversely, other Western countries must find a way to pay for their national health insurance programs and may need to raise taxes to accommodate the greater number of people using them.
- The general state of the economy will influence prices for everything, including healthcare. If wages or prices go up, healthcare costs will, too.

What does this mean for you? Basically, you are part of an aging population that is facing higher healthcare costs than previous generations did. Healthcare is a necessity, so you can't cut back on it, but you do need to ensure that costs stay under control as much as possible.

One of the biggest challenges involves managing chronic conditions. The National Council of Aging has found that 95% of people over the age of 55 have, at least, one chronic condition (NCOA, 2023). Chronic conditions are more costly to treat because they require ongoing monitoring and treatment. For example, diabetes costs an average of $20,000/year per patient, while Alzheimer's and dementia cost about $49,000.

However, there are some solutions:

- **Online monitoring of some conditions:** It may be cheaper for people to track conditions like diabetes from the comfort of their homes and upload information to their patient portal for their doctors to see. Similarly, some conditions require only virtual visits rather than seeing the doctor in person.
- **Community-based care services:** They can reduce the need for long-term care, which will save money. Long-term care is costly, so anything that can reduce people's dependence on it can help cut costs.
- **Focus on preventative services:** The more people can take action to stay healthy, the lower the costs will be. Treatment of serious conditions is far more costly than wellness visits, after all.

The best way to reduce healthcare costs in the future involves using digital technology, but paradoxically, many older people find it difficult to use these innovative options. Thus, it is incumbent upon leaders in the healthcare industry to ensure that all tech is user-friendly, and that there are services available to help older people learn how to use these new technologies.

Variables Influencing Healthcare Spending

Healthcare costs are rising in the United States and have been for decades. Probasco (2023) theorizes that one reason for the rising costs is the existence of services like Medicare, as providers are aware that government-paid insurance will pay any amount. However, this theory does not explain why the United States has higher healthcare costs than other Western nations, when it's the only one without a national health insurance plan for all citizens.

The state of the American healthcare system is grim. In 2020, Americans spent more than their peers on healthcare, yet had the highest COVID mortality rate, the highest rates of infant and maternal mortality, and lower life expectancies (Probasco, 2023). Thirty one percent of those increased costs came from hospitalizations, suggesting that preventative care can help cut costs. Some of the factors influencing healthcare costs therefore include:

- a rising population
- a larger number of aging seniors, including those with greater longevity than earlier generations
- an increase in chronic conditions
- an increase in how many people are using medical services

COVID-19 contributed initially to many of these costs; however, long term, the disease's presence isn't expected to dramatically increase healthcare costs.

The No Surprise Act of 2021 may help lower costs, as it outlaws surprise medical bills and requires transparency on the part of insurance companies about how costs are calculated.

Strategies to Cope With Unexpected Medical Expenses

No matter how healthy you are, you may face a medical emergency or other unexpected healthcare expenses. While you can't control the costs of healthcare, there are things you can do to minimize the financial impact of unplanned medical treatment. One of the most powerful tools in your financial arsenal is your "emergency fund." This is a savings account specifically for emergencies—once you put money into it, you should not take it out unless you are in dire need.

If you're going to use an emergency fund, it's important for you to have clear definitions of what constitutes an emergency. It can be tempting to remove money from the account for "emergency" needs that are really just wants, such as not being able to afford tickets to a once-in-a-lifetime experience, but if you do this, you won't be covered during a bona fide emergency.

Here are some typical examples of emergencies:

- You or your partner unexpectedly lose a job and need to pay bills.
- You lose wages because you have a serious illness and are out of work for a month.
- Your car breaks down, and you have no other way to pay for repairs.
- A global event disrupts your livelihood for an indefinite period of time, such as the COVID-19 lockdowns in early 2020.

These types of unforeseen circumstances require you to spend money you don't have on basic needs. Thus, without an emergency fund, you may be left with little recourse. It's best to save money regularly for emergencies. Many financial advisors suggest saving three to six months' worth of income. But how do you do it?

One way is to budget a certain percentage of every check you get for emergencies. For example, if you are receiving Social Security income, you could put 10% of each check into savings. If you use this method, make sure you still have enough money in your checking account to cover your expenses so that you won't have to take money out of your emergency fund any time soon. If your budget allows, you could set up an auto transfer on certain days of the month. That way, your bank automatically moves money into your savings. Just make sure you have the money in your account on the day of the transfer so that you don't incur overdraft fees.

If money is tight, look closely at your budget to see where you can cut back on your spending. You could also look for ways to increase your income, such as selling unneeded items or getting a second job, so that you can afford to put good money into emergency savings.

Should You Consider Long-Term Care Insurance?

If you're concerned about paying for nursing homes or other long-term healthcare needs, you might want to consider purchasing insurance to cover it. Although many people think of nursing homes when considering long-term care, that's far from the only thing this type of insurance covers. Seventy three percent of people receive long-term care services at home (US Bank, 2022), and this type of insurance covers the cost of home health aides as well as assisted living facilities or nursing homes. If you should become ill or disabled enough to require this kind of care, having insurance can help defray costs so you don't need to use your retirement savings or depend on your family to take care of you.

While you may not want to pay for an additional insurance policy on top of your Medicare, the fact is that Medicare does not cover most long-term care. Medicare Part A will cover a short-term stay in a nursing facility, following treatment in a hospital, but if you need more than 100 days' worth of care, you or your family will have to pay out-of-pocket unless you have long-term care insurance.

Even if you are in perfect health, you may still want to consider long-term care. Sadly, the majority of people end up needing it as they approach the end of their lives, and if you don't have insurance, this type of care can eat into your savings, and if you run out of money, you won't be able to pay for your care.

Costs vary depending on your age and health, the policy, and what it covers. Many policies offer limited benefits; however, you can purchase policies that are more expansive. You might also consider a hybrid life/long-term care policy that allows you to make claims against the policy for long-term care and offers your beneficiaries a cash benefit from what's left after you pass away.

Using Medigap or Medicare Advantage to Lower HealthCare Costs

Depending on your Medicare plan, you might be able to use it to lower your healthcare costs. If you have Original Medicare, you may also want to purchase Medigap supplemental insurance. As we discussed in Chapter 5, there are various Medigap plans available to cover needs that Medicare does not. It's important to examine all available plans and choose the one that best meets your needs, as not all plans cover the same services.

You do not need Medigap insurance if you have Medicare Advantage—in fact, you cannot use both at once, and it is illegal for anyone to try to sell you Medigap if you are already enrolled in Medicare Advantage. Medicare Advantage is similar to private insurance and covers many services Original Medicare does not, so it would be redundant to also purchase a Medigap policy (even if you could do so).

If you already have Medigap insurance and switch to Medicare Advantage, you won't be able to use your Medigap plan anymore. You can cancel it even if you're unsure whether you will stay with Medicare Advantage. If, within the first 12 months, you decide not to stay with Medicare Advantage, you have the right to switch back and get the same Medigap plan you had before.

Create Your Healthcare Cost Worksheet

Now that you understand a bit more about the different factors contributing to rising healthcare costs and how to manage them, it's time to create your healthcare cost worksheet.

Fill in the following to figure out what your current and future healthcare costs may be:

CURRENT EXPENSES

<u>Health Insurance</u>

Primary Insurance Premium: _____

Secondary Insurance Premium: _____

Annual deductibles (medical): _____

Out-of-Pocket Expenses

Co-pays for routine visits: _____

Co-pays for prescription drugs: _____

Non-covered medicines: _____

Non-covered dental care: _____

Non-covered vision care: _____

Non-covered hearing care: _____

Other non-covered medical care (e.g., specialists, experimental treatments, etc.):

_____

Total current expenses:

PREDICTED FUTURE EXPENSES

Chronic-condition-related care:

_____

Cost of long-term care (should I need it):

_____

Total predicted future expenses:

SAVINGS OPTIONS

Amount of medical expenses 100% covered by Medicare or other insurance: _____

Amount currently saved in Emergency Fund:

_____

Total Savings:

SUBTRACT Total Savings from (Current + Future Expenses). This is how much you must save to prepare for future healthcare costs.

Check savings from various insurance programs to see how this number changes.

Summary

Healthcare is expensive, especially if you are a senior citizen living in the United States. Costs rise every year and will continue to rise, and it's hard to cut back spending on these types of expenses since you need health care for your survival.

There are many reasons for health care to be as expensive as it is today. One of the biggest reasons is that people are living longer. This means there are more people in need of services; in addition, older people may need more healthcare than younger people. Older people often need more medical treatment for various diseases, including chronic conditions such as diabetes. However, they may also take greater advantage of preventative services, adding to the cost of healthcare.

Another reason for rising healthcare costs may be that government programs give people greater access to healthcare, which puts a bigger burden on the system. However, Americans pay far more for healthcare than countries that have a national healthcare system, so government programs can't fully explain this phenomenon. Indeed, the United States has poorer healthcare outcomes than many other countries despite far higher costs for healthcare. Greater utilization of services is only one factor contributing to the cost of healthcare; the bigger reasons are linked to the fact that today's population is larger than it has ever been before.

If you want to lower your healthcare costs, the best thing you can do for yourself is start an emergency fund. You can start this fund anytime during your life, but the sooner you begin, the better. The key to successful emergency savings is understanding what you can and cannot use the money for. It's important to keep it in the fund unless you have a true emergency, such as losing a job or your wages being reduced due to an extended hospital stay.

In addition to having an emergency fund with three to six months' worth of income inside, it's helpful to purchase the correct insurance. You may want to consider Medigap to cover services your Original Medicare does not cover. You need to check the plans carefully before signing up, as not all plans cover the same things. Conversely, you could choose to enroll in Medicare Advantage, which covers more services than Original Medicare. Remember that you cannot use Medical Advantage and Medigap at the same time. Finally, you should consider whether you want to invest in long-term care insurance. This insurance will cover your needs if you ever need a home health aide or to reside permanently in an assisted living or nursing home—some of the few things that Medicare does not cover.

Now that you have a clear understanding of your options for saving money on healthcare, let's look together at another important aspect of retirement planning: your government pension. Make sure to check out the next chapter when you're ready to learn about pensions!

The Golden Years - Understanding Your Government Pensions

Retirement is wonderful if you have two essentials: much to live on and much to live for.

Unknown Source

Throughout this book, we've been talking about retirement planning as your key to creating the life of your dreams. We've already talked about how to use Social Security and Medicare to help you achieve that ideal life. Now we're going to talk about government pensions.

What are Government Pensions?

Government pensions are retirement plans set up for all federal employees. If you worked for any branch of the federal government, no matter what your job was, you are entitled to benefits under the Federal Employee Retirement System (FERS).

FERS covers all federal employees, regardless of what branch you worked in. So, if you were a receptionist for a legislator, a federal prosecutor, or were on the White House staff, you're covered. However, it does not cover military personnel or non-federal employees. Public school teachers, for example, are considered government employees, but at the state or local level, so they would not receive FERS benefits.

There are three types of benefits via FERS: the Basic Benefit Plan; Social Security; and the Thrift Savings Plan. The Basic Benefit Plan is likely what you are thinking of when you consider the idea of a government pension. This plan is a "defined benefit plan," which means it offers you a set amount of income per month, based on how much you made while you were working. It is calculated using the length of time you were employed by a federal employer and your three highest years of earnings. The Basic Benefit Plan doesn't take into account things like overtime or bonuses; it just looks at your base salary for the three highest-paid years.

To calculate the pension amount, the agency multiplies the average salary (using the high-three data) by the years of service, then multiplies that by one percent. For example, if you worked for 25 years and your average salary was $65,000/year, your annual pension amount would equal 25 x $65,000 x .01, or $16,250/year. This would then be divided by 12 to give you a monthly pension payment of $1,354.17. If you are over the age of 62, and have been in service for, at least, 20 years, your multiplier rate is 1.1 percent instead of 1 percent. Using the example above, you would get $17,875 per year or $1,489.58 per month.

Although some government pension plans cancel out Social Security, FERS is not one of them. Federal employers pay Social Security tax on your earnings. Thus, you are entitled to the same Social Security retirement benefit as private employees.

The Thrift Savings Plan, or TSP, is similar to a 401k. Your employer automatically deposits one percent of each paycheck into your TSP and you can voluntarily contribute more than that. Contributions are tax-deferred. Unlike Social Security or your Basic Benefit Plan, your TSP is a "defined contribution plan." This means that you are required to make contributions to the plan, but it doesn't offer you a set amount each month. You will receive a list of potential investments when you set up your TSP and must choose where to invest your funds. The amount in your account at any given time depends on the investments you've made, and you can lose money if you are not careful.

There are various types of retirement benefits that you can take as a government employee. You can receive full retirement benefits if you are disabled; you can also take early retirement, beginning at age 57. You may also be entitled to benefits if you are laid off from your job.

To begin receiving benefits, you need to file an application with the Office of Personnel Management (OPM). It's best to apply about two months before retirement.

There are various types of government pensions. Social Security retirement benefits are a government pension. So are any funds you receive from your state or local government as a retirement benefit.

FERS pension eligibility requirements are similar as those for Social Security retirement benefits. However, federal employees become eligible for full retirement at 57, whereas you do not become eligible for any Social Security retirement benefits until your 62nd birthday, and are further not able to claim full retirement benefits unless you wait until you are 67. When we discuss FERS eligibility at age 57, we mean only that you are able to receive any money from the program. Your FERS benefits are the money you receive each month once your application is processed.

Managing Your Pension Among Other Income Sources

As a retiree, it's important to manage all your income appropriately so that you continue to pay your living expenses, save money for emergencies, and continue doing things you enjoy with whatever's left over. Managing your money, as a retiree, is not that different from managing it during your working years, but there are some special considerations.

There are several types of budgets you might want to consider:

- **The envelope method:** This type of budgeting requires you to create an envelope for each type of expense you anticipate. For example, you might have envelopes for rent, food, clothing, and so on. You then withdraw the amount of cash you have budgeted for each category and place it in the appropriate envelope. When the cash in an envelope is gone, you cannot spend any more in that category. This method is very tactile—you feel the money in your hand and see the amount in each envelope go down over the course of the month. However, it requires you to use cash for all purchases, which may not be feasible. For example, your landlord may not accept cash for rent payments. However, if a vendor who does not accept cash accepts cashier's checks or money orders, you could convert the requisite amount of cash to one of these instruments.
- **The zero-budget method:** While using this method, income and expenses must be perfectly balanced, meaning that after you complete your plan, you should have a balance of $0 that is not accounted for. If you find you have extra money after listing all your expenses, you must decide what to do with it. You can allocate it to a combination of savings, spending, and donations to charity, but you must

account for all money so that you don't mindlessly spend your surplus without forethought.
- **The ratio method:** This method requires you to allocate a certain percentage of your income to savings and a certain amount to discretionary spending, with the rest allocated for expenses. This method encourages you to "pay yourself first" by transferring money to your savings account and putting money aside for discretionary spending before you pay your bills. It's important to ensure that you leave enough money to cover your expenses if you use this method; you may have to adjust the percentage of your income that "you pay yourself" to ensure your bills are paid.

Whatever budget method you use, you should strive to save three to six months' worth of income in your emergency savings fund, so that you have enough to keep you afloat should you experience a major hit to your finances, such as the loss of a job.

Once you have sufficient money saved, it's a good idea to pay off any debts you still owe, such as student loans or balances on your credit cards. Paying back debt often takes significant time, but it can free up money in the long run. If you can afford to do so, you should pay more than the minimum required payment so that you can pay off your debt sooner and pay less in interest. This is especially important for retirees. Not only will you have more disposable income if you pay off your debt, but you will also protect your heirs—your estate's debts must be paid before any inheritances can be distributed from what is left over.

Some people also invest excess money once they are debt-free and have a secure financial foundation. If you have a 401k, you are already making choices about how to invest your savings; in addition, if you learn how to invest wisely or hire a financial planner to help you, you might be able to create a nest egg for your children and grandchildren.

Retirees can also employ some of the following special strategies to manage their finances:

- **Delay claiming your Social Security benefits for as long as possible.** The longer you wait, the more money you will receive each month after you begin collecting.
- **Create a separate account for your healthcare costs.** You may have greater healthcare needs as you get older, and Medicare won't cover everything. Saving money in a separate account for healthcare can help defray the costs. You might also want to consider enrolling in a medical savings account.
- **Analyze your home equity.** Knowing how much equity you have in your home can help you plan your finances. If needed, you can take a loan out against your home equity line of credit (but make sure you pay it back in a timely manner!).
- **Consider downsizing.** If you own your home outright, selling it and moving to a smaller place might be a wise financial move. Many older people purchase a condo or move to a rental unit, especially if your partner has passed away and your kids no longer live with you. If you don't need so much space, downsizing may make both emotional and financial sense.

Meet George

George has served his country his entire adult life. After 15 years of exemplary service to the military, he shifted gears and got a job in the public sector so that he could continue to be of service as a civilian. He remained at his job for over three decades, retiring at the age of 63.

Once George retired, he felt lost and confused for the first time in his life. He knew he was entitled to two pensions from his two careers, but he wasn't sure how to get the maximum benefit or how to begin receiving them. He also had begun contributing to a Roth IRA when he was in the military and had some investment income.

Working with a financial advisor helped George figure it all out. His financial planner examined his pensions and explained how they were calculated, and how and when to request to receive them. He learned that it made financial sense to request his military pension immediately, as the amount wouldn't change if he deferred reception, but that he should delay getting his civilian pension to receive larger benefits later, and that he could use his retirement savings and investment income to help him pay his bills in the meantime.

By being willing to ask for help, learning about his different income sources, and creating a concrete plan, George has ensured the best financial outcome possible for his retirement.

Pension Checklist

Here's what you need to do to maximize your pension benefits. Check off each item as it is completed.

- Learn what pensions you may be entitled to. You may be able to get this information online, by speaking to someone who works in the appropriate department, or by speaking to your financial planner.

- Learn the benefit amounts you are entitled to, and whether any benefits will grow larger over time so that you can decide when to claim your pension.
- Before applying for a pension, gather all necessary documents, such as your birth certificate, documentation of who is in your family, proof of years of service, proof of any name change, any certificates of death or divorce (needed to prove you are no longer living with the partner you were with at your time of service), and any required endorsements or recommendations. You may need to get certified copies of some documents if they must be attached to your application form or if you don't have the originals.
- Fill out your application for pension and attach copies of necessary documents.
- Communicate, as needed, with the department handling your pension to make sure your application is processed correctly and you get the correct amount owed to you each month.

Summary

If you are a current or former federal employee, you must have a solid understanding of government pensions.

Federal employees are entitled to a government pension (except for military personnel, who receive pensions under their own system). This pension supplements your Social Security retirement benefit; it does not replace it. Thus, you need to understand the different rules governing government and Social Security retirement benefits. For instance, it's possible to retire from government service at an earlier age than when you become eligible to receive Social Security benefits. If you are a state employee, such as a public-school teacher, you will receive a state pension, which may be governed by different rules from federal pensions.

In any case, it's important to understand when you become eligible for a pension and how your benefits are calculated. You also need to manage your retirement income, including pensions, so that you can save money for emergencies, pay off any debt you owe, and have money available for the type of experiences you want to have during your retirement.

To drive the point home, consider the anecdote about George, the military and civil servant described in this chapter. George was confused about his pension benefits prior to speaking to a financial planner; his willingness to seek help and be proactive about managing his retirement income allowed him to develop a plan, thus maximizing his benefits.

The checklist at the end of the chapter is designed to help you get ready to claim your pension. Government pensions are only one part of retirement planning. In the next chapter, we will go into more detail about how to plan your finances before and during retirement.

9

Securing Your Retirement - Building a Financial Fortress

Nearly 46% of retirees leave the workplace earlier than planned because of some illness or job loss (Employment Benefit Research Institute, 2023). The COVID pandemic accelerated this problem; many people lost their jobs or chose not to return to them because of fear of illness, which made their lives more difficult because they didn't have the financial security they needed.

Don't let something similar happen to you. You never know when something might happen that leaves you jobless. But if you've planned for retirement correctly, you'll have money in your emergency fund and retirement savings account to tide you over until you put the rest of your plan into place.

In this chapter, we'll talk about all the components of retirement planning and how to ensure that you have the financial stability to retire even if unexpected events throw a monkey wrench into your plans.

What Is Retirement Planning?

Don't let the words scare you. Retirement planning simply means deciding how you will support yourself and your family financially after you retire, and how you will ensure you have enough money to retire comfortably.

Retirement planning often includes things like:

- How long you will continue working—you may need to work until you are 67 or older to ensure you maximize your Social Security benefits and put enough money in your retirement account to be able to afford your post-retirement goals.
- Deciding when to claim Social Security retirement benefits and other pensions. In earlier chapters, we discussed the benefits of delaying your claims; remember, each individual or family's circumstances are different, so you'll need to make the choice that is right for you.
- Understanding what sources of income will be available to you post-retirement and planning your finances accordingly.
- Seeing what expenses you will have after retirement and deciding whether to cut back on some of them.
- Planning for how to cover current and anticipated healthcare costs.
- Determining whether your retirement goals are feasible and what you need to do to reach them.
- Saving money while you are still working so that you will have it when you retire.

The earlier you can begin retirement planning, the better. Retirement savings grow over time if you or your financial planner make good investments, so if you start early, you'll build a bigger nest egg than if you wait until later. However, it's never too late! Even if you are near your retirement age, it's better to start saving now than to not do it at all. Retirement planning might not sound like much fun, but you'll be glad you did it after you retire and are able to enjoy yourself... thanks to your careful planning.

Steps to Consider

Everyone's retirement plan looks slightly different. But in general, there are a few steps you want to consider. However, before you create any other plan, decide how much money you will need for your retirement. This will give you a savings goal to work toward as well as help you understand what it'll take to make your dream a reality.

Think about the various things you want to do and find out how much they cost on average. Don't forget to consider your living expenses, too—you'll still need to be able to pay for food, shelter, and transportation after you retire. You may want to budget a little more for these than you currently pay to take possible inflation into account. If this is too overwhelming, you can also use a formula to help you decide how much to save. Many people set a goal of putting 12 years of pre-retirement income away; others like the idea of their expenses adding up to no more than four percent of their retirement savings each year (Investopedia, 2023).

Depending on your life circumstances, you might need to consider certain factors when thinking about how much money you need to save:

- **Do you have children or grandchildren, or are you expecting some in the future?** New generations come with extra expenses. If you have adult children who are planning their own families, keep in mind that you may want to give gifts to your future grandchildren or pay for things for them that their parents couldn't ordinarily afford. These extra expenses will affect how much you need to save for your retirement.
- **What are your plans for retirement?** If you want to travel, you'll have different expenses than someone who wants to stay at home. If you're planning on selling your house and moving into a retirement community, consider how that will affect your finances.
- **Do you have your family nearby?** If you have no ties to your local community, you might consider moving to a cheaper city or even to another country with a lower cost of living.
- **What taxes will you have to pay?** Talk with your accountant or financial planner to find out the tax consequences of withdrawing money from your retirement accounts.

Once you understand your expenses and financial needs, the next step is to understand your "time horizon." In other words, how much time do you have to save this money? If you have 30 years before you reach retirement age, you can save at a slower pace than someone who first starts saving at the age of 60.

In addition, if you have lots of time. you can afford to take bigger risks with your retirement savings. Most retirement accounts, such as IRAs or 401(k)s, grow your money by investing it in stocks, bonds, or mutual funds. You decide which vehicles to invest your funds in; if you have lots of time to save, you might choose higher-risk investments with possibly higher returns than if you'll need the money fairly soon, as you will have time to recoup your losses. You'll also want to consider inflation and ensure your returns outpace it. The closer to retirement you are, the more secure your investments should be. You'll need the money soon, so focus on keeping as much of it as possible and on stable investments, such as bonds, that may grow at a slower rate, but guarantee excellent returns.

Don't assume your expenses will be less when you retire. That's often not the case—you can't anticipate healthcare costs, expenses related to grandchildren who have not yet been born, or changes to the economy, after you retire. Make sure you budget with the idea that your expenses will be comparable to what you are spending now, if not higher. In addition, consider your potential longevity. Your health and the age your parents lived to can help you predict how long you are likely to live. This is important because someone who expects to live into their 90s, or beyond, will need their retirement savings for far longer than someone with a life expectancy of 75 or 80.

Estate Planning Is Also Important

In addition to planning your post-retirement life, you'll need to make some decisions about what you want to happen to your assets after your death. You'll need the help of a lawyer for estate planning. Your lawyer can draft a will and advise you as to the tax implications of various types of bequeathments. That way, you can ensure that you leave your heirs with extra money and not a big tax burden.

You'll also want to consider life insurance as part of your estate planning. Life insurance will provide your beneficiaries with some money after your death, which will help with funeral costs.

Key Factors in Retirement Planning

There are four key factors you must consider in your retirement planning.

- **Inflation:** It is important to consider inflation because it can seriously damage your retirement savings' ability to cover your expenses. A three percent inflation rate might not seem like much, but $100 today will only be worth $34.44 after 30 years! To counteract this, ensure your retirement vehicles offer a growth rate that outpaces inflation.
- **Taxes:** Taxes can be complicated when it comes to retirement. You may have to pay taxes on withdrawals from retirement savings, and if your Social Security benefits cause you to take in more than $25,000/year ($32,000 for married couples filing jointly), you will have to pay taxes on those benefits as well. There are also tax considerations in play when saving for retirement. For example, contributions to your retirement income are tax-deferred, which means that you don't pay payroll taxes on them, but they also can't be used, which may leave you with less money in your paycheck.
- **Compound interest:** It is something that helps your money grow. A thorough understanding of how it works will help you realize how much money you will have at retirement, if you put money away in various types of savings now. Compound interest is interest on both the principal (your current balance) and prior contributions. Thus, the more consistently you deposit money in retirement savings, the more interest you will earn on your savings.
- **Personal savings:** They should be part of your retirement plan, too. Social Security retirement benefits aren't meant to cover all your expenses, so you'll need to have other

sources of income during your retirement. And if you live a lot longer than expected, or discover you didn't save enough for your retirement, you might need to depend on personal savings to make up the difference. Make sure that you are saving regularly while working so that you'll have sufficient personal savings at and after retirement.

Top Ways to Prepare

If all this information about what you need to do feels overwhelming, take a deep breath. There are some steps you can take right now to ensure a successful retirement:

- **Start saving ASAP:** Ideally, you should save three to six months of income in your emergency savings so that if you're laid off or suffer some other financial crisis before your retirement, you have the money to cover for it. Keep saving every paycheck even after you reach this goal.
- **Figure out what your financial needs will be during retirement:** Make your retirement budget and set some savings goals for your personal and retirement accounts.
- **Contribute to the savings plan set up by your employer:** Begin making regular contributions to the 401(k) or other plan offered by your job. In many cases, your employer will match contributions, so you can save twice as much for retirement if you arrange for a portion of your paycheck to be saved each pay period.
- **Talk to your employer about options:** If your employer doesn't currently offer a retirement savings plan, approach them about the possibility of starting one. Similarly, if your employer doesn't match your contributions, discuss the issue with them and see if it can be changed.

- **Save money in an individual retirement account (IRA):** In addition to your employer plan, put some money away for retirement in an IRA to increase your nest egg. There are different types of IRAs available with different rules, so be sure to talk to your financial advisor before opening an account.
- **Find out what kind of pension you'll be entitled to upon retirement:** Talk to your HR department or look online to read about pensions. It's helpful to know the eligibility requirements and whether there is any benefit to delaying your request to begin getting a pension after you retire from your job. Estimate the benefits you'll get from your pension so that you can include them in your retirement plan.
- **Learn how to invest wisely:** Study investment basics and learn about risks and returns, how to choose investments, and the different investment vehicles available. Understanding this can help you invest your retirement savings wisely. In addition, if you have enough extra income, consider investing some of it to increase the amount of money available to you in retirement.
- **Leave your retirement savings alone until after you reach retirement age:** Not only are there penalties for early withdrawal, but the money won't be there when you need it if you withdraw it now! Find some other ways to handle emergencies, such as using emergency savings, taking out a bank loan, or using credit cards with low interest rates. If you find you are regularly scrambling for money, examine your budget closely and cut expenses so that your retirement savings can stay where they belong until you retire.

- **Ask questions:** Hire a financial planner to assist you with your retirement planning—but don't sit back and let them do everything. Ask questions to ensure you understand your options and the reason behind the planner's advice before consenting to their plan.

Balancing Various Sources of Retirement Income

A key part of your retirement planning is understanding how the various sources of retirement income work together.

After retirement, you may have many sources of income:

- Social Security retirement benefits
- State or federal pension if you worked a government job
- Military pension, if you served
- Private pension from any private employer
- Withdrawals from retirement accounts
- Paychecks from any jobs you take post-retirement

It can be confusing to figure out how much money you're getting, what money comes when, and how much to take from your retirement savings. The best way to balance these things is to use the tips in the above section to prepare for retirement. Specifically, you need to understand how much you will get from Social Security, which varies depending on when you choose to take it; how much you will get from any public or private pension; and how much you plan to withdraw from retirement savings each month.

This is where hiring a financial planner comes in handy. Choose someone who understands retirement planning and who will work with you to set and achieve financial goals for your retirement. Your financial planner can help guide your savings and investment strategy while you are still working, go over options for when to claim pensions and other retirement benefits so that you get the maximum benefits due, and help you create a withdrawal strategy for your retirement savings that will allow them to last as long as possible.

Remember George, the hypothetical retiree we met in Chapter 7? Let's look together at how he approaches his retirement planning to help you understand the process better.

- George learned he was entitled to a military pension. With the help of his financial planner, he discovered that he was entitled to 2.5% of his final monthly pay for every year of service. Since he served for 15 years, he is entitled to 37.5% of his final monthly pay (to calculate this, he multiplied 2.5 X 15). He also learned that there was no advantage to delaying his claim for these benefits, and took them as soon as he retired.
- George was also entitled to a civil pension for his job in the public sector, which he worked at for 30 years. Since this pension is calculated based on the average of his three highest annual salaries, he remained with this job longer than originally planned to maximize his benefits, while simultaneously getting his military pension. He was also careful to take as few sick days as possible during his final three years of work, as unused sick leave is added to the pension calculation.
- George asked his financial planner if he was allowed to take both pensions at the same time. He learned that he was, but there was a caveat: he could not get two pensions for the same year. In other words, he could not ask for his years of military service to be counted toward his federal

pension amount unless he waived his right to his military service pension. After going over his options, George decided the best thing to do was ask the federal government not to count his military service when calculating his federal pension. That way, he could draw both pensions, which would give him more money per month than if he rolled them both into his FERS pension.
- Next, George had to decide what to do with his Social Security benefits. George's wife had passed away, so he was entitled to survivor benefits, which he would have to give up to claim his retirement benefits. He was still in good health and able to work when he turned 62, so he decided to continue getting his survivor benefits and delay getting his retirement benefits until later in order to get more of his retirement benefits. He re-evaluated at age 67. He could have delayed his benefits until age 70 to get the maximum amount, but he was beginning to get fatigued and had recently been diagnosed with diabetes, so he decided to retire from his job. However, he had rental income from some real estate investments coming in as well as his pensions, so he did not need to take his Social Security benefit until age 70, which gave him the maximum benefit.
- George had retirement savings from both a 401(k) and Roth IRA, and discussed with his financial planner how best to use these savings, taking into account that he was likely to live into his late 80s, based on his health and his family history. He also had a year's worth of income saved in his emergency savings as a backup. He also had a life insurance policy that he had purchased when he was in the military.
- After he turned 65, George enrolled in Medicare Part A, but kept his VA insurance for other types of medical treatment.

However, after his diabetes diagnosis at age 67, he examined his options and decided that Medicare Advantage gave him the best coverage for his healthcare needs and switched his Medicare insurance to that program.
- George's grandson was born soon after his retirement, so George consulted his attorney about updating his will to ensure his grandson would be provided for after his death.

Retirement Bucket Strategy

One popular strategy for retirement planning is the bucket strategy. This is an investment strategy that takes all of your needs into account by considering:

- immediate cash needs
- intermediate needs (e.g., you'll need the money in the near future)
- long-term needs, such as saving for retirement years in the future

The idea behind this strategy is to help you create long-term investments with your retirement funds that you need by also attending to your immediate and short-term needs, so that you don't have to quickly sell off investments to gain cash.

To use this strategy, you'll need to invest in a variety of instruments. You can use certificates of deposit, high-yield savings accounts, and Treasury bonds; these are all liquid investments that can easily be converted to cash. You'll want two years' worth of income to be tied up in these types of investments so that you can have peace of mind that your immediate needs will always be covered. For example, if you need to pay $50,000/year in expenses after retirement, you should have $100,000 worth of investments in this bucket.

Your intermediate bucket should give you access to funds to cover years 3 through 10 of retirement. You'll also want some long-term investment vehicles such as preferred stock options, longer-term bonds, and utility stocks. Finally, your long-term investments should include riskier assets that may lose money in the short term and gain it in the longer term.

If you are not well-versed in different types of investments, your financial planner can help you understand your options and create a portfolio that includes all three buckets. One type of investment you might want to consider is a Treasury Inflation-Protected Security bond (TIPS). This bond is protected against inflation, which means that the value of the bond rises when inflation occurs. This ensures that the bonds are worth the same amount when cashed in as they would be if inflation rates had not made money worth less over time. For example, if inflation causes a dollar in 2023 to be worth only 70 cents, TIPS bonds will rise in value to account for the change.

Staying Informed About Policy Changes

It's important to stay up-to-date about policies related to your Social Security retirement benefits and other types of retirement planning. Having the most up-to-date information can help ensure that you don't miss new deadlines and maximize your benefits.

One of the most important laws you should be aware of is the "Employee Retirement Income Security Act" (ERISA). First passed in 1974, this Act governs private employee retirement plans, spelling out eligibility requirements, protecting you against some losses, and requiring employers who offer retirement plans to fund them.

As of 2023, ERISA does not require any employer to provide a private retirement plan (Findlaw, 2020). However, it does require employers who do choose to offer such a plan to follow some guidelines. For example, employers who offer retirement plans must regularly provide employees with information about the plan, such as features and funding methods. It is not required to make all such information free of charge. Employers must also provide a minimum level of funding and have clear rules for how long an employee must work to become eligible for benefits after they retire. Fiduciaries are held accountable for some losses to retirement accounts under ERISA, and employees may sue if they don't receive the benefits they are entitled to.

ERISA applies to any retirement plan established after 1975.

There are several types of plans employers may provide under ERISA:

- **Defined benefit plans:** They provide you with a set monthly sum after retirement. For example, a plan that gives retirees $1000/month, or one that gives them five percent of their last year's salary each month, upon retirement would be a defined benefit plan.
- **Defined contribution plans:** These provide you with the balance in your account upon retirement. These types of plans often involve investing retirement funds, so it's possible you'll lose money if your investments don't pay off. 401k plans and profit-sharing plans are both defined contribution plans.

- **Money purchase plan:** It requires your employer to contribute a fixed amount to your individual account each year.
- **Simplified employee pension (SEP):** It is a type of employee pension plan that requires you to set up an Individual Retirement Account (IRA) and your employer to contribute regularly to it. Your employer contributes the lesser of 25% of your pay or $40,000 each year.
- **SIMPLE IRAs:** They are employer-matched contribution plans. Under these plans, employers match your contributions to your IRA. SIMPLE IRAs are for businesses that have less than 100 employees but make more than $5,000. This plan is meant to make retirement plans affordable for small businesses; employees can contribute up to $15,500 in 2023, while employers match contributions up to three percent of the employee's salary. Employers cannot offer a SIMPLE IRA if they sponsor other retirement plans.
- **Profit-sharing plans:** Also known as "stock bonus plans," they are defined contribution plans where each participant gets a certain percentage of the entire contribution to the plan. For example, if employees collectively contribute $5,000 to the plan, each employee will get a small percentage of that contribution.
- **401k plans:** They are defined contribution plans in which you put away pre-tax dollars from each paycheck, which are then invested according to your directions. The money must stay in the account until you reach retirement age or separate from the employer (although some 401k plans are portable and can be transferred to a new employer). If you need the money before retirement, you can take a loan out against your 401k balance. In some cases, you may be able to withdraw funds in case of hardship, but remember: if

you do that, you won't have them available when you retire.
- **Employee stock ownership plans (ESOPs):** They are defined contribution plans where the investments are primarily in employer stock. These types of plans are meant to encourage employees to own stock in the companies they work for.

The federal government oversees all of these plans; however, some types of employment are exempt from ERISA. Specifically, federal or state government jobs, jobs in churches or other houses of worship, and plans meant specifically to cover disability, unemployment, or workers' compensation are exempt. In addition, ERISA does not cover plans based in foreign countries for non-residents of the United States or unfunded excess benefit plans.

The Labor Department oversees eligible private pension plans, while the IRS ensures these plans are run in accordance with tax laws. The Pension Benefit Guaranty Corporation (PBGC), on the other hand, guarantees pension benefits if a defined benefit plan is terminated due to a lack of sufficient funds to pay retirees (Findlaw, 2023).

Make Your Budget

To put what you've learned into action, make your first retirement budget. Use your favorite spreadsheet. On one side, record each planned type of retirement income, estimating how much per month you'll get:

- pensions
- Social Security retirement
- retirement savings

- other sources of income
- Use the spreadsheet to total your income.

Next, list all your expected expenses. Don't forget to consider things that may not have happened yet, such as new grandchildren or health issues that may arise later in life. Add up your expenses and have the spreadsheet also calculate your expenses minus your retirement income to see how much is left over.

Play around with the numbers, focusing especially on changing how much you have available per month from your retirement savings, and see how it makes your budget change. This will help you see what, and how, you need to save to achieve your financial goals.

Summary

Retirement planning can be complicated, but it's very important. You need to know how much money you'll need to support your planned lifestyle after retirement, how much time you have to save for retirement, and what your options are for collecting retirement benefits and pensions once you retire. You also should consider estate planning, including making out your will and deciding what type of life insurance you need. Paying down debts will also aid in your estate planning, as you don't want your loved ones burdened with a lot of debt after you die.

It can be helpful to consult a financial planner to help you see how various aspects of your retirement plan can come together to create stable finances. For example, your financial planner can help you understand when the best time to take each of your pensions and your Social Security retirement is, how much you need to save for retirement, and how much to withdraw from retirement accounts each month after you retire. Finally, you will want to learn about investing and place retirement funds in various types of investments so that you have short-, medium-, and long-term investments to cover you during retirement.

Now with the hard part out of the way, we're almost done! In the next chapter, we'll explore how to implement your plan.

10

From Planning to Action - Putting Your Retirement Plan Into Motion

Don't simply retire from something. Have something to retire to.

Harry Emerson Fosdick

Throughout this book, we've discussed the importance of retirement planning. Now, we're almost at the finish line—it's time to discuss putting our plan into action!

Applying for Social Security and Medicare

In order to get the benefits, you are entitled to, you must first apply for them. The application process can be confusing; so, here's what you need to know.

There are three ways to apply for Social Security and Medicare:

- Online
- Calling the national toll-free number: 1-800-772-1213 (TTY 1-800-325-0778)
- Visiting your local Social Security office

Before you apply, gather all the documents and information you will need:

- Documents about yourself and your family
- Your Social Security Number
- Any other Social Security number that you've used in the past
- Your date and place of birth
- Your citizenship status
- Whether you or anyone else has filed for Social Security on your behalf. If so, you'll need the Social Security number and name of the person who applied and the date of application
- The names and Social Security numbers of any spouses, including former or deceased spouses (if relevant, you'll also need their death certificate or your divorce decree)
- The names of any unmarried children under the age of 18, children between the ages of 18 and 19 who are still in secondary school, and children of any age who became disabled before the age of 22
- Certified copy of your birth certificate
- Bank or other financial institution's routing and accounting numbers
- The month you want retirement benefits to begin from, if you are applying for them

- Whether you want to enroll in Medicare Part B (only if you are within three months from turning 65)

Employment Documents

- The name and address of your employers for the last two years
- Your earnings for the last two years (if you apply between September and December, you will also need to provide an estimate of your next year's earnings)
- A copy of your Social Security statement (you can get this online)
- Beginning and end dates for active military service before 1968
- Information about whether, and when, you became unable to work due to illness or injury during the past 14 months
- Whether you or your spouse has ever worked for the railroad industry
- Whether you have earned any Social Security credits under a foreign country's system
- Whether you expect to earn a federal or state pension
- Photocopies of your W-2s or self-employment tax return

If you mail documents to the Social Security Administration, attach a cover letter with your Social Security number so that the SSA can more easily match the documents with your application. Your application for Social Security also entitles you to Medicare Part A; if you qualify for both, you will receive both. You need to separately apply for Medicare Part B through the Social Security office if you want to get this coverage.

If you are younger than 65 and have ESRD, you can apply for Medicare via telephone by calling **1-800-772-1213** (TTY **1-800-325-0778**).

If you are applying for a government pension, this requires a separate application. Obtain the application through your employer or union about six months before you intend to start collecting it. You will need most of the same documents you need for Social Security to apply for a government pension.

Seeking Professional Advice

Throughout the book, we've discussed the possibility of getting help from a financial advisor or planner. It's important to ensure you get the right advisor if you go this route; a financial planner or advisor who isn't familiar with retirement accounts and related issues might steer you in the wrong direction.

Retirement financial advisors help you plan and manage your finances both before and after retirement, but their main objective is to assist you with meeting your retirement goals. Your retirement financial advisor might be a certified public accountant, certified financial planner, or investment manager.

Retirement planners assist you in several ways, including:

- developing a budget and plan to save
- estate planning, including plans for long-term care (should it become necessary)
- investing money to increase your retirement portfolio
- minimizing tax liability

It's not mandatory to use a retirement planner, and many people don't. For some people, the cost can be prohibitive; others dislike the feeling of loss of control or being dependent on their financial advisor. However, using a financial planner can give you peace of mind or a place to turn to if you have any questions or concerns about your retirement plans.

It's important to ask questions and to work in partnership with your financial planner rather than allowing them to call all the shots. Remember: it's your money, and you are the one who will have to deal with the consequences if your planner makes poor investments or steers you in the wrong direction. Some financial advisors may try to sell you products or services they get commissions on, and it might not be in your best interest to buy these. Paying attention and asking relevant questions can help you avoid making mistakes when dealing with a financial planner.

Tips for Keeping Track of Your Pension

The most important thing you can do for yourself is keep records of how much your pension is supposed to be, and how much you get paid each month. That way, if there are any questions or discrepancies, you will have the documentation you need to get them resolved. You should also keep all your W-2s and paystubs (in case there are any questions).

Make sure you keep any information you are given about the rules of the plan so that you understand how much you need to contribute, how long you have to work, and what benefits you can expect to receive. Keep any benefits statements you get, and make sure to ask your plan administrator any questions that you may have. It's especially important to understand the rules governing the reduction of benefits.

Ask your plan manager for the plan's annual reports as well as look at its Form 5500 to see its current status. This will allow you to understand how the plan is funded and what the funding looks like. Find out whether you are entitled to "cost of living increases" in your benefits. Many plans do not offer this, which could significantly impact the funds you have available after retirement. Finally, you should ensure any former employers have your current contact information, in case they need to send the benefits to you or your beneficiaries.

What if My Plan Is Terminated?

If your plan is terminated, you will receive a notice 60 days in advance. You will need to find out whether a private insurance company or the PBGC is handling payouts to beneficiaries, as this will affect what you are able to get, and you will need to know who to contact with questions or concerns.

If your 401k is terminated, you will receive all benefits you are owed. If, for some reason, you don't, you can check with PBGC to see if they have any information. You can also look into whether your state is holding any unclaimed funds for you.

Action Plan Worksheet

Let's plan your retirement together! Complete this worksheet.

- List total expenses after retirement: _____
- List sources of expected income: _____
- What date will I apply for Social Security and Medicare?
- What date will I apply for my pension(s)?
- What documents am I missing that I need?
- What information do I need about my private pension?

Summary

Now that you know all about Social Security, Medicare, and pensions, it's time to plan your retirement. It's important to make sure you have all of your documentation available so that you can apply for Social Security and Medicare whenever you are ready. You will need information about yourself, your spouse, any former spouses, and your children, as well as information about your most recent work history and earnings. You will also need your statement of benefits from the Social Security office. Be sure to apply for Medicare Part B and D (or Medicare Part C) if you want the coverage, as it is not automatic. Medicare Part A may be.

You'll also want information about any private pensions or retirement plans you have participated in, especially about the type of plan you're enrolled in, how much you need to contribute, and what benefits you can expect. Most private pensions are covered under ERISA, and your employer is required to provide you with information about your eligibility and benefits.

Once you begin getting your pension, you should keep good records so that you can address it promptly if there is any type of discrepancy. If your pension is terminated by the pension holder, you have the right to benefits. Find out who is managing the benefit process after termination so that you know who to contact. If your 401k is terminated, you should immediately receive all of your benefits; if, for some reason, you don't, you'll have to contact the PBGC or the Labor Department to find out what happened to them.

You've come a long way! When you opened this book, you might have been confused or overwhelmed about retirement planning. Now you have a solid understanding of Social Security, Medicare, and pensions, and are equipped to plan the retirement of your dreams. The things we've talked about in this book aren't just theoretical; they're facts and ideas that light your path forward so that you can confidently move toward a financially independent and fulfilling retirement. Let's take a moment to reflect on the journey we've taken together.

Turn the page for some concluding thoughts.

Conclusion

As you've learned throughout this book, retirement planning can be exciting when you know what you're doing.

The federal government wants everyone to have the same chance at a fulfilling retirement. Programs like Social Security and Medicare exist to ensure that you can live comfortably after you retire, and don't have to work longer than what is healthy for you. But these programs aren't automatic; you have to apply for them. Now that you've learned about the different options available to you, you can make a plan to do that, ensuring that you take full advantage of everything the government has to offer its retirees.

We've also discussed other aspects of your retirement planning, such as public and private pensions, and offered alternative Social Security programs for people who are not yet ready to retire but may have special needs. If you are a widow, divorcee, disabled person, or spouse who does not work outside the home, hopefully, you now understand all the benefits available to you.

Conclusion

Retirement planning involves a lot of moving parts, but you don't have to be overwhelmed while doing it. No matter how young or old you are, it's never too late to start creating the retirement plan that will give you the life you deserve. But don't stop there, though. Make sure you stay up-to-date on policies and programs that can help you and your family during this stage of your life. Subscribe to reputable retirement planning publications, talk with your financial advisor, and join retirement planning forums online so that you're always connected to the latest trends and won't be blindsided by economic surprises.

If you found this book helpful, please leave a review so that other people who are searching for answers to their questions about retirement can benefit from it, too.

Congratulations on your successful retirement!

References

7 things to know about long-term care insurance. (2022, March 29). US Bank. https://www.usbank.com/financialiq/plan-your-future/health-and-wellness/costs-and-benefits-of-long-term-care-insurance.html

AARP. (2022, December 20). *How are Social Security disability benefits calculated?* https://www.aarp.org/retirement/social-security/info-2021/ssdi-benefit-calculation.html

Addressing healthcare costs of an aging population through digital transformation. (2023, June 16). Wolters Kluwer. https://www.wolterskluwer.com/en/expert-insights/addressing-healthcare-costs-of-an-aging-population-through-digital-transformation

Anderson, S. (2019, September 1). *A brief history of Medicare in America.* Medicare Resources. https://www.medicareresources.org/basic-medicare-information/brief-history-of-medicare/

Ball, R. M. (2020, October 13). *The nine guiding principles of social security: Where they came from, what they accomplish.* Social Security Works. https://socialsecurityworks.org/2020/10/13/nine-guiding-principles-of-social-security/

Fontinelle, A. (2023, February 19). *When to take Social Security: An overview.* Investopedia. https://www.investopedia.com/retirement/when-take-social-security-complete-guide/

Fonville, M. (2020, February 2). *9 reasons why retirement planning is important.* Covenant. https://www.covenantwealthadvisors.com/post/9-reasons-why-retirement-planning-is-important#:~:text=Retirement%20planning%20is%20important%20because

Chen, J. (2023, April 24). *Treasury Inflation-Protected Securities (TIPS) explained.* Investopedia. https://www.investopedia.com/terms/t/tips.asp#:~:text=Key%20Takeaways-

Daugherty, G. (2021, April 6). Early retirement: *The pros and (mostly) cons.* Investopedia. https://www.investopedia.com/articles/personal-finance/073114/pros-and-mostly-cons-early-retirement.asp#:~:text=Pros%20of%20retiring%20early%20include

Department of Labor. (2019). *Top 10 ways to prepare for retirement.* https://www.dol.gov/sites/dolgov/files/ebsa/about-ebsa/our-activities/resource-center/publications/top-10-ways-to-prepare-for-retirement.pdf

Dushi, I., Iams, H. M., & Trenkamp, B. (2017). The importance of Social Security benefits to the income of the aged population. *Social Security Bulletin, 77*(2), 1-12. https://www.ssa.gov/policy/docs/ssb/v77n2/v77n2p1.html

FindLaw. (2020, December 17). *Your retirement plan: What you should know.* https://www.findlaw.com/employment/wages-and-benefits/your-retirement-plan-what-you-should-know.html

Gigante, S. (2022, June 22). *Social Security filing strategies for the widowed.* MassMutual. https://blog.massmutual.com/retiring-investing/what-the-widowed-should-consider-when-filing-for-social-security

Hager, T. (2023, February 8). *Claiming Social Security benefits - early or late?* Forbes. https://www.forbes.com/sites/tomhager/2022/02/08/claiming-social-security-benefitsearly-or-late/?sh=33bf4642a984

Hayes, A. (2022, March 28). *Benefit-cost ratio (BCR): Definition, formula, and example.* Investopedia. https://www.investopedia.com/terms/b/bcr.asp

Huffman, L. (2023, January 13). *What is the retirement bucket strategy?* Smart Asset. https://smartasset.com/retirement/retirement-bucket-strategy

Investopedia. (2022, November 2). *How are Social Security benefits affected by your income?* https://www.investopedia.com/ask/answers/102714/how-are-social-security-benefits-affected-your-income.asp

Investopedia. (2023). *Pension plan definition.* https://www.investopedia.com/terms/p/pensionplan.asp

John Hancock. (n.d.). *Social Security's role in retirement planning.* https://www.johnhancock.com/ideas-insights/factoring-social-security-into-retirement-planning.html

Kagan, J. (2021, November 18). *5 key retirement planning steps to take.* Investopedia. https://www.investopedia.com/articles/retirement/11/5-steps-to-retirement-plan.asp

Kagan, J. (2022, March 25). *Employee retirement income security act (ERISA), history, purpose.* Investopedia. https://www.investopedia.com/terms/e/erisa.asp

Kagan, J. (2023, January 9). *What is retirement planning? Steps, stages, and what to consider.* Investopedia. https://www.investopedia.com/terms/r/retirement-planning.asp#:~:text=Retirement%20planning%20includes%20identifying%20income

Kagan, J. (2022, October 13). *What are Social Security benefits? Definition, types, and history.* Investopedia. https://www.investopedia.com/terms/s/social-security-benefits.asp

Key factors in retirement planning. (2023). Richwood Investment Advisors. https://www.richwoodia.com/key-factors-in-retirement-planning

Konish, L. (2022, November 1). *This social security quiz can help test how much you know about benefits before you claim.* CNBC. https://www.cnbc.com/2022/11/01/social-security-quiz-tests-how-much-you-know-about-benefits.html

Konish, L. (2023, February 1). *Wait until age 70 to claim Social Security: The return on being patient is huge, says economist.* CNBC. https://www.cnbc.com/2023/02/01/why-it-pays-to-wait-to-claim-social-security-retirement-benefits.html

Kurt, D. (2022, February 9). *Emergency fund.* Investopedia. https://www.investopedia.com/terms/e/emergency_fund.asp#:~:text=You%20establish%20an%20emergency%20fund

Learn how Medigap works. (n.d.). Medicare.Gov. https://www.medicare.gov/health-drug-plans/medigap/basics/how-medigap-works#:~:text=Medigap%20%26%20Medicare%20Advantage%20Plans

Lockett, E. (2021, January 15). *What are the advantages and disadvantages of Medicare Advantage plans?* Healthline. https://www.healthline.com/health/medicare/what-are-the-advantages-and-disadvantages-of-medicare-advantage-plans

Married couples have Social Security options. (n.d.). Vanguard. https://investor.vanguard.com/investor-resources-education/social-security/strategies-for-married-couples

McKenna, J. (2021, July 26). *Medicare Parts A, B, C, and D explained.* WebMD. https://www.webmd.com/health-insurance/medicare-21/medicare-parts-explained

Medicare. (n.d.). *How do I sign up for Medicare?* https://www.medicare.gov/basics/get-started-with-medicare/sign-up/how-do-i-sign-up-for-medicare

Medicare Interactive. (2019). *The parts of Medicare (A, B, C, D).* https://www.medicareinteractive.org/get-answers/medicare-basics/medicare-coverage-overview/original-medicare

Medicare Made Clear. (2023). *What is the difference between Original Medicare and Medicare Advantage?* United Healthcare. https://www.uhc.com/news-articles/medicare-articles/what-is-the-difference-between-original-medicare-and-medicare-advantage#:~:text=Medicare%20Advantage%20plans%20cover%20everything

Peck, B. (2023, February 4). *How to increase Social Security disability payments (7 ways).* Evans Disability. https://evansdisability.com/blog/how-to-increase-social-security-disability-payments/

Pension Rights Center. (2023, May 10). *Tips for keeping track of your pension: Additional detail.* https://pensionrights.org/resource/tips-for-keeping-track-of-your-pension-additional-detail/

Probasco, J. (2019). *9 ways to boost your Social Security benefits.* Investopedia. https://www.investopedia.com/articles/retirement/112116/10-social-security-secrets-could-boost-your-benefits.asp

Probasco, J. (2023, June 20). *How to manage income during retirement.* Investopedia. https://www.investopedia.com/retirement/how-to-manage-timing-and-sources-of-income-retirement/

Probasco, J. (2022, June 22). *Why do healthcare costs keep rising?* Investopedia. https://

www.investopedia.com/insurance/why-do-healthcare-costs-keep-rising/#:~:text=A%20Journal%20of%20American

Promotion of sustainable employment - A. basic principles. (n.d.). International Social Security Association (ISSA). https://ww1.issa.int/guidelines/pse/174760

Ross, S. (2022, December 18). *Yes, you can manage your own retirement!* Investopedia. https://www.investopedia.com/articles/personal-finance/081715/yes-you-can-manage-your-own-retirement.asp#:~:text=Some%20good%20tips%20to%20manage

Rubin Law. (2013, October 3). *The Pickle Rule article.* https://www.rubinlaw.com/resources/the-pickle-rule-article/

Seladi-Schulman, J. (2021, May 28). Medicare and private insurance: Can you have both? Healthline. https://www.healthline.com/health/medicare/can-you-have-private-insurance-and-medicare

Social Security Administration. (2019). *Apply for disability benefits - child (under age 18).* https://www.ssa.gov/benefits/disability/apply-child.html

Social Security Administration. (n.d.). *Form SSA-1: Information you need to apply for retirement benefits or Medicare.* https://www.ssa.gov/forms/ssa-1.html

Social Security Administration. (n.d.). *Introduction to Social Security.* https://www.ssa.gov/section218training/basic_course_3.htm#:~:text=To%20provide%20for%20the%20material

Social Security Administration. (n.d.). *Social Security credits and benefit eligibility.* https://www.ssa.gov/benefits/retirement/planner/credits.html

Social Security Administration. (n.d.). *Social Security history.* https://www.ssa.gov/history/50ed.html#:~:text=Roosevelt%20signed%20the%20Social%20Security

Social Security Administration. (n.d.). *Social Security history - Ida May Fuller.* https://www.ssa.gov/history/imf.html

Social Security Administration. (2020). *Survivors benefits.* https://www.ssa.gov/benefits/survivors/

Substance Abuse and Mental Health Services Association. (n.d.). *Overview of Social Security disability programs: SSI and SSDI.* https://soarworks.samhsa.gov/article/overview-of-social-security-disability-programs-ssi-and-ssdi

Substance Abuse and Mental Health Services Association. (n.d.). *Social Security Administration programs for expediting disability claims.* https://soarworks.samhsa.gov/article/social-security-administration-programs-for-expediting-disability-claims

Substance Abuse and Mental Health Services Association. (n.d.). *SSI/SSDI and employment: A brief overview of SSA work incentives.* https://soarworks.samhsa.gov/article/ssissdi-and-employment-a-brief-overview-of-ssa-work-incentives

Tisdale, S. (2015, September 29). *Why your family is probably owed $120,000 in unclaimed social security benefits.* Black Enterprise. https://www.blackenterprise.

com/why-your-family-is-probably-owed-120000-in-unclaimed-social-security-benefits/

Treece, D. D. (2023, June 7). *What to know before hiring a retirement financial advisor.* Forbes. https://www.forbes.com/advisor/investing/financial-advisor/what-to-know-before-hiring-a-retirement-financial-advisor/

Turner, T. (2022, August 17). *How to choose a Medicare plan.* RetireGuide. https://www.retireguide.com/medicare/compare/how-to-choose-a-plan/

What widows and widowers need to know about Social Security survivor benefits. (2020, October 13). Prudential. https://www.prudential.com/corporate-insights/widows-widowers-approaching-retirement-social-security-survivor-benefits

Whitelocks, S. (2015, January 30). *Meet Ida May Fuller, recipient of 1st Social Security check.* Daily Mail. https://www.dailymail.co.uk/news/article-2932568/Meet-Ida-May-Fuller-recipient-1st-Social-Security-check.html

You may be able to claim on your ex's earnings record. (n.d.). Vanguard. https://investor.vanguard.com/investor-resources-education/social-security/benefits-for-divorced-spouse

Your retirement readiness assessment in 31 questions: An action checklist to help you plan for your transition to retirement. (2005, January 1). ICMA. https://icma.org/documents/your-retirement-readiness-assessment-31-questions-action-checklist-help-you-plan-your-transition-retirement

Estate Planning
SIMPLIFIED

SAFEGUARD YOUR LEGACY WITH WILLS, TRUSTS, AND INHERITANCE FOR EFFECTIVE ASSET MANAGEMENT

RETIREWISE

Introduction

Welcome to a journey that is as inevitable as it is imperative: the journey into estate planning. It is a path paved with decisions that shape the legacy we leave behind, a testament to our lives and the care we have for those we cherish.

Understanding the importance of planning your estate cannot be overstated. It involves ensuring that you respect your wishes, protect your assets, and provide for your loved ones as you intend. It is about peace of mind, knowing that you have taken the steps to safeguard the future, regardless of life's unpredictable nature.

Yet, we recognize that the complexity of estate planning can be daunting. Legal terms can seem labyrinthine, the tax implications are often intricate, and the emotional weight of these considerations is indisputably profound. Unsurprisingly, many feel overwhelmed, perhaps even tempted to postpone this crucial task.

We understand that clarity is the antidote to complexity. Each chapter will break down estate planning into its most fundamental components. We will guide you through the essentials of wills and trusts, explain the nuances of various estate planning instruments, and provide you with practical steps to take control of your financial future.

This book offers information and a series of stepping stones to help you build a bridge to your legacy. The following pages aim to serve as your companion, offering the knowledge you need and encouraging you to apply it.

So, let us step forward together. Through real-life scenarios, specific recommendations, and actionable advice, this book will equip you with the tools you need to navigate the process confidently. Your legacy deserves nothing less.

1

Estate Planning: The What, Why, and How

In the tapestry of life, the threads of financial planning and personal wishes intertwine to form the fabric of one's estate. This tapestry, rich with the hues of assets, memories, and desires, is one we weave throughout our lifetime. The act of estate planning, often perceived as a task reserved for the wealthy or the elderly, is, in truth, a practical step that holds significance for every adult. Individuals can ensure that their personal and financial matters are handled according to their wishes upon their passing or incapacitation.

An estate is not solely the sum of one's financial assets; it is an all-encompassing term that includes your possessions, real estate, investments, insurance policies, and digital footprint. To some, it may encompass a collection of fine art; to others, it could mean a cherished family home, or it might simply be a heartfelt letter written to a loved one.

Estate planning is the process of arranging for the management and distribution of a person's estate during and after their life. It encompasses a range of tasks, from drafting a will, setting up trusts, appointing beneficiaries, and making healthcare directives. These steps aim to ensure that an individual's health, wealth, and personal wishes are honored while easing the legal and financial burdens on the bereaved family.

Defining Estate Planning

"Estate" refers to everything you own or control that can be passed on to your heirs or beneficiaries. It is not exclusive to cash, property, and personal belongings but also includes your investments, life insurance proceeds, and even your debts and liabilities. An estate reflects the narrative of your life and the financial footprint you leave behind.

Estate planning is the blueprint for your story once you're no longer here to tell it yourself. It directs who will inherit your assets and how your affairs should be managed. At its core, it represents your voice in decisions that impact the financial well-being and emotional stability of those you care about. This planning involves legal structures and financial tools but is driven by your values, priorities, and the relationships you cherish.

The role of estate planning stretches far beyond deciding who gets what. It is a critical process that can significantly impact the financial security and emotional comfort of your loved ones. It can shield them from the complexities of probate, the legal process where a court oversees the distribution of your estate. With a well-structured plan, you can minimize the taxes levied on your estate, ensuring that your beneficiaries receive more of your assets. Moreover, it can prevent disputes among family members, which often arise during the stressful time following a loss.

The scope of estate planning is broad and dynamic. It is not a one-time event but an ongoing process that evolves with you. Your estate plan should adapt to life's milestones—marriage, the birth of children, significant financial changes, and even shifts in your values and priorities. This plan should be revisited and refined in response to the changing legal landscape and your unique circumstances.

For instance, consider the implications of the digital age on estate planning. In an era where our lives are increasingly online, digital assets such as social media accounts, online banking, and cryptocurrency holdings have become significant components of our estates. These digital assets require the same planning and care as physical assets, ensuring access and control are passed on according to your wishes.

Estate planning also includes making decisions about your healthcare should you become unable to communicate your wishes. Through documents like a living will or a healthcare power of attorney, you can provide instructions on the medical treatment you desire or appoint someone to make decisions on your behalf. This aspect of planning alleviates the burden on family members to make difficult healthcare choices during times of emotional distress.

In reality, estate planning is a form of care—a way to show concern for your own well-being and the welfare of those you may leave behind. It is a tangible expression of love, a method to alleviate potential burdens, and a strategy to preserve your legacy. To illustrate, reflect on a family business that has been the livelihood of multiple generations. Without a comprehensive estate plan, the sudden loss of the owner could plunge the business into uncertainty, affecting not only the immediate family but also employees and customers. By implementing a succession plan and clear directives for the continued operation or sale of the business, the owner can secure the company's future and the financial stability of those dependent on it.

Considering the multifaceted nature of estate planning, it becomes evident that this practice is not an esoteric ritual meant only for those with vast wealth. It is a crucial step for anyone who wishes to take responsibility for their financial and personal legacy. Through planning, you can ensure that your estate—a reflection of your life's work and personal values—is preserved and passed on as you see fit.

The Importance of Estate Planning

Estate planning is fundamental to the financial and emotional well-being of those we care about. It's the process of arranging the management of your estate, and it impacts everyone—regardless of the size of the estate or the age of the individual. Let's discuss the significance of estate planning and the inherent benefits it brings.

Ensuring Financial Security

Financial security is a significant concern for many, and rightly so. Estate planning plays a pivotal role in safeguarding the financial future of your heirs. The process involves designating beneficiaries for your assets, which can range from savings accounts to retirement funds; by clearly outlining who receives what and when you minimize the risk of assets being tied up in lengthy court procedures. Moreover, properly designating beneficiaries on life insurance policies and retirement accounts ensures the direct transfer of these funds, bypassing the time-consuming and costly probate process.

Reducing Legal Complications

The absence of an estate plan often leads to legal entanglements that can drag on for years, draining resources and causing unnecessary stress for your loved ones. A well-crafted estate plan includes a valid will, trusts when appropriate, and other legal documents clearly stating your intentions. This plan reduces ambiguity and the likelihood of legal challenges. For instance, a trust can manage your assets effectively, providing a legal structure that outlines how to handle and distribute your assets, with the trustee ensuring the execution of your wishes.

Preserving Family Harmony

Disagreements among family members over inheritance can be emotionally charged and potentially cause long-lasting rifts. Estate planning addresses this by communicating your wishes clearly, thereby reducing the chances of misunderstandings and conflicts. Such planning is about distributing assets, your values, and the relationships you want to nurture even after you're gone. For example, using a personal property memorandum can be effective; it's a document that accompanies your will, allowing you to specify which personal items go to which beneficiaries, thereby preventing potential disputes over sentimental items.

Minimizing Tax Burden

Taxes can take a significant bite out of an inheritance. Strategic estate planning can minimize the tax impact on your estate and your beneficiaries. Techniques such as gifting during your lifetime, establishing specific types of trusts, and taking advantage of tax exemptions can preserve more of your estate for your heirs. It's crucial to stay informed on the ever-evolving tax laws to maximize the benefits of these strategies. The federal estate tax exemption is adjusted for inflation, and it's essential to understand how this impacts asset distribution.

Leaving a Legacy

Estate planning involves considering your legacy and the impact you leave behind. It provides an opportunity to support the causes and organizations that are important to you through bequests. Planning could mean setting up educational funds for grandchildren, donating to a cherished charity, or ensuring the continuation of a family business. A legacy is not solely defined by the financial assets left behind but also by the values and traditions passed on.

A comprehensive estate plan can include an ethical will, a non-binding document allowing you to share your values, experiences, and life lessons with your family. Unlike a traditional will, which focuses on the distribution of assets, an ethical will is about the intangible aspects of your legacy. It's a way to articulate the values you wish to impart, the family traditions you hope will continue, and the personal and moral guidance you want to provide.

In essence, the estate planning process is a clear statement of your financial and personal intentions. It is a testament to your concern for the well-being of those you leave behind, ensuring that your final wishes are respected and that your legacy endures as you envision. It's about putting the pieces in place today so that your story unfolds as you wish tomorrow, providing a sense of continuity and stability in the lives of your loved ones.

The Process of Estate Planning

Embarking on estate planning is akin to preparing for a significant voyage. You wouldn't set sail without a map or a clear destination, and similarly, you should not navigate your financial future without a well-thought-out plan. This process involves several key steps, each building upon the last, to ensure your estate is managed and distributed according to your wishes.

Initial Assessment of Assets

The first step in estate planning is to take stock of what you own. The assessment forms the basis of your plan. It involves listing all your assets, including but not limited to your home, other real estate, bank accounts, investment accounts, retirement funds, life insurance policies, and personal property of value, such as jewelry, art, or collectibles. In addition, you must consider your digital assets, such as social media accounts, online storage, and cryptocurrency holdings.

Equally important is understanding your liabilities—mortgages, loans, credit card debts, and other obligations. An accurate and comprehensive inventory is a snapshot of your financial situation, highlighting the assets that will form part of your estate and those that may require settlement with your estate's assets.

This detailed inventory is not a one-time task. Still, it should be updated regularly to reflect changes such as acquisitions or disposals of assets, fluctuations in value, or changes in your financial situation. Such diligence ensures that your estate plan remains relevant and aligned with your current circumstances.

Setting Estate Objectives

Once your assets and liabilities are clear, the next step is to consider your goals. What do you wish to achieve with your estate? Your objectives might include:

- Ensuring the financial security of a surviving spouse.
- Providing for children's education.
- Supporting a charitable cause.
- Passing on a family business.

Your goals will likely reflect the unique dynamics of your family and life circumstances.

In this stage, it is vital to prioritize your objectives. Sometimes, the goals may conflict, such as wanting to leave a substantial gift to charity while also providing for your family's financial needs. Prioritizing helps in making decisions that align with your most important objectives.

Your objectives will guide the tools and strategies you employ in your estate plan. For instance, if minimizing taxes is a primary goal, specific types of trusts might be appropriate. A special needs trust could be the right tool to ensure a special needs child is cared for. Clearly defining your objectives allows for tailored solutions most effective for your unique situation.

Drafting Essential Documents

Armed with a comprehensive understanding of your assets and a clear set of objectives, you now create the essential documents that will form the backbone of your estate plan. These documents typically include a will, various types of trusts, a power of attorney, and healthcare directives, if applicable.

A will is the fundamental document most people consider when estate planning comes up. It states your wishes regarding the distribution of your assets and can nominate guardians for any minor children. State law dictates asset distribution without a will, which may not align with your preferences.

Trusts are versatile tools that can help achieve various estate objectives, from avoiding probate to reducing estate taxes. There are many kinds of trusts, each serving different purposes. A living trust can manage assets during your lifetime and distribute them after your death without probate.

A power of attorney is a legal document granting someone you trust authority to handle your financial affairs if you become incapacitated. This document can be as broad or as narrow as you wish, granting total control or limiting to specific actions.

Healthcare directives such as a living will, and healthcare power of attorney ensure that your medical preferences are honored if you are unable to communicate them. A living will outlines the types of medical treatment you do or do not want, while a healthcare power of attorney appoints someone to make medical decisions on your behalf.

It is crucial to draft these documents with legal expertise, precision, and clarity to comply with state laws, which vary significantly, and express your wishes unequivocally.

Regular Review and Update

Finally, the fluidity of life necessitates regular reviews and updates to your estate plan. Changes such as marriage, divorce, birth, death, and significant financial shifts can all impact your plan. Additionally, changes in laws may affect various components of your estate plan, especially those related to taxes and asset distribution.

A regular review, ideally annually or after any major life event, ensures that your estate plan remains current and effective. During these reviews, revisit your asset inventory to account for any changes. Reflect on your objectives to ensure they still align with your current wishes. Evaluate the individuals you've designated in roles such as executor, trustee, or healthcare proxy, and consider if these choices still reflect your best interests.

It's crucial to consult with estate planning professionals during this review process. Their expertise helps identify any legal or financial shifts that necessitate adjustments to your plan. They can also guide new strategies or tools that may benefit your estate.

By diligently following these steps—assessing your assets, setting clear objectives, drafting essential documents, and conducting regular reviews—you create a robust estate plan that serves as a blueprint for your legacy. This plan reflects your financial assets and embodies your values and wishes, ensuring they are honored and respected.

2

Decoding the Legal Lexicon of Estate Planning

Picture a foreign city with its bustling streets, vibrant markets, and intricate architecture—a place rich in culture and history but where the local tongue is unfamiliar to you. Navigating this city without understanding its language can be both challenging and intimidating. Similarly, the realm of estate planning is replete with its own language, a specialized lexicon that can seem just as foreign and daunting to many. But fear not; with the right guide, you can become fluent in this critical vernacular, transforming what once seemed like legal gibberish into clear, actionable information.

To traverse the landscape of estate planning effectively, one must first become acquainted with the key terms that serve as signposts along the way. These terms are the building blocks of your estate plan—the nouns that name your players and the verbs that drive your actions. Let's introduce and demystify these pivotal terms, giving you the clarity needed to make informed decisions about your estate.

Beneficiary

The beneficiary is the individual or entity you designate to receive the fruits of your labor—the assets and property from your estate. It's like handing over the keys to a treasure chest; the beneficiary is the person you've chosen to open it and benefit from what's inside. Your beneficiaries can include family members, friends, charities, or institutions, and you can specify what you want each to receive, be it a sum of money, a piece of real estate, or a treasured family heirloom.

Executor

The executor is the conductor of your estate's symphony—the person you entrust to orchestrate the fulfillment of your final wishes, as outlined in your will. They are responsible for handling the affairs of your estate, paying off any outstanding debts or taxes, and guaranteeing that your assets are distributed according to your wishes. Choosing the right executor is crucial; this person should be responsible, organized, and willing to commit time to the task. They'll be the ones standing at the helm, guiding your estate through the probate process, acting as the steward of your legacy.

Trustee

A trustee is akin to a guardian of your assets held in trust—a role of honor and obligation. When you set up a trust, you're placing your assets under the trustee's care, who manages and protects these assets for the benefit of the trust's beneficiaries. The trustee wears many hats: an investor, a custodian, and often, a mediator. They must act with the utmost integrity and in the best interest of the beneficiaries, adhering to the trust's terms and navigating the complexities of trust administration.

Power of Attorney

Imagine having a stand-in, someone to step into your shoes and make decisions on your behalf should the need arise. That's the essence of a power of attorney—a legal document that grants another person the authority to act for you, usually in financial or medical matters. This proxy can be granted broad powers, such as handling all your financial affairs, or limited powers, such as selling a specific property. Durable powers of attorney remain in effect even if you become incapacitated, ensuring that someone you trust makes decisions aligned with your preferences.

Probate

Probate is the official proving ground for your will—a court-supervised process that validates your will and oversees the distribution of your estate. Consider it as a safeguard that guarantees payment of your debts and allocation of your assets as per your documented wishes. Probate can be lengthy and public, often involving paperwork, court appearances, and potential legal fees. Many opt for estate planning tools like trusts, which can bypass this process, allowing for a more private and expedited transfer of assets.

Visual Element: Infographic
Understanding Key Estate Planning Terms

A visual diagram that illustrates the relationships and roles of each key term in estate planning:

- **Beneficiary:** Receives assets from the estate or trust.
- **Executor:** Manages and settles the will's directives through probate.

- **Trustee:** Oversees and administers trust assets for beneficiaries.
- **Power of Attorney:** Acts on your behalf in financial or medical decisions.
- **Probate:** Legal process validating the will and overseeing asset distribution.

With these terms clarified, envision how they fit into the broader picture of your estate plan. Each plays a pivotal role in ensuring your intentions are honored, and your estate is cared for. As you continue to build your understanding, remember that the ultimate goal of familiarizing yourself with this language is to create a document and craft a plan that reflects your wishes and provides for those you care about most.

Understanding Legal Language

The lexicon of estate planning can sometimes feel like a dense thicket of terms and phrases, each with nuanced definition and significance. The precision of this language carves a clear path for your intentions, ensuring they are understood and executed as you desire. Unraveling the complexity of this terminology is akin to translating a legal code that governs the passage of your life's accumulations to the next generation.

Decoding Legal Terminology

In this intricate network of estate planning, specific phrases act as keystones, holding the structure of your plan together. Terms such as "intestate" or "testate" determine how your assets are handled with or without a valid will. Understanding these conditions and their consequences allows you to exert control over the distribution process. When transferring ownership, distinguishing between tangible and intangible assets may impact their management and taxation. When transferring ownership, distinguishing between tangible and intangible assets may affect their management and taxation. Tangible assets are physical objects like real estate and artwork, while intangible assets encompass non-physical rights and interests such as stocks or patents.

To navigate effectively, it's crucial to fully understand terms like "codicil." A codicil is an amendment to a will that can modify, add, or revoke sections of the document without requiring a complete rewrite. It is a tool used in estate planning that allows for adjustments to be made without disrupting the overall structure of the will. Another critical term is "per stirpes," a method of distributing an estate that ensures descendants of a beneficiary receive their ancestor's share should the beneficiary pass before the testator. This concept speaks to the distribution of assets and reflects a commitment to family continuity.

Importance of Clear Language

Using clear and concise language is crucial when drafting estate planning documents. This clarity acts as a safeguard, protecting your plan from misinterpretation or disputes. It's the beacon that guides executors and trustees through the fog of complex directives, illuminating the way forward. When drafting these documents, simplicity, and precision are paramount. For example, "fiduciary" should be clearly defined to establish the standard of care expected from the executor or trustee. This person has a fiduciary duty, a legal obligation to act in the best interest of the beneficiaries, with a level of care that is prudent and diligent.

The specificity of language extends to the designation of heirs. It is essential to name each heir individually in your will to prevent confusion and ensure that your assets are distributed as per your wishes. Similarly, in the context of a trust, the language should unambiguously state the "trust corpus," which refers to the assets placed within the trust, and the "trust instrument," which is the document that outlines the trust's terms.

Commonly Misunderstood Terms

Certain terms frequently trip up even the savviest individuals within the fabric of estate planning. When misunderstood, these terms can potentially unravel the intentions behind an estate plan. "Joint tenancy with the right of survivorship" is one such term. It refers to a form of co-ownership where, upon the death of one owner, their interest automatically passes to the surviving co-owner(s). It's a straightforward concept, yet with proper understanding, individuals may realize that this form of ownership supersedes the directives in a will, leading to unintended consequences for asset distribution.

Another commonly misunderstood term is "durable power of attorney," which remains in effect even if the grantor becomes incapacitated. It's often confused with a "general power of attorney," which becomes null and void under the same circumstances. The durability clause is critical; it ensures that the chosen individual can continue managing your affairs when you cannot.

The term "grantor" holds great importance in the world of trusts. The grantor is the person who creates the trust and transfers assets into it. Understanding the grantor's responsibilities and how they affect the trust's management and taxation is crucial. Similarly, the concept of "funded" versus "unfunded" trusts is pivotal. A funded trust has assets placed into it during the grantor's lifetime, whereas an unfunded trust consists only of the trust agreement with no assets transferred until later, often at the grantor's death.

In the dance of estate planning, even seemingly simple terms like "gift" carry layers of meaning. In legal parlance, a gift is a transfer of property for which no consideration is expected or received in return. The act of gifting can serve as a strategic tool for estate planning, allowing the transfer of wealth during one's lifetime and potentially reducing the taxable estate. Proper documentation and adherence to annual gifting limits are essential to avoid tax liabilities when gifting.

This level of comprehension gives you the power to craft an estate plan that serves as a testament to your life and values. With a firm grasp of the legal language, you can ensure that every clause and codicil of your plan serves its intended purpose, honoring your wishes and providing for your loved ones with the utmost fidelity. As we continue to explore the nuances of estate planning, remember that each term you encounter is more than just a word—it's a vessel carrying the weight of your intentions. This beacon lights the path for your legacy to follow.

The Role of Legal Terms in Your Estate Plan

Navigating the intricate fabric of estate planning necessitates a keen understanding of legal terminology, as the specific words used in your documents can significantly impact their effectiveness and enforceability. Let us explore the critical legal terms that serve as pillars in the architecture of wills, trusts, and powers of attorney. These terms act as the DNA of your estate plan, each sequence encoding vital instructions that will shape its execution.

Legal Terms in Wills

A will is akin to a map that guides your loved ones through the distribution of your estate, and the language employed within it must be precise and unequivocal. One such term is "testator," who creates the will. It is your role as the testator to designate "heirs," who are the individuals entitled to your assets by law, and "legatees," who are specifically named to receive particular property or amounts.

The residue of an estate is what's left after debts, taxes, and specific bequests are paid. It is often left to a residuary beneficiary, typically a close family member or a spouse, who will receive the balance of your assets. To avoid any potential confusion, it is vital to clearly identify this party and any alternates in case your primary choice predeceases you.

A will may also contain a "no-contest clause" intended to deter beneficiaries from challenging your will. Such a clause, however, must be drafted with care, as its enforceability varies from state to state.

Furthermore, including a "simultaneous death clause" guides asset distribution should you and a beneficiary die concurrently or within a short period of one another. This term ensures that your estate plan contemplates even the most unforeseen events, thereby preventing your assets from becoming subject to default state laws that may not reflect your intentions.

Legal Terms in Trusts

In trusts, the terminology shapes the vessel that holds and protects your assets for the benefit of your chosen recipients. A "settlor" or "grantor" is the person who establishes the trust, transferring assets into it. The "trust property" or "principal" refers to the assets that fund the trust. At the same time, "income" describes the earnings generated from these assets, which may be distributed to beneficiaries according to the terms you set forth.

The "trust instrument" is the trust's governing document, and within it, terms like "irrevocable" and "revocable" determine the degree of control retained over the trust. An irrevocable trust generally cannot be altered once established, while a revocable trust permits modifications during the settlor's lifetime.

A "spendthrift clause" protects a beneficiary from creditors by prohibiting the beneficiary's interest from being assigned or reached by creditors before the trust distributes the assets. It is a safeguard for the assets within the trust, ensuring that they are used as intended for the benefit of the beneficiary rather than to pay off the beneficiary's debts.

When distributing trust assets, terms like "discretionary distributions" grant the trustee the power to decide when and how much to allocate to beneficiaries, often based on a standard, such as health, education, maintenance, and support. This flexibility allows the trustee to manage the trust assets in response to the beneficiaries' changing needs and circumstances.

Legal Terms in Power of Attorney

A power of attorney is a robust tool in estate planning, allowing you to appoint an "agent" or "attorney-in-fact" to act on your behalf in financial or healthcare matters. The "principal" in this context refers to the person granting the power, which is you.

The "capacity" of the principal is a critical term, as it relates to the individual's ability to understand and make decisions. The power of attorney document must specify the circumstances under which it becomes effective or ceases to be in effect, especially in the case of a "springing power of attorney," which only becomes active upon the occurrence of a specific event, typically the principal's incapacitation.

The "scope" of authority granted to the agent can be as broad or as narrow as the principal desires, delineated by terms such as "general," giving wide-ranging powers, or "limited," confining the agent's authority to specific matters.

Understanding these terms and their nuances is vital to creating a power of attorney that accurately conveys your intentions and gives your agent appropriate control. It is an instrument of delegation that, when crafted with precision, can provide peace of mind and continuity in managing your affairs should you be unable to do so yourself.

The words we choose in our estate planning documents are more than mere placeholders; they are the messengers of our deepest wishes and directives. They carry the weight of our intentions and the power to enact them. As you reflect upon the legal terms that will form the cornerstone of your estate plan, consider them your allies—tools that, when wielded with understanding and precision, build a fortress around your legacy, ensuring that it stands firm against the tides of time and change.

As you turn these pages, you continue to fortify your knowledge, layering brick upon brick until the structure of your estate plan stands complete and resolute. It is a plan that, in its final form, will not only speak with your voice but will do so with the clarity and authority that your legacy deserves.

3

The Keystone of Estate Planning: Wills Explained

Imagine you're about to paint a picture that illustrates your life's achievements, values, and care for loved ones. Instead of relying on brushes and colors, you possess something far more powerful and enduring: your will. This document, often perceived as the cornerstone of estate planning, is not a mere formality but an expression of your life's narrative, ensuring that your story doesn't end with your last breath but continues as you envisioned.

A will is your voice in a future where you won't be present to speak. It's a declaration of your intentions, a protective shell around your assets, and a guide for those you leave behind. With it, you chart a course for the future, one that honors your wishes and upholds your legacy.

What Exactly is a Will?

Purpose of a Will

The primary purpose of a will is to communicate your wishes regarding the distribution of your assets after your passing. Think of it as the director of an orchestra, guiding each instrument to play its part at the right time, ensuring the harmony of the final piece. A will can be as straightforward as bequeathing everything to a single person or as intricate as assigning specific items to various individuals and organizations. It's not just about who gets what; it's also about who will manage the process, care for your minor children, and look after your pets.

Basic Structure of a Will

The will is a legal document that provides clarity and direction by identifying the person it belongs to, known as the testator. It typically follows a specific order of instructions, starting with a declaration of intent, followed by revoking previous wills, and ending with the appointment of an executor responsible for carrying out the instructions. The main body of the will outlines the distribution of assets, including bank accounts and family heirlooms, and may also include the appointment of guardians for minor children. Finally, the will concludes with the testator's and witnesses' signatures, signifying validity.

Imagine you're crafting a recipe that your family will follow to recreate your favorite dish. Your will, like that recipe, details the essential ingredients (your assets), the method (instructions for distribution), and the preferred outcome (your intended beneficiaries enjoying the meal). It's a blend of precision and personal touch that results in a lasting legacy.

Legal Requirements for a Valid Will

For a will to hold up as a binding legal document, it must meet specific criteria. These vary by jurisdiction but commonly include the testator being of legal age and sound mind, meaning they understand the nature of the will and its consequences. The will should be written willingly, without any external pressure or influence from others. It usually requires the testator's signature and those of witnesses who attest to the testa or's capacity and free will in signing the document. Some states allow for "holographic" wills handwritten by the testator; in some cases, these may not even require witnesses.

Consider the act of securing your signature on an important contract. It's a moment that signifies agreement, intent, and commitment. Similarly, signing a will is a pivotal event that cements your decisions and sets them into motion.

Visual Element: Checklist
Essentials of a Valid Will

- Testator's full name and statement of intent
- Revocation of previous wills or codicils
- Appointment of an executor
- Detailed asset distribution
- Guardianship designations (if applicable)
- Testator's signature
- Witnesses' signatures
- Notarization (depending on state requirements)

A will's power lies in its details— the specificity with which it outlines who gets what. For example, leaving a family business to a child who has shown interest and aptitude can ensure the enterprise's continuing success, reflecting your pride in the legacy you've built. Or, assigning a cherished piece of jewelry to a dear friend can serve as a tangible reminder of a bond that transcends time.

Understanding the purpose and structure of a will and the legal requirements for its validity forms the bedrock of effective estate planning. In the following sections, we'll explore how to create a will that faithfully reflects your intentions and safeguards your legacy, ensuring that your final wishes are honored and your loved ones are cared for according to your plan.

The Role of a Will in Estate Planning

A will serves as the blueprint for orchestrating one's estate after one's departure, providing explicit directions to ease the transfer of assets, the care of minors, and the responsibilities bestowed upon the chosen executor. This document ensures that personal wishes are executed precisely for estate planning.

Distribution of Assets

The allocation of one's assets is a personal affair reflective of relationships, affections, and the legacy one wishes to leave. A will delineate who inherits property, monetary ass ts, family heirlooms, and other personal belongings. In this document, you may detail the division of assets with granularity, assigning particular items or specific monetary amounts to individuals or organizations. This assignment can include leaving particular pieces of real estate to heirs or bequeathing donations to favored charities.

Without a will, the state assumes control over the distribution process, applying a one-size-fits-all approach to a situation that often requires a tailored fit. This formulaic division of assets ignores personal connections and stories, potentially conflicting with the deceased's desires and beneficiaries' needs. A will, therefore, is essential to ensure that each asset is passed on according to the owner's express instructions, reflecting their decisions and values.

Appointment of Guardians for Minors

For parents and guardians, the well-being of their minor children is paramount. In the unfortunate event of the parent's untimely demise, a will becomes the vehicle for expressing their wishes regarding the children's future care. Within its clauses, parents can appoint a guardian they trust to raise their children with the same values and care they would provide.

Determining guardianship within a will is a thoughtful process, often involving heartfelt discussions with potential guardians to ensure they are willing and able to take on such a responsibility. This consideration also extends to the financial arrangements made for the children's upbringing, which can be addressed by establishing trusts within the will. By making these decisions, parents offer their children stability and continuity of care, even in their absence.

Naming an Executor

An executor is the individual entrusted with the duty of enacting the provisions of the will. This role extends beyond merely distributing assets; it encompasses managing the estate's affairs, settling debts and taxes, and, often, making pivotal decisions during the probate process. Selecting an executor is a decision imbued with trust and foresight, as this person will be at the helm, steering the estate through the intricacies of fulfillment.

When naming an executor, consider the individual's capability, integrity, and willingness to commit time and energy to the task ahead. The executor must navigate the legal landscape, coordinate with beneficiaries, and sometimes resolve conflicts that arise. Selecting someone equipped with both the insight for the administrative aspects and the empathy to handle delicate family dynamics is crucial for the smooth execution of the will.

In assigning this role, the testator can provide the executor with guidance and resources through a letter of instruction or by establishing clear lines of communication with the estate's attorney and financial advisor. This foresight eases the executor's burden, allowing them to act confidently and align with the testator's intentions.

Each of these elements—the distribution of assets, the appointment of guardians for minors, and the naming of an executor—plays a vital role in the tapestry of estate planning. Together, they ensure that the testator's wishes are not left to interpretation or chance but executed with the care and precision they deserve. A will, therefore, is not a mere document but a testament to one's life and values, a final act of consideration for those left behind, and a definitive statement of one's legacy.

How to Create a Will

Inventory of Assets

The first step in creating a w ll is compiling a thorough inventory of your assets. This task is akin to assembling the puzzle pieces that, when complete, will reveal the full picture of your estate. List tangible assets such as real estate, vehicles, jewelry, and artwork. Remember items of sentimental value; these often hold immeasurable worth to those you love. Next, detail your financial assets: bank accounts, stocks, bonds, retirement accounts, and life insurance policies. Make sure to securely document usernames and passwords for online accounts for the executor, as digital assets are also a part of your estate. Consider liabilities as well, such as mortgages, loans, and credit card debts, as these will impact the net value of your estate.

Creating a comprehensive list of assets and liabilities provides a clear starting point for distributing your estate and assists your executive in accurately managing and settling your affairs. Please don't rush this step; it ensures you account for everything you own and pass it on according to your wishes.

Decision on Beneficiaries

Selecting your beneficiaries is the next pivotal step after accounting for your assets. Reflect on those who have touched your life and whom you wish to acknowledge or support. Beneficiaries include family, friends, charitable organizations, or educational institutions. When deciding on beneficiaries, consider the impact of your legacy. For some, a financial inheritance can provide educational opportunities or be a foundation for future security. For others, a particular item may hold deep emotional significance, serving as a lasting reminder of your relationship.

In making these decisions, it's essential to be clear and specific to avoid ambiguity and potential conflict. If a particular asset has multiple prospective beneficiaries, contemplate the division carefully. Discussing with these individuals to gauge their feelings and expectations regarding potential inheritances might be prudent. These conversations can also help avoid surprises and ensure your decisions align with the beneficiaries' circumstances and needs.

Drafting the Will

With a comprehensive asset inventory and a clear decision on beneficiaries, you are ready to draft the will. This step is where the elements of your estate plan merge into a formal legal document. Engage the services of an estate planning attorney to ensure that yours will adhere to state laws and truly reflect your intentions. An attorney can also advise on complex situations, such as providing for a special needs beneficiary or structuring your estate to minimize tax implications.

Approach the drafting process with thoroughness and attention to detail. Craft each clause to convey your wishes unambiguously. Consider including alternate beneficiaries in case your primary choices predecease you. If you have minor children, the will should nominate a guardian and establish a trust to manage any inheritance until they reach adulthood. Remember to periodically review your will to ensure it reflects your current situation and desires. Remember, you can continually update it as circumstances change.

Witnessing and Signing the Will

The final step in creating a will is the formal signing and witnessing process, essential for the document's legal validity. Witnesses to a will are typically required to be disinterested parties —meaning they do not stand to benefit from the will. One must maintain impartiality to ensure fairness and prevent potential disputes regarding the will's authenticity.

When you sign the will, do so in the presence of your witnesses, who must also sign the document, attesting to your capacity and voluntary action. The number of witnesses required can vary by jurisdiction, so following your state's specific regulations is critical.

In some cases, the signing may also need to be notarized, adding a layer of certification to the document's authenticity.

Signing the will is more than a formality; it is an affirmation of your decisions and a pivotal moment that sets your estate plan into motion. Once signed and witnessed, your will stands as a legally binding document that articulates your final wishes and provides the blueprint for the distribution of your estate. It is an enduring expression of your life's narrative, crafted to ensure your legacy is honored and your loved ones are supported as you intended.

What Happens If You Die Without a Will?

Without a will, an individual's estate becomes an open narrative, with endings not authored by the deceased but written by state laws. Intestate succession laws govern the distribution of assets when a person dies without leaving behind a will. These laws may result in outcomes that differ significantly from the individual's preference.

State Laws on Intestate Succession

A set of regulations specific to each state dictates the division of assets when there is no will. These laws create a default distribution plan, typically favoring the closest relatives—spouses, children, and parents. Without immediate family, the estate may pass to more distant kin, following a hierarchy that the state deems equitable. The rigidity of these laws does not account for the nuances of personal relationships or individual circumstances. Intestate succession does not recognize a lifelong friend or a charitable cause close to the deceased's heart.

To illustrate, if a single individual with no children passes away, their parents might inherit the estate, even if the individual had a more distant relative or friend they would have preferred to benefit. Depending on the jurisdiction, married individuals may pass on the entirety of their estate to their surviving spouse or divide it among their spouse, siblings, and parents. These outcomes can vastly differ from what the deceased might have intended, highlighting the importance of drafting a will to fulfill personal wishes.

Potential Disputes Among Heirs

When potential heirs need the guidance of a will, they often engage in disputes over the estate. In the face of unclear directives, emotions can run high, and disagreements may arise regarding the rightful recipients of assets.

When questioning the fairness of state-mandated distributions, disputes can become more intense, especially when sentimental or valuable assets are involved. The potential for conflict extends beyond the immediate aftermath of a person's death, as the effects of a contentious probate process can leave lasting scars on relationships and tarnish the memory of the deceased.

Probate Process Without a Will

The probate process without a will is a public affair where the court oversees the distribution of the estate. This procedure can be time-consuming and costly, diminishing the estate's value through legal fees and court costs. The court appoints an administrator, a role similar to an executor, to manage the estate's affairs. This individual may not have intimate knowledge of the deceased's wishes or relationships, which can lead to decisions that may not align with what the deceased would have wanted.

The administrator's duties include locating legal heirs, managing and liquidating assets, paying debts and taxes, and distributing the remaining assets according to state laws. Without the deceased's input, this process can become a mechanical distribution of assets, void of the personal touch that a well-crafted will provides.

The impersonal statutes will be responsible for distributing the deceased's estate without a will, and the deceased's true intentions may never surface. This underscores the significance of taking the reins of one's estate planning to ensure that the legacy left behind is one of choice, not chance.

Ultimately, the absence of a will can result in a narrative far removed from one's life story, with final chapters that may not reflect the bonds and values held dear. It is a stark reminder of the pivotal role estate planning plays in preserving one's wishes and the harmony of those left to remember and honor a life lived. With careful planning and a clear will, the legacy left behind can be a true testament to the life and love shared rather than a tale of unintended consequences and legal dictates.

The next chapter will build upon this foundation, exploring the intricate weave of trusts. This tool offers control over asset distribution and potential benefits in privacy, tax planning, and managing complex family dynamics. The discussion will illuminate the types of trusts available and their advantages, guiding you to make informed choices that align with your estate planning goals.

4

Fortifying Your Legacy with Trusts

Imagine a treasure chest, ornate and timeless, safeguarding precious jewels and heirlooms. This chest is not hidden away but entrusted to a guardian who ensures your treasures are protected, managed, and ultimately gifted to those you've chosen. In estate planning, this chest is not a figment of pirate lore but a trust—a powerful instrument designed to hold and secure your assets with the same commitment to safeguarding your legacy as you would.

Trusts are not merely tools of the wealthy; they are adaptable instruments that can serve many purposes, from charitable giving to special needs planning, offering benefits that extend beyond the simplistic division of assets. In this chapter, we'll explore what a trust is, the roles of those involved, and the various types of trusts, providing an understanding of how they can be integrated into your estate planning to serve your unique objectives.

The Concept of Trusts

Definition of a Trust

At its core, a trust is a fiduciary arrangement, a relationship bound by trust and confidence. It allows a third party, or trustee, to hold assets on behalf of a beneficiary or beneficiaries. It's a legal entity you create to take title to your assets, but it's more than just a holding space. You set forth specific guidelines for managing assets in a trust with a commitment and promise to benefit those you choose.

Think of a trust like a legal greenhouse, where you carefully plant your assets, and a chosen gardener—the trustee—tends to them. Like delicate seedlings, these assets can grow and flourish under the trustee's care until it's time to pass them on to your beneficiaries, just as you've directed. This process can occur during your lifetime or after your passing, depending on the type of trust you establish.

Parties Involved in a Trust

Establishing a trust brings together three critical roles: the grantor, the trustee, and the beneficiary. Each has a distinct part to play in this legal relationship.

- The Grantor: Also known as the settlor or trustor, the grantor is the person who creates the trust, sets the terms, and transfers assets into it. You, the artist, paint the future of your assets and decide how and when they will be distributed.
- The Trustee: The individual or institution the grantor appoints to manage the trust's assets. The trustee's role is

vital; they must act with prudence and loyalty, putting the beneficiaries' interests above all else. It's a role that requires a steadfast commitment to the grantor's intentions.
- The Beneficiary: These are the individuals or entities the grantor designates to benefit from the trust. Beneficiaries may receive income from the trust during its term, distribution of assets at a specified time, or other benefits as directed by the grantor.

The trust document governs the roles of each party, as they are integral to the function of the trust. The terms laid out in the document direct this legal ensemble.

Types of Trusts

Trusts come in many shapes and sizes, each with features and benefits. Here's a glimpse into the variety:

- Living Trusts (Inter Vivos): Created during the grantor's lifetime, these trusts can be either revocable or irrevocable. They enable the management of assets while the grantor is alive and stipulate the distribution after death.
- Testamentary Trusts: These are established through a will and come into effect after the grantor's death. They provide a way to manage and protect beneficiaries' assets over time.
- Charitable Trusts: These trusts are designed to benefit a charitable organization or cause and may offer the grantor tax benefits.
- Special Needs Trusts: Tailored trusts for beneficiaries with disabilities ensure they qualify for government assistance programs.
- Spendthrift Trusts: These protect the trust's assets from being claimed by a beneficiary's creditors.

- Marital or "A" Trust: Beneficial for a surviving spouse, this trust often provides income and principal as needed and may offer estate tax benefits.

Visual Element: Chart
A Snapshot of Trust Types and Their Functions

Type of Trust

- **Description**
- **Primary Benefit**

Living Trust (Revocable)

- Created during the grantor's life and can be altered.
- Flexibility and control during the grantor's life.

Living Trust (Irrevocable)

- Cannot be altered once established.
- Asset protection and potential tax benefits.

Testamentary Trust

- Established through a will after death.
- Management of assets for beneficiaries over time.

Charitable Trust

- Established to benefit a charitable organization.
- Charitable giving and tax advantages.

Special Needs Trust

- Provides for a beneficiary with disabilities.
- Ensures government assistance eligibility.

Spendthrift Trust

- Protects assets from beneficiaries' creditors.
- Asset protection for beneficiaries.

Marital Trust

- Provides for a surviving spouse.
- Income for spouse and potential estate tax benefits.

The selection of a trust type is as personal as choosing a home. You must consider the size, structure, and location—all attributes that align with your needs and goals. Just as you would select a cozy cottage for its charm and warmth or a modern loft for its efficiency and style, you choose a trust based on the protection, management, and benefits it offers to your estate.

In the following sections, we will delve further into the distinct types of trusts, providing insights to determine which one or combination best aligns with your estate planning objectives. The choices are varied and valuable, from revocable living trusts that offer flexibility and control to irrevocable trusts that provide asset protection and tax advantages. We'll explore how each trust functions and its unique advantages, empowering you with the knowledge to select the perfect trust to fortify your legacy.

Different Types of Trusts

Revocable Trusts

A revocable trust is a dynamic estate planning tool, offering the grantor flexibility that other trusts do not. The grantor can alter, amend, or even dissolve this type of trust entirely at their discretion as long as they are alive and mentally competent. The adaptability of a revocable trust makes it an attractive option for those who seek to maintain control over their assets while also planning for the future.

Imagine a revocable trust as a living, breathing document that grows and changes with you through various life stages. It allows you to appoint yourself as the trustee, overseeing the assets and making changes as circumstances evolve—whether that's the birth of a grandchild, the acquisition of new property, or a change in marital status. Upon the grantor's death, the revocable trust typically becomes irrevocable, securing the assets for beneficiaries and often bypassing the public and meticulous probate process.

Irrevocable Trusts

In contrast to their adaptable counterparts, irrevocable trusts are steadfast agreements. Once established, they cannot be modified or rescinded. This permanence offers distinct advantages concerning asset protection and potential tax benefits. By transferring assets into an irrevocable trust, you effectively remove them from your estate, shielding them from future creditors and reducing your taxable estate.

Crafting an irrevocable trust is a gesture of forward-thinking commitment. It requires a level of certainty about the disposition of one's assets that is not necessary with revocable trusts. However, for those looking to mitigate estate taxes, protect wealth from legal judgments, or preserve assets for specific purposes such as special needs planning or philanthropy, an irrevocable trust can be an invaluable component of their estate strategy.

Testamentary Trusts

A testamentary trust, often called a will trust, emerges from the provisions outlined in a will. This trust does not exist until after the grantor's death, at which point it is irrevocable. Testamentary trusts serve many purposes, including providing structured support to beneficiaries who may not be prepared for a lump-sum inheritance or ensuring that a surviving spouse is taken care of before the remaining assets are distributed to other beneficiaries.

The creation of a testamentary trust is a thoughtful process. To form the trust, you must include a clause in your will that specifies the assets to fund it and the beneficiaries who will receive support. Testamentary trusts offer a tiered approach to asset distribution, often used to stagger inheritances over time or until certain conditions are met, such as a beneficiary reaching a specific age or milestone.

Living Trusts

Living trusts, formally inter vivos trusts, are established during the grantor's lifetime. Depending on the grantor's goals and needs, they can be either revocable or irrevocable. Living trusts are a proactive approach to estate planning, allowing you to place assets within the trust while you're still alive, with the option to benefit from them before they pass on to your heirs.

One of the primary advantages of a living trust is its ability to bypass probate. Assets within a living trust can be transferred directly to beneficiaries without court involvement, expediting the distribution process and maintaining privacy. Living trusts also provide an avenue for managing your assets should you become incapacitated, as you can name a successor trustee who will manage the trust's affairs according to your established terms.

Each type of trust serves a specific purpose and offers benefits tailored to different situations. Whether seeking flexibility and control, asset protection, tax efficiency, or planning for incapacity, there's a trust structure that can align with your estate planning objectives. These trusts' careful selection and customization create a fortified legacy, ensuring that your assets are preserved, protected, and passed on according to your most profound intentions.

Setting Up a Trust

Establishing a trust is akin to preparing a tailored suit; the fit must be perfect for the intended purpose. The meticulous process involves several steps, each critical to ensuring that the trust operates effectively and aligns with your long-term intentions.

Choosing the Right Type of Trust

The initial stage in setting up a trust is akin to selecting the right material for that suit. It requires thoroughly understanding the various trust fabrics available and their properties. You must assess your circumstances, financial goals, and the needs of your beneficiaries.

For instance, if your priority is to retain the ability to modify the trust, a revocable trust might suit your needs, offering the flexibility to adjust terms or dissolve the trust entirely. On the other hand, if asset protection and estate tax reduction are your primary goals, an irrevocable trust could provide a sturdy framework, insulating your assets from claims and reducing taxable estate size.

The choice becomes more nuanced when considering specialized trusts. Should you wish to set aside funds for a beneficiary with a disability, a special needs trust ensures they receive the care they require without jeopardizing their eligibility for public assistance. Alternatively, if philanthropy is close to your heart, a charitable remainder trust could fulfill your desire to give back while delivering certain tax advantages.

This stage demands careful consideration and, often, the guidance of an estate planning professional who can illuminate the paths each trust type offers and help you select the one that aligns with your unique tapestry of needs and aspirations.

Naming the Trustee

Once the type of trust is selected, attention turns to appointing the trustee, a critical decision that shapes the trust's operation. The trustee's role is multifaceted, encompassing asset management, distribution to beneficiaries, and adherence to the trust's terms. Remember that this individual needs to be trustworthy and competent, as they will manage your assets and carry out your instructions.

In selecting a trustee, evaluate candidates based on their integrity, financial acumen, and ability to navigate complex legal and fiduciary responsibilities. For some, a family member or close friend may embody these qualities, offering a personal connection to the beneficiaries and an intimate understanding of your wishes. Others may opt for a professional trustee, such as a trust attorney or a financial institution, which can bring neutrality, expertise, and experience to the role.

It is also prudent to designate a successor trustee who can step in should the original trustee not fulfill their duties. This ensures the continuation of managing and distributing the trust's assets, thus preserving the integrity of your estate plan.

Transferring Assets into the Trust

With the trustee in place, the process moves to transferring assets into the trust and establishing the trust's funding. This transfer is not merely a transaction but a deliberate placement of your chosen assets under the trust's protection.

The trust must transfer the deed of tangible assets, like real estate, into its name. The account holder must re-title financial accounts and formally assign personal belongings. For certain assets, such as life insurance or retirement accounts, the trust must be named as the beneficiary to ensure that these assets flow into the trust upon your passing.

The transfer is a detailed operation that demands accuracy to prevent oversights that could lead to assets being left outside the trust's purview, potentially subjecting them to probate or disputes. Creating a comprehensive list of assets and methodically working through each, confirming their integration into the trust is advisable.

Securities, for example, may require coordination with financial institutions to ensure proper transfer. Similarly, business interests might necessitate agreements that respect existing ownership structures while aligning with the trust's terms.

It may be beneficial to transfer some assets into the trust incrementally, especially if there are potential tax implications to consider. Engaging with tax advisors or estate planning attorneys can provide clarity and ensure that you execute the transfers in a manner that supports your financial strategy. This step may be complex, but seeking professional advice can help simplify the process.

Each asset transitioned into the trust weaves another thread into the fabric of your estate plan. This careful integration ensures that the trust is fully prepared to safeguard your assets and, when the time comes, to transfer them seamlessly to your beneficiaries.

Establishing a trust is a process that demands thoughtful deliberation, meticulous planning, and strategic execution. It reflects your attention to detail and commitment to effectively providing for your beneficiaries. With the correct type of trust in place, a reliable trustee at the helm, and a thorough transfer of assets, the trust stands ready to fulfill the vital role it plays in your estate plan.

Trusts and Tax Implications

Various tax threads interweave the fabric of estate planning, shaping your financial tapestry's overall design and impact. Trusts, in particular, play a pivotal role in this regard, offering mechanisms that can alter the tax landscape of your estate. Navigating these waters with an informed mind is crucial, recognizing how trusts can interact with different tax obligations and possibly turn the tide in your favor.

Estate Tax Considerations

Estate taxes can significantly affect the value of your beneficiaries' inheritance when they subject the transferred assets upon death.

Trusts can serve as strategic vessels, skillfully navigating these tax-infused waters. For example, certain irrevocable trusts can remove assets from your taxable estate, potentially lowering the estate tax liability.

Consider a bypass trust, which can shelter assets up to the estate tax exemption amount upon the first spouse's death. This can create a safe harbor for these assets and prevent them from being swept into the surviving spouse's taxable estate. The benefit is twofold: it preserves the exemption for the first spouse while securing assets for beneficiaries, often the couple's children, independent of the surviving spouse's estate.

Income Tax Considerations

The currents of income tax also flow through the world of trusts, with distinct considerations for the grantor, the trust itself, and the beneficiaries. Trusts can generate income through their assets, and this income is subject to taxation. However, the responsibility for payment can vary.

In the case of revocable trusts, the grantor typically bears the income tax responsibility as they retain control over the assets. Conversely, irrevocable trusts often pay their income taxes, which can be at higher rates than individual taxes. However, if such a trust distributes income to beneficiaries, that income shifts to their tax returns, potentially creating a tax-saving windfall if they are in lower brackets.

Therefore, the strategic use of trusts can influence the flow of income taxes, either directing them to the trust itself or allocating them to beneficiaries to optimize the overall tax impact on the estate.

Gift Tax Considerations

When transferring assets into an irrevocable trust, it's essential to consider gift tax, as it becomes another factor in the trust equation. Many consider these transfers taxable gifts, but you can structure them to utilize annual gift tax exclusions and lifetime exemption amounts.

The careful timing and structuring of asset transfers into a trust can maximize these exemptions. For instance, spreading out transfers over multiple years can leverage the annual gift tax exclusion, reducing the overall gift tax burden. Additionally, by applying a portion of the lifetime gift tax exemption to larger transfers, you can mitigate the gift tax impact while funding the trust.

Generation-Skipping Transfer Tax Considerations

The generation-skipping transfer (GST) tax is a tax on assets transferred to individuals two or more generations below the grantor, such as grandchildren. Using trusts can help navigate these GST tax waters with agility.

Specifically designed trusts, like the dynasty trust, can provide for multiple generations while minimizing the impact of GST taxes. By allocating the GST tax exemption to transfers into the trust, the grantor can protect assets as they cascade down through the family lineage, often bypassing GST taxes for generations.

With each twist and turn in the tax landscape, trusts offer options to shield your assets and ensure your beneficiaries receive the full benefit of your legacy. Understanding these tax implications is essential in charting a course that minimizes tax liabilities and aligns with your vision for your estate.

Navigating the intricate tax implications of trusts resembles a captain steering a ship through a maze of channels and currents. Each decision can significantly alter the course, dictating the final destination of your assets and the legacy they represent. It requires vigilance, knowledge, and the foresight to anticipate how each move can affect the future of your estate.

In trust planning, the tax element is a dynamic force that shapes the structure and effectiveness of the trust. It is an area where expert guidance can be invaluable, providing the clarity to make informed decisions and the strategies to optimize your estate for tax purposes. This knowledge makes designing a trust that guides your assets safely to your chosen beneficiaries more accessible.

As we continue to weave the narrative of estate planning, it becomes clear that trusts are more than mere vessels for asset management—they are powerful instruments that can shape your estate's tax narrative, offering opportunities for preservation and growth. By understanding how trusts interact with taxes, you can ensure that your legacy stands strong and resilient against the burden of tax obligations. Remember that understanding this knowledge can help you create a tax-efficient plan to ensure that you fulfill your wishes as intended.

The journey through estate planning continues, and as the path unfolds, the focus shifts to other crucial elements of your plan. Each step builds upon the last to create a cohesive and robust strategy that honors your legacy and secures your beneficiaries' futures.

5

Estate Strategies for Every Stage of Adult Life

The tapestry of life is rich with individual threads, each representing a different path, a unique story. Many people believe that estate planning is only essential for those who have spouses or children, which can overshadow its significance for single adults. But the truth is, regardless of marital or parental status, every adult has a legacy—assets, decisions, and healthcare preferences—that needs a voice. This chapter highlights the often-overlooked essentials of estate planning for the single adult, mapping out strategies that affirm one's autonomy and secure one's interests.

Planning for Single Adults

Asset Distribution

Asset distribution for the single adult isn't about dividing wealth among a spouse and offspring; it's about honoring personal relationships and supporting the causes close to one's heart. It's also about transferring assets smoothly and efficiently to avoid additional burdens on loved ones.

- Designate Beneficiaries: Review all your accounts, especially retirement plans and insurance policies, to ensure beneficiaries are updated. This simple act can prevent your assets from being tied up in probate, the legal process that can otherwise decide where your assets go if beneficiaries are not designated.
- Consider a Living Trust: A living trust can be an intelligent choice for singles. You can control your assets while alive and specify how they should be handled after you pass away. If you have a cherished collection, property, or investments, a trust can ensure they go exactly where you intend.

Guardianship Decisions

For single adults, "guardianship" may conjure images irrelevant to their life stage. However, the concept extends beyond the care of children—it also applies to your care should you become unable to make decisions.

- Choose a Proxy: Appointing a durable power of attorney for finances and healthcare ensures that someone you trust can manage your affairs if you cannot. This person can pay your bills, manage your investments, and make decisions about your medical care according to your wishes.

Healthcare Directives

Healthcare directives are your medical voice when you cannot speak. They're about making your medical preferences known and designating someone to oversee these wishes.

- Living Will: A living will is where you document your wishes regarding life-sustaining treatments. Would you want aggressive treatment for a terminal illness? What about a "do not resuscitate" order? These are tough questions, but addressing them head-on ensures your healthcare preferences are respected.
- Medical Power of Attorney: This document appoints someone to make healthcare decisions on your behalf. It complements your living will, as this person interprets and implements your wishes as medical situations arise.

Visual Element: Checklist
Estate Planning Essentials for Single Adults

- Review and update beneficiaries on all accounts.
- Consider establishing a living trust for asset management and distribution.
- Choose a reliable power of attorney for finances and healthcare.
- Create a living will to document your healthcare preferences.
- Appoint a trusted individual with a medical power of attorney.

Estate planning for single adults is less about tradition and more about personal legacy. It's a proactive stance, a declaration of independence and responsibility. Just as one might take pride in purchasing their first home solo, crafting an estate plan is a statement of self-reliance and foresight—a plan that stands as a testament to the life you've built and the relationships you've cherished.

These strategies are not one-size-fits-all; they require personalization. Tailoring a suit to fit your unique measurements is similar to customizing your estate plan to fit your life circumstances. It's about making informed, strategic decisions that reflect your current situation and anticipated future changes.

This section lays the groundwork for single adults to take charge of their estate planning. The following chapters will address the nuances of estate strategies for married couples, blended families, and unmarried partners. The intention is to ensure that each thread in the fabric of adult life weaves together with care and purpose.

Estate Planning for Married Couples

In the sphere of marriage, the union of two lives extends beyond daily companionship to include the intertwining of financial and legal affairs. Estate planning within the bonds of matrimony necessitates a nuanced approach reflecting the shared life you've built and the individual legacies you contribute to that partnership. Ensuring both parties' wishes are honored, protecting their assets, and realizing the couple's joint intentions is a delicate balance.

Joint Ownership

Married couples should revisit the decision of holding assets jointly through the lens of estate planning instead of making it the default ownership mode. Joint ownership, where both spouses own the property together, can simplify the management of assets and provide a clear path of succession. However, it also means that the asset is not solely yours or your spouse's but belongs to you both legally.

- Titled Assets: Both spouses frequently hold titles for homes, vehicles, and bank accounts. This approach can offer several advantages, such as facilitating the smooth transfer of these assets to the surviving spouse without the need for probate.
- Considerations: When opting for joint ownership, it's vital to understand the implications. For instance, should one spouse encounter legal difficulties, jointly owned assets may be at risk. Additionally, if both spouses pass away simultaneously, the question of the following beneficiaries becomes paramount.

Survivorship Rights

The term "survivorship rights" is particularly resonant for married couples. It denotes the principle that upon the death of one spouse, ownership of certain jointly held assets automatically transfers to the surviving spouse. This provision in joint tenancy agreements bypasses the probate process, allowing immediate asset access.

- Joint Tenancy with Right of Survivorship (JTWROS): This form of ownership is common among married couples, ensuring that assets like real estate and bank accounts transition smoothly to the surviving spouse.
- Tenancy by the Entirety: In some states, this particular form of joint tenancy is available only to married couples, providing an added layer of protection against individual creditors of one spouse.

Tax Considerations

Taxes are an inevitable element that married couples must navigate in estate planning. The interplay between estate planning and taxation can be complex, yet strategic planning offers opportunities to minimize the tax burden on the surviving spouse and eventual heirs.

- Unlimited Marital Deduction: A cornerstone of estate tax planning for married couples, this provision allows for an unlimited amount of assets to be transferred to the surviving spouse tax-free, provided the spouse is a U.S. citizen.
- Portability: The concept of portability allows a surviving spouse to utilize any unused portion of their deceased spouse's federal estate tax exemption. This can effectively double the amount the couple can pass on without incurring estate taxes.
- Gift Splitting: Couples may elect to split gifts made to others, effectively doubling the annual gift tax exclusion amount and reducing their taxable estate without incurring gift tax.

Married couples need to execute an intricate dance in estate planning, where they harmonize individual desires with joint aspirations, and the legal framework must accommodate love and loss. When assessing how assets are held, it is important to carefully consider the surviving spouse's rights and strategically approach any potential tax implications. Engaging in this planning process is not just a financial exercise but an act of love and responsibility, ensuring the life you've built together is honored and preserved for the future.

Addressing Needs of Blended Families

In the mosaic of modern family structures, blended families reflect a rich amalgamation of past and present relationships, each with their own emotional and legal intricacies. Estate planning in this context requires a sensitive touch—a careful calibration that respects previous commitments while honoring current bonds.

Stepchildren Considerations

When families blend, stepchildren often become as dear as one's biological offspring. They may share your home and your life, yet without legal adoption; they do not automatically share in your estate. The absence of a biological link can create unintended barriers to inheritance, making intentional inclusion in estate planning documents critical.

- Explicit Inclusion in Wills and Trusts: Ensure that your stepchildren are not overlooked by naming them in your will or creating specific provisions within a trust. This act can also mitigate assumptions arising from standardized language in estate planning documents that traditionally favor biological relationships.
- Education and Trust Funds: For stepchildren, specially designated funds can provide educational opportunities or financial support that mirrors what you might set aside for biological children, ensuring equitable treatment among all children in the family.

Ex-Spouse Obligations

Navigating the obligations to an ex-spouse while balancing the needs of a current family can be akin to walking a tightrope. When you weave financial responsibilities stipulated in alimony, child support, or divorce agreements into your estate plan, you actively ensure that your financial obligations are met.

- Life Insurance Policies: Ensure your current family's security while structuring ongoing support commitments appropriately. It's a strategy that maintains the integrity of your financial obligations without disrupting the estate's distribution to other beneficiaries.
- Clear Documentation: Maintaining meticulous records of your commitments and how you address them in your estate plan is essential. This clarity can prevent future disputes and ensure all parties understand the rationale behind certain asset allocations.

Fair Asset Division

Achieving fairness in asset division within a blended family is a delicate endeavor. It is not merely a matter of mathematics but a balance of emotional equities, past contributions, and future needs.

- Prenuptial Agreements: These can be instrumental in clarifying the intentions for asset division, particularly for assets brought into the marriage. They provide a predetermined roadmap for asset allocation, which can be a valuable reference point in estate planning.

- Dynamic Trust Structures: Blended families can customize trusts to suit their specific dynamics. A marital trust, for example, can provide for a surviving spouse during their lifetime, with the remaining assets then flowing to children from a previous marriage.

Crafting an estate plan that encapsulates the essence of a blended family requires a nuanced approach—one that considers the emotional and financial threads that bind the family tapestry. It is about creating a plan that feels just and equitable to all members, recognizing that each has played a role in the family's story.

In blended families, the estate plan becomes a narrative that weaves divergent histories into a cohesive story of unity and respect. It demands diplomacy and foresight, ensuring each member's role and rights are acknowledged and preserved. With careful planning and clear communication, the estate plan for a blended family can be a testament to the strength and love that binds its members together.

Estate Planning for Unmarried Partners

In modern society, couples who are not married may face legal challenges due to the lack of recognition of their union. Estate planning for unmarried partners is crucial in affirming their commitment and ensuring that both are protected and provided for according to their mutual intentions.

Legal Protections

Unlike their married counterparts, unmarried partners cannot rely on the legal system to automatically intercede on their behalf in the event of one partner's incapacity or death. This makes establishing legal protections a priority.

- Durable Powers of Attorney: Partners can make critical decisions on each other's behalf and ensure their voices are heard when it matters most by creating durable powers of attorney for healthcare finances.
- Cohabitation Agreements: These contracts can outline each partner's rights and responsibilities, providing a semblance of the legal structure that marriage offers. They can include details on property division, support obligations, and more, tailored to fit the unique contours of the couple's relationship.

Property Ownership

Property and real estate pose particular challenges for unmarried partners, as the default legal presumptions that benefit married couples do not apply.

- Joint Tenancy with Right of Survivorship: This form of co-ownership ensures that upon the death of one partner, the property in question passes directly to the surviving partner without the need for probate. It provides a smooth transfer of ownership, reflecting the shared life the couple has built.
- Tenancy in Common: For those who wish to maintain individual ownership stakes or pass their share to someone other than their partner upon death, tenancy in common offers an alternative. A beneficiary of their choosing can receive a specified share of each partner's property.

Beneficiary Designations

Unmarried partners can ensure that the surviving partner is provided for by naming each other as beneficiaries on life insurance policies, retirement accounts, and other financial instruments.

- Payable on Death (POD) and Transfer on Death (TOD) Accounts: These designations allow unmarried partners to name each other as beneficiaries on bank and investment accounts. They are straightforward tools that facilitate the transfer of assets outside the probate process.
- Retirement Plans and Insurance Policies: Regularly reviewing and updating beneficiary designations on retirement plans and insurance policies is imperative. These designations should reflect the couple's current wishes and can be crucial in supporting the surviving partner financially.

For unmarried partners, estate planning is not an abstract concept; it's a tangible way to protect each other in a world where legal recognition of their relationship is not a given. It's a declaration that their mutual support, shared dreams, and life together are equally valid and worthy of protection as those within a marriage. With thoughtful planning and legal tools, unmarried partners can create a safety net that honors their relationship and secures their shared future.

As we close this chapter, we recognize the importance of intentionality and foresight in estate planning. Whether navigating life's path solo, alongside a spouse, within a blended family, or with an unmarried partner, the strategies and protections you put in place today serve as the framework for the legacy you'll leave tomorrow. This thoughtful preparation ensures that your wishes are not left to the winds of chance but are anchored firmly in your care and consideration for those you hold dear.

Our exploration continues, evolving with each new life change and adapting to meet the needs of every unique situation. The next chapter will further expand on estate planning principles, guiding you through the complexities and bestowing you with the knowledge to secure your legacy, no matter what the future holds.

6

Safeguarding Your Digital Legacy

The distinction between the tangible and the intangible blurs as we increasingly live our lives online in this era. Your digital footprint, a mosaic of online interactions and assets, is as much a part of your legacy as the physical items you bequeath. Yet, regarding estate planning, these digital assets are often left in a nebulous state of oversight, floating in uncertainty. It's vital to anchor them down, ensuring they are as meticulously cataloged and managed as your material possessions.

Consider the digital world a vast ocean, with every email, tweet, or transaction a single droplet. Over a lifetime, these droplets accumulate into a personal sea of data, a digital estate that requires careful navigation. Without a map and compass—tools to define and manage your digital assets—your online life risks becoming adrift, susceptible to the currents of chance.

Defining Digital Assets

Digital assets are not just bits and bytes but the repositories of our personal stories, creative expressions, and financial endeavors. Let's explore three critical categories of digital assets that, without question, should feature in your estate planning.

- Social Media Accounts Social media platforms are the 21st-century scrapbooks of our lives. They chronicle everything from momentous occasions to the daily minutiae that, collectively, tell the story of 'you.' Think of each post as a page in an autobiography you're writing in real-time. Facebook, Instagram, Twitter, and LinkedIn accounts can contain decades of personal history, connections, and insights into your interests and activities. These accounts may hold sentimental value for loved ones or serve as a record of your personal and professional legacy.
- Digital Currencies Cryptocurrencies, like Bitcoin and Ethereum, are the modern-day treasure chests. They can be highly valuable and, crucially, they're assets that exist outside traditional banking systems. Given their decentralized nature, access hinges on specific keys—passwords and codes that, if lost, render the currency as good as sunken treasure: irretrievable. Their volatile nature also means their worth can fluctuate dramatically, making timely management and transfer crucial.
- Online Businesses An online business is akin to a ship you've built and set sail in the digital ocean. It carries your entrepreneurial spirit, financial investments, and professional reputation. Whether it's an e-commerce platform, a freelance portfolio, or a digital content creation hub, this asset requires proactive stewardship to ensure its continuity or smooth transfer in your absence.

Visual Element: Infographic
Mapping Your Digital Assets

A visual representation showing the different types of digital assets and their place in your digital estate:

- Social Media Accounts: Connect the dots between various platforms to illustrate the web of your online presence.
- Digital Currencies: Depict a vault with different cryptocurrency symbols representing value and security considerations.
- Online Businesses: Show a ship navigating digital waters, symbolizing the ongoing management and potential growth of the business.

Understanding your digital assets is the first step in reining them under your estate plan's umbrella. It's about taking the nebulous and grounding it in the concrete, transforming your digital existence from a transient stream into a well-charted river that flows according to your design.

In recognizing the value of these digital assets, you begin to understand the necessity of including them in your estate plan. They are not merely ancillary components but integral parts of your legacy that require the same attention as any physical asset you own. Their management demands a proactive approach, ensuring they are not left to languish in the digital expanse but are preserved, protected, and passed on as you intend.

As we navigate the following chapters, we'll harness the tools and strategies to identify and secure your digital assets within your estate plan. Let's explore why including these assets is essential, how to inventory them accurately, and the steps required to integrate them into your estate planning with the same level of care as your physical assets.

Your digital legacy is a testament to your era—an era where the line between real and virtual is increasingly intertwined. By bringing your digital assets into the fold of your estate planning, you ensure that every aspect of your legacy—online and off—is accounted for and protected.

The Importance of Including Digital Assets in Your Estate Plan

Navigating the digital landscape requires foresight. You should shield your digital assets, like safeguarding a house or a family heirloom. The tapestry of our online lives, woven from emails, photos, blogs, and more, demands protection. It is not just about preventing loss; it's about ensuring that the essence of who we are, as etched into the digital realm, is preserved and that our online endeavors continue to flourish or conclude with dignity, per our wishes.

Asset Protection

Treat digital assets with the same level of vigilance as physical property since they carry both monetary and sentimental value. Investors should take online investment portfolios and revenue streams from digital platforms seriously, as they are tangible assets. Safeguarding these assets means ensuring they are not vulnerable to cyber threats or legal ambiguities. Establishing clear directives within your estate plan for how these assets are to be managed or transferred can preclude potential financial losses that might otherwise occur through oversight or mismanagement.

Privacy Concerns

In the digital sphere, privacy is paramount. Our online interactions, from communication to transactions, often contain sensitive information that, in the wrong hands, could lead to privacy breaches or identity theft. Including digital assets in your estate plan demands a strategy to protect this information. It is about delineating who should gain access to your digital life and under what circumstances. An estate plan that addresses digital assets can help maintain the confidentiality of personal data, ensuring that only designated individuals familiar with your privacy expectations can control these assets.

Legacy Preservation

The story of our lives today is told in pixels as much as in paper and ink. Digital assets constitute a narrative of our existence, capturing moments, ideas, and interactions that map our journey through life. Preserving this legacy means considering how you want your digital life handled posthumously. Will social media profiles remain as memorials, or should they be deactivated? How will personal blogs, websites, or creative works be maintained? The answers to these questions form the blueprint for preserving a digital legacy that respects your memory and reflects your life's narrative.

When you weave digital threads into your estate plan, you ensure that you capture the full extent of your assets and treat the digital manifestations of your life with the same care as the physical ones. This inclusion is not merely a precaution but a reflection of our interconnected world—where our digital presence continues to echo beyond our physical existence.

How to Inventory Your Digital Assets

In an age where our digital footprints are as significant as our physical ones, taking stock of online assets is paramount. To inventory your digital assets is to lay down the map of your online world, marking each treasure chest and noting the paths to reach them. In this meticulous process, we detail the contents of a safety deposit box, ensuring that we account for each item and know its worth.

Listing Online Accounts

The first step in taking inventory is to compile a list of your online accounts. A detailed and structured inventory must note each item and identify its specific location, similar to how a librarian catalogues books.

- Email Accounts: These are often the keys to your digital kingdom, as they can be used to reset passwords and access other accounts. Record each email address, the provider, and any notes on its primary use.
- Financial Accounts: Include banking, investment, and retirement accounts, detailing the institution, account types, and any relevant online customer IDs or usernames.
- Social Networks: List each platform where you maintain a presence, from professional networks like LinkedIn to personal ones like Facebook and Instagram.
- Online Retail Accounts: Document any sites where you shop or sell goods, including marketplaces like eBay or Etsy, and retail giants like Amazon.
- Subscription Services: Note down subscription services for entertainment, software, news outlets, and any other recurring digital service.

- Utility and Service Providers: Remember to manage accounts related to utilities, phone services, and internet providers online.

Documenting Digital Properties

Beyond the list of accounts lies the realm of digital properties that may include domains, blogs, or any other online real estate you own. These properties often hold value both in monetary and intellectual terms and should be cataloged with care.

- **Domains:** For each domain, note the registrar, expiration date, and any associated hosting services.
- **Blogs and Websites:** Document where you have hosted these files, provide details about your content management system, and specify any associated revenue streams.
- **Digital Media:** Keep a tally of your digital creations, whether photographs, videos, or written works, and where they're stored or published online.
- **Online Business Interests:** If you operate or have stakes in online businesses, record the business structure, partners, and digital assets associated with these enterprises.

Recording Access Information

A map is only as good as its ability to guide one to the destination. To ensure that you can manage your digital assets according to your wishes, you must include access information in your inventory of digital assets.

- Passwords: Store passwords securely, whether in a password manager or encrypted digital vault, and provide a means of access to someone you trust.

- Security Questions and Two-Factor Authentication: Record the answers to security questions and details of any two-factor authentication methods in place, such as a mobile device or authentication app.
- Encryption Keys: Ensure that any keys or seed phrases are securely recorded and stored for digital currencies or other encrypted assets.
- Access Permissions: Remember to detail any permissions that may be required to access certain assets, particularly if you share them with business partners or family members.

Take your time in creating a thorough inventory of your digital assets. It requires the same attention and diligence as auditing a complex financial portfolio. Each entry is a commitment to the future management of your online presence and the legacy you choose to leave behind. It's a living document, one that should evolve as your digital life grows and changes.

With every account listed, every property documented, and every piece of access information securely recorded, your digital estate stands in clear view. This clarity simplifies the management of your online assets and provides a beacon for those handling your digital legacy. Your digital inventory, with its detailed entries and careful annotations, becomes a guidebook for the stewardship of your online life, ensuring that your digital assets are as respected and maintained as the physical world you inhabit.

Steps to Include Digital Assets in Your Estate Plan

In the meticulous task of estate planning, incorporating your digital assets ensures that the full spectrum of your estate is acknowledged and prepared for future transitions. It's about taking affirmative action to weave these assets seamlessly into the legal fabric of your will and trust while also designating a trustworthy individual as the custodian of your digital life.

Update Will and Trust

Updating your will and trust to include digital assets safeguards your online presence and ensures a smooth transition of these assets to your beneficiaries. It's an act that acknowledges the evolving nature of asset ownership and the importance of digital holdings within your estate.

- Explicit Instructions: When creating your will and trust, be clear about handling each of your digital assets. Each decision should be unambiguous, whether about continuing online business, distributing digital art collections to loved ones, or memorializing social media accounts.
- Asset Allocation: Assign each digital asset to a beneficiary or specify a trust to manage the assets. For instance, if you have a valuable online business, you could create a separate trust to manage the company's assets, providing detailed guidelines on how the business should be run or dissolved.
- Legal Compliance: Ensure that your will and trust comply with online platforms' and digital service providers' Terms of Service Agreements. Tailoring your estate plan to the terms outlined in these agreements is paramount since they often specify what can legally be done with accounts after the owner's death.

Assign Digital Executor

A digital executor is someone you appoint to manage your online presence after you pass away. This role carries significant responsibility, as it involves navigating both the technical and sentimental aspects of your digital life.

- Role Definition: Define the role of the digital executor in your will or trust, outlining their responsibilities and the scope of their authority. This person must access, manage, and close online accounts, safeguard digital assets, and execute your digital estate plan.
- Skill Considerations: Choose an individual with the necessary technical skills and understanding of digital platforms. You must find someone who respects your privacy and whom you can trust with sensitive information.
- Legal Authority: Provide your digital executor with the legal authority to act on your behalf. This text clarifies the legal right to access digital assets, including electronic communications, online accounts, and digital files, as permitted under state law and federal legislation such as the Revised Uniform Fiduciary Access to Digital Assets Act (RUFADAA).

Provide Access Instructions

Access instructions are the keys to your digital estate, offering a clear path for your digital executor to fulfill their role. These instructions should be precise, secure, and updated regularly.

- Secure Storage: Keep access instructions in a secure location, such as a safe deposit box or with an attorney, and ensure your digital executor knows how to access them when needed.

- Detailed Access Methods: Provide instructions for accessing digital assets, including login credentials, security questions, and guidance for accessing encrypted data or devices.
- Regular Updates: Digital access credentials can change frequently. Establish a routine for updating your access instructions to reflect changes to accounts, passwords, or security features.

Don't take incorporating digital assets into your estate plan lightly. It is an essential step that demands attention to detail, foresight, and an understanding of the digital landscape. To ensure that your digital assets receive the same level of care and diligence as the rest of your estate, update your will and trust, assign a digital executor, and provide comprehensive access instructions.

As we conclude this chapter, it's clear that digital assets are as integral to our legacy as tangible property. Managing these assets effectively requires a blend of technical understanding and thoughtful planning, ensuring that our online identities and possessions are respected and transferred according to our wishes. In the next chapter, we'll shift our focus to another crucial aspect of estate planning: navigating the complexities of family dynamics and ensuring that your estate plan serves as a unifying force rather than a source of discord.

7

Navigating the Waters of Estate Taxes

Imagine standing at the edge of a sprawling vineyard that you've nurtured over the years. Each grapevine is a financial asset; together, they form the wealth you'll eventually pass on. But as with any harvest, there's a portion owed back—to the land, in the form of care and maintenance, and to the state, through taxes. Estate taxes, often called the "death tax," are the government's share of the bounty you've accrued over a lifetime. Understanding these taxes is crucial to ensuring the fruits of your labor benefit those you intend rather than being consumed by tax liabilities.

Understanding Estate Taxes

Federal Estate Tax

The federal estate tax is a levy on transferring the "estate" of a deceased person. It's calculated based on the net value of the property owned at the time of death after accounting for debts and expenses. Simply put, if your estate is worth more than a certain threshold—the federal estate tax exemption amount—your estate may owe taxes to the federal government.

- Exemption Amounts: The IRS sets exemption amounts, which have historically fluctuated. As of my knowledge cutoff in 2023, estates valued under approximately $11.7 million for individuals and $23.4 million for married couples may not be subject to federal estate taxes. It's vital to stay updated, as tax laws and exemption amounts are subject to change.
- Tax Rates: For estates that exceed the exemption amounts, the tax rates can be steep, often starting at around 18% and climbing to as high as 40% for the portion of the estate that exceeds the maximum threshold.

State Inheritance Tax

Not all states impose state inheritance tax, as it is separate from federal estate tax. The government imposes an inheritance tax on the beneficiaries of an estate according to the value of the assets they inherit. The rate and applicability vary widely from state to state, with some states collecting no inheritance tax at all. In contrast, others impose rates that can significantly dent your beneficiaries' inheritance.

- Varied Rates and Exemptions: Each state that imposes an inheritance tax sets its own rates and exemption levels. For instance, some states have lower exemption thresholds than the federal level, meaning that even if your estate doesn't owe federal taxes, it might still be liable for state taxes.
- Consider the Beneficiary's Relationship: The inheritance tax rate owed in many states can depend on the beneficiary's relationship to the deceased. Spouses are often exempt,

while distant relatives or non-relatives may face higher rates.

Gift Tax

Gift tax is the federal tax applied to transferring money or property to another person while you're still alive without receiving something of equal value in return. It's a way for the government to ensure that individuals don't simply give away their wealth before death to avoid estate taxes.

- Annual Exclusion: An annual exclusion amount allows you to give away a certain sum to any number of individuals each year without incurring gift tax. As of my last update, this amount is $15,000 per recipient per year.
- Lifetime Exemption: In addition to the annual exclusion, a lifetime exemption coincides with the federal estate tax exemption. This means you can give away a certain amount over your lifetime without owing taxes—once you exceed this amount, the gift tax kicks in.
- Direct Payments: It's worth noting that certain types of gifts, such as direct payments for someone's medical expenses or tuition, are exempt from the gift tax altogether.

Visual Element: Chart
Understanding Estate and Gift Tax Exemptions

Year

    Federal Estate Tax Exemption
    Annual Gift Tax Exclusion
    Lifetime Gift Tax Exemption

2023

$11.7 million
$15,000
$11.7 million

Understanding these taxes and their implications can be as intricate as chess; each move has consequences, and your strategy will determine the outcome. Knowing the rules is the first step, but playing the game well requires foresight and planning. Understanding how federal and state taxes will impact the family business or valuable piece of property can influence your decisions today, especially if you're considering passing them on to someone else.

Estate planning is about more than just drafting documents—it's about crafting a strategy that encompasses not only the distribution of your assets but also the preservation of your wealth against the erosive potential of taxes. Remember that understanding these taxes can equip you with better decision-making abilities that align with your financial goals and the legacy you wish to leave behind.

How to Minimize Estate Taxes

Trusts

A Cloak of Protection for Your Assets

The strategic use of trusts can serve as a shield, guarding your estate against the potential siege of taxes. Imagine fortifying your assets within an impenetrable fortress-like trust. When structured astutely, trusts can significantly reduce the taxable estate, thus easing the potential tax burden upon your heirs.

- Irrevocable Life Insurance Trust (ILIT): An ILIT is a type of trust specifically designed to own a life insurance policy. When you transfer a life insurance policy into an ILIT, the proceeds from the policy are not considered part of your estate and are, therefore, not subject to estate taxes. This can offer sizable savings, especially for estates that hover around the tax exemption threshold.
- Grantor Retained Annuity Trust (GRAT): A GRAT allows you to transfer appreciating assets to beneficiaries while retaining a right to annuity payments for a term of years. Any appreciation of the assets over a set interest rate—known as the Section 7520 rate—passes to your beneficiaries tax-free. This can be an effective tool for transferring growth potential out of your estate with little to no gift tax cost.
- Qualified Personal Residence Trust (QPRT): A QPRT enables you to transfer a personal residence to a trust while retaining the right to live there for a term of years. Post-term, the residence transfers to the trust beneficiaries, often at a reduced tax cost. The transfer freezes the value of the gift at the time of transfer rather than when the beneficiaries receive the residence, making this trust advantageous.

Each trust serves as a strategic bulwark, crafted to protect specific assets from the reach of estate taxes. Transferring assets into these trusts removes them from your estate, thereby decreasing its value and the corresponding tax liability.

Gifting Strategies

The Art of Generosity

Gifting can be a proactive tactic in estate tax reduction, allowing you to disperse portions of your wealth to beneficiaries during your lifetime, thus diminishing the taxable estate. The artistry lies in gifting assets that have the potential for significant appreciation, thereby transferring the future growth out of your estate.

- Annual Exclusion Gifting: Utilize the annual gift tax exclusion to give up to the allowable amount per recipient each year. Using this exclusion regularly allows you to transfer wealth incrementally without tapping into your lifetime gift and estate tax exemption.
- Education and Medical Expenses: Payments made directly to an educational institution for tuition or to a healthcare provider for medical expenses are exempt from gift tax. These are strategic avenues for reducing your estate while investing in the well-being and future of your beneficiaries.
- Family Loan Strategy: Lend money to family members at the minimum interest rates required by the IRS, known as the Applicable Federal Rates (AFRs). If the family member then invests that money in a way that outperforms the AFR, the excess growth is effectively transferred out of your estate.

Through gifting, you can lighten your estate tax load while enriching the lives of your beneficiaries. When executed precisely, these transfers can create immediate joy and long-term benefit for those you care about, all while adhering to an intelligent estate tax strategy.

Charitable Donations

The Legacy of Altruism

Charitable giving can be a cornerstone of estate tax minimization, offering a dual benefit of fulfilling philanthropic desires and reducing the size of your taxable estate. When you earmark assets for charity, you forge a legacy of altruism and craft an estate plan that benefits from tax deductions and exemptions.

- Charitable Remainder Trust (CRT): A CRT allows you to convert a highly appreciated asset into lifetime income. It reduces your taxable income by allowing a deduction for the charitable contribution and eliminates capital gains taxes on the sale of the asset. At the end of the trust term, the remaining assets go to the charity, reflecting your philanthropic legacy.
- Charitable Lead Trust (CLT): In a CLT, the charity receives income from the trust for a term of years, after which the remaining assets revert to you or pass to your beneficiaries. This arrangement can provide significant gift and estate tax savings, particularly if the assets in the trust appreciate beyond the IRS-assumed rates.
- Donor-Advised Funds (DAF): A DAF is a philanthropic vehicle that allows you to make a charitable donation, receive an immediate tax deduction, and recommend grants from the fund over time. It's an effective way to create a lasting impact while receiving a tax benefit upfront.

Employing charitable strategies within your estate plan serves the greater good and aligns your financial legacy with your personal values. Incorporating charitable giving into your estate can achieve a more favorable tax position, ensuring your generosity extends beyond your lifetime.

In each of these strategies—trusts, gifting, and charitable donations—the goal remains constant: to minimize the impact of estate taxes on the wealth you've worked so hard to accumulate. These approaches offer avenues to transfer your assets in ways that reflect your priorities and preserve your estate for the benefit of your heirs and the causes you champion. Using these instruments, you can sculpt your legacy and ensure that your estate reflects your life's work and enduring values.

Estate Planning and Income Taxes

The realm of income taxes is a landscape every estate must traverse. As you strategize your estate plan, it's imperative to consider the assets you will bequeath and the income taxes that will continue to play a role for your beneficiaries. The nuances of capital gains tax mark the path here, as do the intricacies of retirement account distributions and the particulars of life insurance proceeds. Each element demands attention to mitigate the tax burden on your heirs.

Capital Gains Tax

- Asset Appreciation: When an asset appreciates in value and is sold, capital gains tax comes into play. This tax is applied to the difference between the purchase price, known as the 'basis,' and the sale price. Understanding the basis is crucial for beneficiaries as it determines the tax implications of selling inherited assets.

- Step-Up in Basis: One significant advantage for heirs is the 'step-up in basis' rule. This means that the valuation of an inherited asset is 'stepped up' to its fair market value at the time of the decedent's death. Consequently, if the heir later sells the asset, the capital gains tax is calculated based on this stepped-up basis, potentially reducing the tax owed.
- Holding Periods: Differentiating between long-term and short-term capital gains can impact the tax rate. Assets held for more than a year before being sold are subject to long-term capital gains tax rates, which are generally lower than short-term rates. For inherited assets, the holding period automatically qualifies for long-term treatment, providing another layer of tax efficiency for beneficiaries.

Retirement Account Distributions

- Tax-Deferred Accounts: Retirement accounts like traditional IRAs and 401(k)s are often central to estate planning. Contributions to these accounts are typically tax-deferred, meaning taxes are only paid on the money once it is withdrawn. Beneficiaries inheriting these accounts are responsible for the taxes due upon distribution.
- Required Minimum Distributions (RMDs): Beneficiaries of retirement accounts are usually required to take minimum distributions over their lifetime. These RMDs are taxed as ordinary income, and failing to take them can result in hefty penalties.
- Roth Accounts: In contrast, Roth IRAs and 401(k)s are funded with after-tax dollars, allowing for tax-free growth and distributions. However, beneficiaries must adhere to specific withdrawal rules to maintain the tax-free status of these accounts.

Life Insurance Proceeds

- **Generally Tax-Free:** Life insurance proceeds are typically free from income tax when paid to beneficiaries. This attribute makes life insurance a pivotal component in estate planning, as it provides a tax-efficient means of transferring wealth.
- **Estate Inclusion:** While life insurance proceeds are usually income tax-exempt, they may still be included in the decedent's estate for estate tax purposes, depending on the policy ownership. Proper structuring, such as ownership through an irrevocable life insurance trust, can avoid this inclusion, thereby sidestepping the potential estate tax hit.
- **Accelerated Benefits:** In some cases, policy owners can access life insurance proceeds before death, known as 'accelerated benefits,' if they meet specific criteria like a terminal illness diagnosis. When planning for potential healthcare expenses, it's important to consider that these funds may be taxable depending on the situation.

Addressing these aspects of income taxes within your estate plan is not just about preparation; it's an ongoing strategy that adapts to the ever-flowing current of tax laws and rates. It requires a vigilant eye on legislative changes and a hand ready to adjust the sails to maintain course for the most tax-efficient transfer of wealth to your heirs.

Understanding the impact of income taxes on your estate is akin to planting a garden with an eye toward the seasons ahead. Just as a gardener prepares the soil and selects plants that will thrive in future conditions, so must you lay the groundwork for an estate that will weather the changing tax climate. It's a proactive approach, planting today the seeds that will grow into a robust legacy for your beneficiaries tomorrow.

Each decision made in the context of income taxes—whether to sell an asset now or later, how to manage retirement account distributions, or the best way to incorporate life insurance into your plan— is a deliberate step on the path of estate planning. It's a path that meanders through a landscape of tax implications, with each turn offering opportunities to optimize your estate's financial health. With careful planning and a clear understanding of income taxes, you can ensure that the legacy you leave is not diminished by tax burdens but is instead a testament to your life's work and foresight.

State-Specific Estate Tax Laws

The laws of the land, particularly the states where you possess assets, color the tapestry of regulations in estate taxes. These local nuances can shape the tax landscape of your estate in significant ways, much like regional climates can influence the growth patterns in a garden. Some states mirror the federal approach to estate taxes, while others chart their own course, creating a patchwork of tax environments that can impact your estate planning.

Community Property States

In states that recognize community property, a unique set of rules applies to married couples. These rules consider all property acquired during the marriage, barring inheritances and gifts, as jointly owned. Both spouses jointly own this community property, each holding an undivided half-interest.

- Impact on Estate Tax: When one spouse passes away, the community property is effectively divided into two equal shares. This can be advantageous for tax purposes, as only the deceased spouse's half is subject to estate tax, potentially leading to a lower estate tax liability.
- Benefits of Joint Ownership: The inherent structure of community property simplifies the transfer of assets upon the death of one spouse, often streamlining the estate administration process. However, it's vital to consider this in conjunction with your overall estate plan to ensure it aligns with your wishes and maximizes tax efficiency.

States recognizing community property include Arizona, California, Idaho, Louisiana, Nevada, New Mexico, Texas, Washington, and Wisconsin, with Alaska offering an opt-in community property system. Each has its own flavor of the law, requiring attention to detail when planning your estate.

Inheritance Tax States

A subset of states imposes an inheritance tax, which, unlike estate tax, is paid by the beneficiaries of an estate rather than the estate itself. The rate at which this tax applies can significantly influence your estate planning strategies.

- Varied Rates: Inheritance tax rates can vary widely depending on the state and the beneficiary's relationship to the deceased. Spouses are often exempt, but other close relatives may face lower rates than distant relatives or unrelated individuals.
- Strategic Planning: In states with inheritance tax, careful planning can help manage the tax impact on your beneficiaries. This might involve redistributing assets

during your lifetime or using life insurance policies to provide beneficiaries with the means to pay the inheritance tax without dipping into their inheritance.

If you reside or own property in a state with an inheritance tax, it's essential to consider how this can affect your heirs and to plan accordingly to mitigate the tax burden they may face.

No Estate Tax States

Conversely, several states have chosen not to levy an estate tax. In these states, residents can pass on their wealth without the concern of state-level estate taxation, which can simplify estate planning and administration.

- Tax Planning Simplified: Without the need to plan for state estate taxes, individuals in these states can focus on other aspects of their estate planning, such as asset protection and beneficiary designations.
- Residency Considerations: Residency becomes a critical factor for those with properties in multiple states. Establishing domicile in a state with no estate tax can be a strategic move, potentially saving a significant amount in taxes upon death.

States that do not impose an estate tax provide a favorable environment for preserving wealth for future generations. However, residents must remain vigilant about federal estate tax laws and consider how changes at the national level might affect their estate planning.

Each state's approach to estate taxation can influence the strategies and tools you employ to craft your estate plan. Like a navigator reading the stars, understanding the tax landscape in which your estate resides allows you to chart a course that ensures your assets reach their intended destination with minimal tax burden. You must combine legal knowledge with strategic foresight to align your estate plan with your state's tax laws and preserve your legacy according to your wishes.

With a firm grasp of state-specific estate tax laws, you stand ready to tailor your estate plan to the unique tax environment in which you reside. It's a process that calls for a sharp eye and a steady hand as you align your assets and legacy with the tax climates shaping their future. This understanding is a vital component of your estate planning, enabling you to ensure that your estate is a reflection of your life's work and a gift that continues to benefit your loved ones according to your intentions.

In conclusion, estate planning is akin to charting a navigational course; each decision, from the distribution of assets to the minimization of taxes, is a calculated step toward the legacy you envision. As we move forward, we'll explore how to protect against the unforeseen and the inevitable, ensuring that your estate plan stands as a testament to your foresight and care for your loved ones' future.

8

Navigating the Waters of Healthcare Directives

Imagine a sailor at sea, navigating through fog and tumultuous waves. The clarity of their destination is obscured, the path uncertain. This is akin to facing a medical emergency without a healthcare directive—without clear instructions, your healthcare preferences may remain shrouded in uncertainty, leaving loved ones and medical professionals to guess your course. A healthcare directive acts as a lighthouse, guiding decisions with the bright light of your wishes, cutting through the fog, and providing direction during the most critical moments.

In the maze of healthcare decisions, a directive serves as your voice when you cannot speak for yourself. It's a means of communicating and affirming your values and choices regarding medical treatment. Here, we will explore the critical elements shaping this vital aspect of estate planning.

Living Will

A living will is not about finances or who gets your cherished watch; it's about the treatments you would want—or not want—when facing a severe medical condition. It's a declaration of your healthcare preferences in situations where you may be unable to express them.

- Treatment Preferences: Details in a living will include your wishes to use life-sustaining measures such as mechanical ventilation, artificial nutrition and hydration, and other forms of medical intervention.
- End-of-Life Care: This document often outlines your desires concerning palliative care—care that focuses on comfort and quality of life, particularly when facing a terminal illness.
- Real-Life Scenario: Consider someone diagnosed with a terminal condition who has detailed their choice to forego aggressive treatments in favor of hospice care. The living will ensures that this individual's healthcare aligns with their wishes, providing dignity and respect for their choices.

Durable Power of Attorney for Health Care

The durable power of attorney for healthcare directs the following of the script, which is the living will. This document appoints someone you trust—an agent—to make medical decisions on your behalf if you're incapacitated.

- Agent Selection: Choosing an agent is a significant decision. This individual should understand your healthcare philosophy and be willing to advocate for your preferences,

even under pressure.
- Scope of Authority: The document should clearly delineate the agent's decision-making power, specifying what they can and cannot do regarding your medical care.
- Where and When: It's crucial to have this document in place before any medical emergency arises. The durable power of attorney for healthcare should be readily accessible to your agent and healthcare providers, perhaps registered with a hospital or primary care physician.

Do Not Resuscitate Orders

- A Do Not Resuscitate (DNR) order is a specific instruction that tells medical professionals not to perform CPR if your heart stops or if you stop breathing. A DNR focuses on this singular, critical event, unlike a living will or a durable power of attorney for health care, which can cover a range of medical decisions.
- Clear Intent: The DNR is explicit; it leaves no room for ambiguity in an emergency. It's a decision that should be made after thoughtful consideration and discussion with your doctor, understanding the potential outcomes.
- State Regulations: DNR orders are governed by state laws, so the process for creating one varies. Generally, they require a doctor's signature and must be readily available to emergency responders, such as on a bracelet or in a visible location within your home.

Visual Element: Checklist
Healthcare Directive Essentials

- Decide on your end-of-life care preferences.
- Choose a trusted individual as your healthcare agent.

- Discuss your wishes in detail with your chosen agent.
- Draft a living will and durable power of attorney for healthcare.
- Obtain a Do Not Resuscitate order if desired, following state-specific procedures.
- Make copies of these documents and inform your agent, family, and healthcare providers of their location.

Creating a healthcare directive is a proactive step that speaks to the heart of who you are and how you wish to be cared for. It's a document that reflects your medical preferences and embodies your autonomy and respect for life. It ensures that your voice echoes in the decisions made, even when you cannot speak them aloud. With a healthcare directive in place, you provide a beacon for those navigating tough choices, offering guidance and certainty amid life's most challenging storms.

The Importance of Having a Healthcare Directive

Medical Decision Making

Empowering others to act on your medical behalf is a profound delegation of trust entrusted to someone who understands your health-related values and desires. It's a safeguard, ensuring that the care you receive aligns with your preferences should you be unable to articulate them. The stipulations you place in your healthcare directive serve as a guiding star for this individual, illuminating the path of choices that respect your autonomy and dignity.

- Clarity in Complexity: Decisions must be made swiftly when health crises erupt with little warning. A healthcare directive provides unequivocal guidance during such

tumultuous times, outlining your preferences for procedures and interventions. It mitigates the risk of unnecessary or unwanted treatments that may not align with your values or improve your quality of life.
- Legally Supported Wishes: With the backing of a healthcare directive, your agent has a legal framework to support the execution of your choices. This legal instrument ensures that healthcare providers hear and respect your voice in discussions, regardless of your capacity to communicate.

End-of-Life Care

The dignity you maintain at the end of life is a reflection of the care you receive. It's essential to articulate your wishes for this final stage—whether it involves seeking every possible treatment or focusing on comfort and quality of life.

- Personalized Care: Each person has unique thresholds for what they consider quality of life, particularly when facing a terminal illness. You can define what quality of life means to you through a healthcare directive, whether you want to sustain life at all costs or ensure pain management and preservation of dignity.
- Specifying Desires: Within your directive, you might identify specific interventions to accept or decline, like mechanical ventilation or artificial nutrition. You can also express wishes regarding palliative care, hospice, and the environment in which you'd like to spend your final days.

Family Dispute Prevention

Families can find themselves at a crossroads without a healthcare directive, with each member bringing their own perceptions of what is best. This can lead to conflicts that strain relationships and complicate decision-making during challenging times.

- Unambiguous Directives: By clearly outlining your healthcare preferences in a legally binding document, you provide a decisive direction for your loved ones. This minimizes confusion and reduces the likelihood of disagreements among family members about the appropriate course of your care.
- Emotional Burden Alleviated: Clearly outlining the course of action relieves your family from the emotional toll of making tough decisions on the fly. It also spares them the burden of wondering if they made the right choice, providing peace in a time of grief.

By considering establishing a healthcare directive, you lay the foundation for medical decision-making that honors your personal philosophies and life choices. It's a gesture that communicates your foresight and care for those you will one day leave behind, ensuring that your health and end-of-life care are managed consistently with your wishes. This directive is a testament to your values, offering clear guidance in the face of life's most uncertain moments.

Understanding Power of Attorney

Power of Attorney (POA) is a legal instrument that grants one individual—the agent or attorney-in-fact—the authority to act on behalf of another—the principal—in specified financial or legal matters. It's a pivotal tool within the toolbox of estate planning, as it designates who will manage your affairs and how they will do so if you're unable to act due to incapacitation or absence. The scope of this authority can vary greatly depending on the type of POA established. Below, we explore the nuances and applications of different POAs to provide a clearer picture of their functions and importance.

Durable Power of Attorney

The term 'durable' relates to the POA's resilience; it remains effective even if the principal becomes incapacitated. This durability is crucial because it ensures that the agent's authority persists precisely when it's most needed—when the principal cannot manage their own affairs.

- Scope of Authority: Typically, a durable POA encompasses a broad spectrum of financial and legal powers, from managing bank accounts and investments to handling real estate transactions and legal claims.
- Activation: It becomes effective immediately upon signing unless stated otherwise, and it endures through the principal's incapacitation, ensuring uninterrupted management of their affairs.
- Considerations: When drafting a durable POA, it's crucial to contemplate the breadth of powers granted. With great authority comes the potential for misuse, so the chosen agent must be someone of unwavering trustworthiness.

Limited Power of Attorney

The limited POA restricts specific situations, tasks, or periods, as suggested by its name. It's a precision tool tailored for particular actions and relinquishes its authority once those are complete.

- **Targeted Functions:** While you're abroad, the agent may sell a property, manage certain accounts, or execute a financial transaction.
- **Time-Bound:** The person who creates the POA usually sets an expiration date or terminates it upon completing the task for which it was created.
- **Advantage:** Its limited nature can provide peace of mind for those who wish to grant authority for a specific purpose without handing over extensive control of their affairs.

Springing Power of Attorney

A springing POA is akin to a contingency plan—it springs into action under predefined circumstances, typically the principal's incapacitation. Those who prefer to maintain control over their affairs until a triggering event necessitates delegation can use it.

- Triggering Events: The conditions that activate a springing POA are explicitly defined, often requiring medical certification of the principal's incapacity. This ensures that the agent only assumes power when absolutely necessary.
- Delayed Activation: Unlike a durable POA that becomes effective immediately, a springing POA remains inactive until the specified conditions are met. This delay can provide a sense of autonomy to the principal but may also lead to complications or delays when urgent decisions are required.
- Clarity is Key: Given the conditional nature of a springing POA, the document must be clear about what constitutes incapacitation and how it will be determined. Ambiguities could lead to disputes or legal challenges at a time when swift action might be critical.

Each type of Power of Attorney serves distinct purposes, tailored to the principal's specific intentions and circumstances. Selecting the right POA requires careful reflection on the level of control and flexibility desired, balanced against trust in the chosen agent. It is an intricate aspect of estate planning that demands precision in its crafting to ensure that your affairs are managed according to your wishes, regardless of what the future may hold.

Implementing a POA lays the groundwork for future scenarios where hindrances may arise, enabling you to act with foresight. It provides a structured approach to safeguarding your legal and financial matters, ensuring they are in capable hands. Your predetermined directives guide the agent acting on your behalf, and the POA serves as a bulwark to protect your interests and maintain the continuity of your affairs. Whether it's the durable, limited, or springing POA, each plays a strategic role in the comprehensive planning of your estate, reflecting the depth of your preparations for the uncertainties of tomorrow.

How to Set Up a Healthcare Directive and Power of Attorney

Selecting an Agent

When you select an agent, you give them significant power over your well-being. Therefore, you should handle their selection with great care and introspection. This individual will stand as your advocate and surrogate decision-maker should you be unable to communicate your healthcare preferences.

- Alignment of Values: Compatibility of beliefs regarding medical interventions and quality of life is essential. Engage in deep conversations with potential agents to

gauge their understanding and willingness to abide by your healthcare philosophy.
- Resilience Under Pressure: The role requires someone who can maintain composure in stressful situations. Assess the person's ability to navigate complex medical systems and advocate firmly for your wishes in the face of adversity.
- Availability and Proximity: Choosing someone readily available and within a reasonable distance is practical. Proximity can be crucial in situations where immediate decisions are required.

Document Preparation

Creating healthcare directives and powers of attorney requires precision in language and legal acumen. To ensure the accuracy and legality of your wishes, it's crucial to draft these documents carefully.

- Professional Guidance: Enlisting the expertise of a legal professional is highly advised. An attorney specializing in healthcare directives can offer invaluable insight into the nuances of state laws and help tailor your documents to your specific situation.
- Incorporating Specific Wishes: Documents should reflect all your medical preferences, from the types of life-sustaining treatments you would accept or refuse to your thoughts on pain management and palliative care.
- Updates and Revisions: As your health and circumstances evolve, so should your healthcare directives. Regularly review and update your documents to ensure they remain relevant and reflect your current healthcare desires.

Legal Execution

For healthcare directives and powers of attorney to hold legal weight, their execution must adhere to state-specific formalities. This final step is crucial to ensure that your carefully prepared documents are recognized and enforceable.

- Witness Requirements: Most states require the presence of one or more witnesses during the signing of these documents. These individuals attest to the signature's authenticity and the signatory's soundness of mind.
- Notarization: Some jurisdictions may also necessitate the notarization of the documents, adding an extra layer of legal validation.
- Filing with Institutions: You should file copies of the documents with your primary healthcare providers, hospitals where you may receive care, and your designated agent once you execute them. These filings ensure all relevant parties know your directives and can access them when needed.

With your healthcare directive and power of attorney, you have taken a decisive step in maintaining control over your medical and personal affairs. The agent you have chosen now has a clear roadmap to follow, reflecting your healthcare preferences and legal wishes. Your proactive approach to personal healthcare management stands as a testament, offering peace of mind that your voice will still be heard even in times when you cannot speak for yourself.

As you consider life's journey, with its inherent unpredictability, the foresight to establish these directives ensures that your wishes for healthcare and personal matters are respected and upheld. This thoughtful planning is a gift to yourself and your loved ones, providing clarity and direction in what may be challenging times ahead. With these measures in place, you can rest assured that your choices will guide future healthcare decisions, aligning with your values and preserving your autonomy.

In our next chapter, we will build upon the foundations laid here, further solidifying our understanding of estate planning as we examine the strategies and tools that can protect and manage your assets for the future.

9

Guardians of Legacy: Executors and Trustees Explained

There's a quiet strength in the steady hands that steer the ship through the storm, a resilience in the calm voice that commands amidst chaos. These are the hands and the voice of an executor or trustee when the seas of life become turbulent. The aftermath of a loss is a storm of emotions, decisions, and legalities. An executor or trustee stands as the beacon of order, guiding the vessel of an estate through the complex waters of asset management, legal representation, and the eventual distribution that honors the decedent's wishes.

In the real world, these roles are often the unsung heroes in the narrative of estate planning. They don't merely execute tasks; they uphold a legacy, carry out last wishes, and navigate the intricate legalities that arise after a person's passing. In this chapter, we grasp the gravity of their responsibilities and the impact of their actions on those who remain.

The Role of an Executor or Trustee

Asset Management

An executor or trustee is entrusted with the helm, managing assets with a duty of care that mirrors a captain's responsibility to their ship. This role demands an intimate understanding of the estate's holdings, from bank accounts to real estate, investments to family heirlooms. It involves safeguarding these assets, ensuring they are neither squandered nor subjected to unnecessary risk. Think of it as a financial caretaker, scrutinizing expenses, maintaining property, and making prudent decisions that preserve the value of the estate.

Legal Representation

Imagine standing before a council where every decision you make is scrutinized. An executor or trustee often finds themselves in similar situations, representing the estate in all legal matters. They must navigate a labyrinth of court proceedings, from proving the will to addressing claims against the estate. They are the voice that speaks on behalf of the deceased, a voice that must resonate with authority and knowledge of legal obligations.

Distribution of Assets

The distribution of assets is a delicate dance of honoring the decedent's wishes while adhering to legal requirements. It involves a detailed understanding of who gets what, when, and how. Executors and trustees must be meticulous, ensuring each beneficiary receives their due share, as outlined in the will or trust. They act as the hand that weaves through the tapestry of the estate, stitching together the final picture that reflects the decedent's desires.

Tax Responsibilities

The realm of taxes is a complex puzzle that executors and trustees must piece together. They are responsible for filing final income tax returns, paying any estate taxes owed, and sometimes managing ongoing tax obligations for trusts. This task requires a keen eye for detail and a comprehensive understanding of tax laws to ensure compliance and minimize the estate's tax burden.

Conflict Resolution

When disputes arise, the executor or trustee must step in as the mediator, balancing emotions with the tenets of the will or trust. They hold the compass that navigates through family disagreements and beneficiary contentions, always aiming to reach a resolution that aligns with the decedent's intentions and maintains peace among the remaining parties.

Visual Element: Checklist
Executor and Trustee Essentials:

- Accurate record-keeping of all estate transactions.
- Regular communication with beneficiaries regarding estate proceedings.
- Ensuring proper insurance is in place for properties and valuable assets.
- Overseeing the appraisal and valuation of estate holdings.
- Strategic planning for tax obligations and potential liabilities.

Understanding the multifaceted role of executors and trustees is paramount in appreciating the magnitude of their duties. They are the steadying force in a time of upheaval, the custodians of an individual's final testament. Their role is grounded in trust and laden with responsibilities that reach far beyond the mere distribution of assets. Executors and trustees safeguard one's legacy by upholding the individual's last wishes and writing the final chapters of their life story with fidelity.

In the face of grief and loss, the executor or trustee's role is to provide clarity and direction, steering the estate through the complexities of asset management, legal battles, and the distribution of wealth. They are the architects of the decedent's final plan, the hands that sculpt the lasting impression of a life well-lived, and the voice that ensures the story told is true to the author's intent.

Factors to Consider When Choosing Your Executor or Trustee

Selecting the right individual to manage your estate is akin to finding a captain for your ship; they must possess the necessary traits to navigate through complex waters with poise and precision. This choice will reverberate through the lives of your beneficiaries and the legacy you leave behind. The following considerations are pivotal in making an informed decision, ensuring that your estate is in competent and reliable hands.

Trustworthiness

At the core of this pivotal role lies the need for unwavering trustworthiness. Your executor or trustee will have access to sensitive information and control over your assets; their integrity is paramount. You must have unequivocal confidence in their ethical standards and commitment to act in your estate's and beneficiaries' best interests. This trust stems from their track record of honesty and moral conduct in personal and professional spheres.

- A history of dependable actions and decisions in past roles or responsibilities.
- A reputation among peers for ethical behavior and upholding promises.
- Absence of any conflicts of interest that may compromise their impartiality.

Organizational Skills

The executor or trustee cannot overstate the importance of managing a multitude of tasks efficiently. They must keep impeccable records, adhere to deadlines, and coordinate various elements of estate administration. Their organizational prowess will ensure everything runs smoothly, from filing court documents to managing estate accounts.

- Proven experience in managing projects or complex tasks with multiple moving parts.
- An eye for detail and a systematic approach to tracking and documenting actions.
- The capacity to prioritize responsibilities effectively, addressing urgent needs while keeping sight of long-term objectives.

Financial Acumen

A sophisticated understanding of financial matters is a cornerstone of the executor or trustee's role. They will make decisions affecting the estate's fiscal health, from investment choices to tax filings. Their financial literacy will guide these choices, aiming to preserve and maximize the estate's assets for the beneficiaries.

- Experience with financial planning, investments, or managing budgets.
- Familiarity with tax laws and estate accounting practices.
- Ability to interpret financial statements and reports to inform sound estate management decisions.

Availability

Your executor or trustee's ability to dedicate the necessary time to manage your estate is essential. The settlement of your estate can be delayed by the time-consuming demands of estate administration and the availability of resources.

- A clear understanding of the time commitment required and willingness to fulfill the role's responsibilities.
- Current obligations, such as career and family, will not hinder their ability to manage the estate.
- Proximity to the estate's assets and the legal jurisdiction where the estate will be administered.

Emotional Stability

Managing an estate is not just a financial or legal endeavor; it is an emotional one as well. The executor or trustee may need to navigate family dynamics and make tough decisions under stressful conditions. Their emotional fortitude is as crucial as their technical skills.

- The capacity to remain composed and make objective decisions, even in emotionally charged situations.
- The strength to handle grief and loss while carrying out the duties of their role.

- Skills in communication and diplomacy to address beneficiary concerns with empathy and clarity.

As you evaluate candidates for these vital roles, consider these attributes as the compass points that will guide your decision. The right executor or trustee will balance these traits, steering your estate with the care and foresight it deserves. By appointing them, you demonstrate trust in their abilities and dedication, ensuring your final wishes are honored and respected.

The Pros and Cons of Choosing a Professional Executor or Trustee

In the theater of estate management, the actors who take on the roles of executors and trustees are pivotal to the performance. Among the cast, there is an option to enlist a professional—a seasoned player who brings a particular set of skills and attributes to the stage. Like any casting choice, this decision comes with its merits and limitations. This section carefully evaluates the nuances of selecting a professional executor or trustee to manage your estate.

Expertise and Experience

Professionals in estate administration often possess a wealth of knowledge garnered from years of specialized practice. Their expertise covers a broad spectrum of necessary skills, from legal knowledge to financial acumen.

- Adept at navigating the complex maze of probate court, understanding the intricacies of tax laws, and managing investments, these professionals can apply their seasoned expertise to safeguard and optimize the estate's value.

- Exposure to a diverse array of estates equips them with the ability to anticipate issues and implement strategies that may not be apparent to a layperson.
- Their experience can be particularly invaluable in estates that involve complicated assets, such as international holdings or business interests, where specialized knowledge is paramount.

Impartiality

One of the intrinsic benefits of a professional executor or trustee is their objectivity. Free from the web of personal relationships and familial dynamics, they can make decisions aligned with the decedent's wishes and the estate's best interests.

- Making decisions without bias can prevent and resolve conflicts among beneficiaries.
- Their neutrality also protects the estate, as heirs are less likely to question or question their actions based on alleged partiality.

Time Commitment

The administration of an estate can demand an immense investment of time and attention. A professional executor or trustee is committed to dedicating the required resources to manage the estate effectively.

- Equipped with an infrastructure that supports estate management demands, they can ensure that all tasks are completed efficiently and within the necessary timeframes.
- Their focus on the estate is unwavering, unencumbered by

the personal obligations that might distract a non-professional from the task.

Cost

To make an informed decision about hiring a professional, it is important to take financial considerations into account. While their services provide value, they also come at a price.

- Professionals typically charge a fee for their services, which can be a percentage of the estate's value or an hourly rate. Depending on the complexity and duration of the administration process, the estate's assets pay a substantial cost.
- For those weighing the cost against the benefits, it is essential to consider the potential for savings in other areas, such as tax efficiencies or reduced legal challenges, that a professional's expertise might afford.

Lack of Personal Connection

The professional's lack of a personal relationship with the decedent or beneficiaries can be seen as a drawback despite the benefits of objectivity.

- The professional may not possess intimate knowledge of the decedent's values or the nuances of family relationships that can be crucial in interpreting the decedent's wishes.
- Beneficiaries might perceive a professional as detached or less empathetic to their sentiments and needs, which can create a sense of alienation or dissatisfaction with the administration process.

The decision to appoint a professional executor or trustee is a balancing act, weighing the scales of expertise and efficiency against cost and personal touch. The scales may tip in favor of professional management in estates with significant complexity, size, or potential for conflict. In contrast, a trusted family member or friend may be the preferred choice for those who prioritize a personal connection and are mindful of costs.

The selection process is nuanced, requiring a careful assessment of the estate's needs and the dynamics of the beneficiaries. It is a choice that can shape the decedent's legacy and the heirs' experience. The performance of the executor or trustee, whether they are a personal or professional acquaintance, plays a critical role in settling the estate.

How to Appoint an Executor or Trustee

Identifying the individual who will manage your estate is a task marked by its gravity. This person's role, pivotal in orchestrating the faithful execution of your final wishes, requires a selection with the utmost discernment and a formal appointment process that ensures legal validity and practical functionality.

Inclusion in Legal Documents

The starting point for appointing an executor or trustee is the explicit designation within your estate planning documents. Within your will or trust, you must name the person or institution you have chosen to serve as executor or trustee. This statement of appointment should be unambiguous, leaving no doubt about your intentions.

- A detailed provision within your will, known as the executor clause, should lay out the name of your chosen executor and any specific powers or responsibilities you wish to grant them beyond the standard scope.
- Similarly, the trust document should name a trustee, outlining the scope of their authority and any specific instructions regarding the management and distribution of trust assets.

Consent and Acceptance

Before finalizing the appointment, obtaining the consent of the individual or institution you wish to appoint is crucial. This step ensures they are willing and able to take on the role's responsibilities.

- Engage candidly with potential executors or trustees about the duties involved and your expectations for how your estate should be managed and distributed.
- Secure their formal agreement to serve in the appointed role. To ensure clarity and evidence of commitment in the event of any future disputes, the person can sign an acceptance document.

Alternate Executors or Trustees

Life's unpredictability necessitates planning for contingencies. It's wise to consider alternate executors or trustees who can step into the role if your first choice is unable or unwilling to serve when the time comes.

- Name one or more successors to the primary executor or trustee within your will or trust, specifying the circumstances under which they would assume the role.
- Ensure these alternates are also informed and have agreed to serve, understanding the duties and responsibilities they may need to undertake.

Legal Formalities

The process of appointing an executor or trustee must adhere to the legal formalities required by your state of residence. These formalities are designed to ensure the enforceable nature of your estate planning documents.

- Sign your will or trust in the presence of witnesses, as state laws dictate. The number of witnesses and additional requirements, such as notarization, can vary, underscoring the need to adhere to local statutes.
- File any necessary paperwork with the relevant court or legal entity if required by law, especially in the case of trusts, which may not go through the probate process like wills.

You lay a strong foundation for managing your estate by meticulously following these steps. The individuals or institutions you choose will carry out your wishes with fidelity and diligence, empowered and prepared to act on your behalf. The process, marked by its formality and consideration, reflects the significance you place on the stewardship of your legacy.

In the winding path of life, the roles of executor and trustee stand out as critical milestones, ensuring that your estate is a lasting tribute to your life and values. With thoughtful selection and formal appointment, these roles are entrusted to individuals or institutions capable of honoring your legacy with the respect and dedication it deserves. Shaped by careful planning, your estate becomes a beacon of your life's journey, guiding your beneficiaries toward a future you have thoughtfully crafted.

As we move forward, we carry with us the knowledge that the guardians of our legacy are well-chosen and well-prepared, ready to act in our stead and ensure that our wishes are realized. Just as a lighthouse guides ships to safe harbor, our executors and trustees will guide our estate to its intended fate.

10

Clear Horizons: The Essentials of Communicating Your Estate Plan

In the tapestry of life, each thread weaves a narrative telling our decisions, values, and the bonds we share with those closest to us. When the time comes to pass on the mantle of our legacy, the clarity with which we communicate our estate plan to our loved ones can mean the difference between a seamless transition and a tangled aftermath. The heart of estate planning is in the documents and legal frameworks we construct and the conversations and understanding accompanying them.

The fabric of a well-communicated estate plan encompasses transparency, foresight, and a proactive approach to sharing information. Through candid discussions and clear directives, we can ensure that the vision for our estate is clear of doubt and misinterpretation. Through this lens of open communication, we aim to illuminate the path for our heirs, providing them with both the map and the compass to navigate the journey ahead.

The Importance of Communicating Your Estate Plan

Sharing your estate plan with your heirs and executors is akin to setting the stage before the curtain rises on a play. The rehearsal precedes the performance, ensuring each actor knows their part and the cues are clear.

- Avoiding Misunderstandings: Misinterpreting your wishes can lead to assets being allocated in ways that diverge from your intentions. Explaining the rationale behind your decisions—such as why certain assets are earmarked for charity or why a business is to remain family-owned—can preempt confusion and ensure that your reasons are understood.
- Reducing Potential Conflicts: Estate matters can often amplify underlying familial tensions. Imagine a family gathered in the living room, the air thick with unspoken questions about an heirloom or a piece of property. By discussing your estate plan openly, you can address these concerns head-on, lessening the likelihood of disputes that can arise from assumptions or rumors.
- Preparing Heirs: Informing beneficiaries about their future responsibilities or inheritances can empower them. If your son is to inherit the family business, giving him insight into your reasoning and expectations can help him prepare for the role. Similarly, if your daughter is to become the caretaker of a family vacation home, discussing this with her allows her to understand the associated responsibilities.
- Ensuring Smooth Execution: An executor who is blindsided by the complexity of their role may feel as though they've been thrust onto a stage without a script. Early communication provides them the opportunity to ask questions and seek clarifications, ensuring that when the

time comes, they can perform their duties with confidence and efficiency.

Visual Element: Checklist
Estate Plan Communication Checklist:

- Draft a summary of your estate plan that outlines key points and decisions.
- Schedule individual meetings with beneficiaries to discuss their roles and share your intentions.
- Provide executors and trustees with detailed instructions and the rationale behind key decisions.
- Organize a comprehensive list of assets, liabilities, and important contacts for easy reference.

The benefit of such openness is an estate plan that functions not just as a legal document but as a clear expression of your life's work and choices. It's a blueprint that guides your loved ones through the fulfillment of your wishes, minimizing the room for error or uncertainty. By setting the stage properly, you can ensure that the narrative of your legacy unfolds as you intended, with each heir playing their part in harmony with your vision.

In crafting your estate plan, the clarity and depth of communication you establish with your heirs are as critical as the legal structures you put in place. It's a proactive measure that honors your wishes and respects the relationships and trust you've built with those who will carry on your legacy. The conversations you initiate today are the threads that strengthen the fabric of your estate, weaving a legacy that stands the test of time and change.

Strategies for Effective Communication

Open and Honest Discussions

Envision communication within estate planning not as a single event but as a series of thoughtful exchanges, each building upon the last to create a mosaic of mutual understanding. It begins with the courage to engage in open and honest discussions, laying bare the details of your estate plan to those it affects. This transparency is the cornerstone of trust and sets the tone for communication.

- Address the realities of your estate, including its limitations and the reasoning behind the distribution of assets.
- Ensure you foster an environment where you welcome questions and respond thoughtfully to concerns. This approach will help ensure that each conversation clarifies everyone's understanding of your estate plan.

Regular Updates

As life unfolds, you can actively update and modify your estate plan since it is a living document. Regularly revisiting and communicating any changes to your plan is crucial in maintaining its relevance and accuracy.

- Schedule periodic reviews of your estate plan, considering life changes such as marriages, births, or the acquisition of significant assets.
- Following each review, update your heirs and fiduciaries on any amendments, reinforcing that your estate plan actively reflects your current circumstances and intentions.

Involvement of Key Stakeholders

The tapestry of an estate plan is most vibrant when woven with the threads of input and insight from those it affects. Involving key stakeholders in the planning process acknowledges their importance and fosters a sense of collective ownership over the eventual outcomes.

- Invite contributions from heirs and executors, allowing them to express their views and preferences, which may provide valuable perspectives that enhance the overall plan.
- Engage with professional advisors in the presence of your heirs, facilitating a holistic understanding of the estate plan's mechanisms and objectives.

Use of Clear and Simple Language

Our chosen language can illuminate or obscure the path we wish others to follow. In communicating your estate plan, opt for simplicity over complexity, ensuring that the terms and conditions of your plan are accessible to all, regardless of their familiarity with legal or financial concepts.

- Eschew legal jargon in favor of plain language that conveys your wishes unmistakably and fosters an understanding that transcends legal expertise.
- When technical terms are necessary, provide clear explanations that demystify the concepts, ensuring that each heir grasps the full scope and implications of the plan.

Through these strategies, effective communication becomes the wind that propels the ship of your estate plan forward, navigating through potential misunderstandings with the compass of openness and the anchor of clarity. It is the guiding light that ensures your legacy is preserved, respected, and understood by those who will carry it forward.

How to Handle Difficult Conversations

When the moment arrives to discuss the specifics of your estate plan, it's not uncommon for the air to grow heavy with the weight of what those conversations imply. The topics may be fraught with emotion and the potential for disagreement. In these discussions, you delve into the heart of your legacy, where a careful, empathetic approach is paramount.

Empathy and Understanding

It is crucial to approach these discussions with a genuine sense of empathy. Recognize that each person will come to the table with feelings, perspectives, and anxieties about the future. Some may grapple with mortality, while others might be concerned about perceived inequalities.

- Acknowledge their emotions and validate their experiences. A simple affirmation of their feelings can build a bridge towards mutual understanding.
- Strive to view the situation through their eyes, even if their viewpoint differs significantly from yours. This act can foster a connection that eases tensions and paves the way for more productive dialogue.

Patience

Patience must be your steadfast companion throughout these discussions. There are times when the complexity of an estate plan requires multiple explanations or when beneficiaries need time to process information and express their thoughts.

- Allow conversations to unfold naturally, resisting the urge to rush through complex subjects or to impose your sense of urgency on the proceedings.
- Be mindful that comprehension and acceptance may not occur simultaneously. Grant your heirs the space to arrive at their understanding in their own time.

Active Listening

Successful communication builds upon the bedrock of active listening. When discussing your estate plan, it becomes especially critical to not just hear but fully comprehend the concerns and questions that arise.

- Focus your attention entirely on the speaker, consciously absorbing every word and the underlying sentiments they express.
- Reflect on what you hear to ensure you understand correctly and demonstrate that you value their input. This technique can also clarify any misconceptions immediately, preventing them from taking root.

Conflict Resolution Techniques

Despite the best-laid plans, conflicts may still surface. Having a toolkit of resolution techniques at your disposal can be invaluable in navigating these choppy waters.

- Identify common ground as a starting point for discussions. Emphasize shared values and objectives that all parties can agree upon, such as the desire to honor your legacy or to maintain familial harmony.
- Encourage everyone to express their viewpoints without interruption. Enabling individuals to express their thoughts actively reduces frustration and leads to viable solutions.
- Seek solutions incorporating elements from different perspectives, crafting compromises that acknowledge and respect the diversity of opinions.
- If necessary, consider the involvement of a neutral third party, such as a mediator or family counselor, who can provide structured guidance and help steer the conversation toward a mutually acceptable outcome.

Empathy, patience, active listening, and conflict resolution contribute to a foundation of respect and care. They are the tools that can smooth the edges of tough conversations, ensuring that the dialogue remains constructive even when the subject matter is complex or sensitive. Through these intentional practices, you can effectively communicate the intricacies of your estate plan, ensuring that your wishes are conveyed and received with the clarity and compassion they deserve.

Navigating these discussions requires a balance of firmness and gentleness, as you must stand by the decisions made in your estate plan while remaining receptive to the emotional responses they may elicit. It is a delicate dance, one that asks you to lead with confidence yet be responsive to the steps of your partners. This balance makes it possible to move through difficult conversations gracefully and emerge on the other side, with relationships not just intact but potentially strengthened by the experience.

With these conversations, you lay the groundwork for a transition that respects your wishes and the needs of your heirs. You equip them with the understanding necessary to carry your legacy forward, and in doing so, you fortify the bonds that form the foundation of your family. Through carefully navigated discussions, the story of your life's work and love continues beyond the final page, reaching into the future with intention and care.

Planning a Family Meeting

Setting the Agenda

A family meeting about estate planning is like an orchestra's rehearsal before a major performance. Every note, every rest, every dynamic shift is purposefully placed on the score for musicians to interpret. Likewise, an agenda for your family meeting acts as this musical score, providing structure and guiding the flow of discussion. It is essential to detail what topics will be addressed, from the basics of the estate plan to the roles each member might play. This agenda promises transparency and sets expectations, ensuring that no topic plays out of turn.

- Itemize key discussion points, prioritizing them so that the most critical issues receive attention first.
- Include time allocations for each topic to keep the meeting on track without rushing important matters.

- Prepare to provide background information on decisions made within the estate plan, equipping your family with the context needed to understand their significance.

Choosing the Right Time and Place

The venue and timing of a family meeting are as crucial as the content. It is akin to selecting the perfect setting for a meaningful celebration—ambiance matters. The environment should encourage open dialogue and foster a sense of safety and privacy. The chosen time should be convenient and minimal stress for all involved.

- Opt for a location free from distractions, where confidentiality can be maintained and comfort is assured.
- Schedule the meeting when participants are not likely to be preoccupied with other pressing engagements or personal stressors.
- Consider the possibility of remote attendance for members who cannot be physically present, ensuring their inclusive participation through video conferencing.

Inviting Relevant Participants

In the same way that you would carefully curate a guest list for a significant event, selecting attendees for your family meeting requires thoughtful consideration. The individuals invited should have a direct interest or involvement in the estate plan.

- Extend invitations to all beneficiaries, key family members, and any individuals named in roles such as executors or trustees.
- Include professional advisors if their presence would contribute valuable insight or clarity to the proceedings.

- Communicate the purpose of the meeting in advance, ensuring invitees understand its importance and their expected contribution.

Facilitating the Discussion

Once the family meeting commences, the role of facilitator becomes central. This task involves guiding the conversation, ensuring it remains productive and adheres to the topics outlined in the agenda. The facilitator must be adept at encouraging participation from all attendees, navigating complex emotional dynamics, and maintaining focus on the objectives of the meeting.

- Start the meeting with a clear reiteration of the agenda and the desired outcomes to orient attendees.
- Invite questions and encourage a dialogue that allows for the expression of thoughts and concerns.
- Be vigilant in steering the conversation back to the agenda if it veers off course while allowing for organic discussion that can yield valuable insights.
- Summarize key points and agreements reached during the meeting to reinforce understanding and consensus among all participants.

The success of a family meeting on estate planning hinges on meticulous preparation and the intentional creation of a constructive atmosphere. It is an opportunity not only to impart information but also to listen, to build consensus, and to reinforce the familial bonds that the estate plan ultimately serves to protect and honor.

As the meeting draws to a close, the family leaves with a clearer vision of the future, a shared understanding of the path ahead, and a collective commitment to uphold the legacy entrusted to them. It is crucial to maintain unity and clarity to ensure that the estate plan truly represents the family's spirit and letter.

As we conclude each family meeting, we strengthen the threads that bind the fabric of our shared story. Each voice heard, each question answered, and each concern addressed adds depth and texture to understanding our legacy. This delicate and deliberate process is a testament to the care and love that shapes our family's narrative, ensuring that as we move forward, we do so with a collective commitment to honor and preserve the story we have woven together.

11

Keeping Your Estate Plan Current and Relevant

Imagine a garden through the seasons: in spring, it burgeons with fresh blossoms; in summer, it flourishes with vibrant greenery; as autumn arrives, leaves turn gold and fall, and when winter casts its chill, the landscape rests, awaiting renewal. Much like this garden, your estate plan must adapt to the ever-changing seasons of your life, accommodating growth, loss, and transformation.

We live in a world that is not static, and our circumstances echo this dynamism. Once aligned perfectly with your life's framework, an estate plan may become disjointed as new financial, familial, and legal climates emerge. It's natural to periodically tend to your estate plan, ensuring it remains a true reflection of your current situation and continues to serve your intentions effectively.

When and Why to Update Your Estate Plan

Changes in Financial Situation

Wealth is not constant; it ebbs and flows with the tides of our personal and professional lives. A promotion at work, a profitable investment, or the sale of a property can substantially alter the financial landscape of your estate. Conversely, a downturn in business, a market crash, or unexpected medical expenses can reduce the assets you once planned to bequeath.

- What: Reassessing the distribution of assets in your estate plan may be necessary to accommodate shifts in your financial situation.
- Why: To ensure your estate plan aligns with your current financial capabilities and continues to support your long-term goals.
- How: Consult with financial advisors to evaluate the impact of economic changes on your estate and adjust your plan accordingly.

Changes in Family Structure

Just as new branches grow and old ones shed in a family tree, our family structures are subject to change. Marriages, divorces, and the reconfiguring of family units necessitate updates to an estate plan to reflect these new realities.

- What: Updating beneficiaries, guardianships, and other provisions to account for changes in family dynamics.

- Why: To prevent outdated allocations from causing familial tensions and to ensure your estate plan benefits the right individuals.
- How: Review beneficiary designations, trustees, and guardians, making changes in your legal documents to match your current family structure.

Changes in Estate Laws

Laws governing estates are as susceptible to change as the leaves in our proverbial garden. Legislators can shift legislation, tax authorities can rewrite laws, and changes can make a once-tax-efficient strategy obsolete overnight.

- What: Adjust your estate plan to adhere to new laws and benefit from beneficial legal environments.
- Why: Compliance with current laws is essential to avoid penalties and maximize your beneficiaries' benefits.
- How: Stay informed on estate law changes through professional legal counsel and adjust your estate planning strategies as needed.

Periodic Review

Regularly reviewing your estate plan is akin to seasonal pruning; it's a way to maintain the health and vitality of your estate intentions. Life can veer in unexpected directions, and your estate plan should be flexible enough to accommodate these deviations.

- What: Scheduling routine check-ups of your estate plan to ensure it remains current and comprehensive.

- Why: To catch any discrepancies or areas needing refinement, ensure your estate plan is always ready for implementation.
- How: Set calendar reminders for an annual review or tie reviews to significant dates, such as the end of the fiscal year, ensuring consistent oversight.

Visual Element: Checklist
Estate Plan Update Checklist:

- Financial Review: Assess the value of current assets and liabilities.
- Family Changes: Note any additions or reductions to the family unit.
- Legal Updates: Keep abreast of estate law changes that may impact your plan.
- Professional Consultation: Schedule annual meetings with your estate planner or attorney.
- Document Revisions: Adjust wills, trusts, and other related documents.

By incorporating these practices in your estate planning, you guarantee that your wishes will be executed precisely as you envision, regardless of life's inevitable fluctuations. It's a commitment to the stewardship of your legacy, a promise to those you love that you've considered the many facets of change and have planned for their well-being with foresight and care.

Updating your estate plan is not just an exercise in legality; it is an act of love and responsibility. You actively ensure that your legacy is not left to chance but rather shape it according to your evolving life story. Your estate plan is the soil from which your legacy will grow long after you've gone, and its cultivation is a testament to your commitment to nurturing the future of those you hold dear.

Common Life Events That Require an Update

Marriage or Divorce

The union or dissolution of a marriage is more than a change in relationship status; it's a significant event that necessitates a fresh look at your estate plan. The entry or exit of a spouse can drastically alter the distribution of your assets and your plans for the future. In the glow of weddings, adding a spouse as a beneficiary in your will or as a joint tenant in property ownership often becomes a priority. Similarly, divorce calls for an urgent revision to remove the former spouse from holding roles or benefits they were previously assigned. This process may involve:

- Adjusting Beneficiary Designations: Life insurance, retirement accounts, and other payable-on-death accounts may need updates to reflect your current marital situation.
- Revising Legal Titles and Deeds: Ownership documents for real estate and other significant assets should be reviewed and amended to reflect your marital status.
- Renegotiating Estate Plans: Post-nuptial agreements or modifications to pre-existing prenuptial agreements might be necessary to clarify how assets should be treated within the estate.

Birth or Adoption of a Child

Welcoming a child into your family is a time of joy and anticipation as you imagine the life and opportunities you hope to provide them. It's also a moment that calls for your estate plan to evolve as you consider the future security of this new family member. You may need to:

- Designate Guardians: Should something happen to you, deciding who will raise your child is paramount. This choice should be legally documented to ensure your child's care aligns with your wishes.
- Create or Update Trusts: Establishing a trust can help manage the inheritance you leave for your child, stipulating how and when the assets will be used, such as for education or personal development.
- Secure Their Future: Life insurance policies may need adjustments to provide adequate coverage for your child's upbringing and educational needs.

Death of a Beneficiary or Executor

The passing of someone designated in your estate plan as a beneficiary or executor is a profound and saddening event. Consider addressing the void in your plan promptly. The following steps involve:

- Reallocating Inheritances: Assets destined for a deceased beneficiary need redirection, perhaps to alternate beneficiaries or through a reevaluation of your estate's distribution.
- Selecting New Fiduciaries: If an executor or trustee has passed away, identifying a new individual or institution to fulfill these duties is crucial to maintaining the integrity of your estate's management.
- Appraising Impact on Trusts: If the deceased was a trustee or a beneficiary of a trust, reviewing the terms of the trust is

necessary to determine how their role and benefits should be reassigned or managed going forward.

Acquisition or Disposal of Significant Assets

The ebb and flow of your portfolio—be it the acquisition of stocks, the purchase of real estate, or the sale of a business interest—reflects the dynamic nature of your asset base. These transactions have a ripple effect on your estate plan, requiring adjustments that may include:

- Updating Asset Lists: Ensure all newly acquired assets are included in your estate plan and that any disposed assets are removed to prevent confusion or disputes during the execution of your estate.
- Evaluating Tax Implications: Acquiring or disposing of assets can have significant tax consequences. Analyzing these transactions with the help of a tax professional ensures your estate plan remains tax-efficient.
- Redefining Distribution Plans: New acquisitions warrant redistributing your assets among your heirs. In contrast, the disposal of assets could necessitate adjustments to planned bequests to account for the change in your estate's value.

In light of these life events, which can arrive on our doorsteps without a moment's notice, maintaining a responsive and up-to-date estate plan is not just a strategic move—it's an act of caring for those you hold dear. It ensures that through all of life's transitions, your estate plan stands as a steadfast declaration of your wishes, ready to support and protect your loved ones no matter the circumstances.

Reviewing and Updating Your Will and Trusts

Revisiting Beneficiaries

Relationships ebb and flow in the continuous flow of life, and the individuals you once placed at the forefront of your bequests might shift positions. This alteration isn't solely about preference changes; it also reflects the natural progression of life's events: marriages, births, and the unfortunate passing of loved ones. Hence, a meticulous reassessment of your beneficiaries is not merely advisable but necessary. It guarantees that you bestow the fruits of your labor upon the people you select and that no unintended consequences arise due to outdated designations.

- Scrutinizing your current list of beneficiaries should be approached with a clear mind and the latest information about each individual's circumstances.
- Consider the implications of each beneficiary's current life stage and financial needs, which may have transformed since your last estate plan review.
- Assess the impact of contingent beneficiaries and whether they still align with your objectives if primary beneficiaries cannot assume their roles.

Updating Asset Distribution

Update the blueprint for passing on your assets as your wealth fluctuates. Regular revisions ensure that your current financial landscape is mirrored accurately in your estate documents.

- Examine each asset's role and relevance within your estate, pondering whether specific allocations still serve your intended purpose.
- Factor in any changes in the value of your assets that could affect the equitable distribution among your beneficiaries.
- Be especially attentive to items of sentimental value or family heirlooms that may require special consideration to maintain family harmony.

Changing Executors or Trustees

The individuals you have entrusted with the execution of your will and the management of your trusts hold significant power in shaping the posthumous narrative of your legacy. They must remain individuals who are not only capable but also willing to undertake such responsibilities.

- Reevaluate your choices for executors and trustees, considering their availability, capacity, and willingness to serve.
- When an executor or trustee may no longer be the best choice due to changes in their life circumstances or your relationship with them, seek alternative candidates better suited to the role.
- Ensure a smooth transition of responsibilities by communicating any changes to all parties involved, including any new appointees and your legal counsel.

Addressing New Assets or Liabilities

As your estate evolves, so might the nature of your assets and liabilities. The acquisition of new property, the start of a business venture, or the incurrence of debt all play critical roles in the composition of your estate. Attending to these changes is essential to maintaining the validity and effectiveness of your will and trusts.

- Integrate any new assets into your estate plan, considering their implications for your overall asset distribution strategy.
- Evaluate how the addition of liabilities might affect the inheritance you leave behind and make provisions to address these debts through your estate.
- Update your will and trusts to reflect new assets or liabilities, ensuring each document represents your current estate.

Maintaining your will and trust is akin to keeping a cherished heirloom—requiring attention to detail, regular care, and timely adjustments. By carefully managing this legacy, you can make your vision a lasting tribute to your planning and commitment.

Updating Your Healthcare Directive and Power of Attorney

Health and personal wishes are the ever-shifting sands upon which we construct some of the most critical elements of our estate planning. Your healthcare directive and power of attorney represent you, speak on your behalf when you are unable to, and execute decisions based on your wishes when you cannot do so. As such, they must evolve as you do, mirroring changes in your health status and personal wishes, ensuring that your healthcare proxy and the powers you have granted remain apt and aligned with your current desires.

Changes in Health Status

With time, your health may transform in unpredictable ways. An agile healthcare directive must adapt to these shifts. A diagnosis, a significant improvement, or a gradual change in your capabilities may necessitate a reevaluation of your healthcare directive to ensure it accurately reflects your current health situation.

- Revisit the conditions and treatments your healthcare directive covers and adjust it to address any new health concerns or changes in your medical condition.
- If your health has improved significantly, certain directives may no longer be relevant and could be revised to reflect your current state of well-being.
- In the event of a decline in health, including more detailed instructions regarding your care preferences and end-of-life decisions may be prudent.

Changes in Personal Wishes

Your thoughts about healthcare choices might evolve as you navigate life's seasons. What once seemed a clear-cut decision may now present itself in a different light, colored by experience, relationships, or shifts in your values.

- Periodically reflect on your existing healthcare directive to ensure it still resonates with your present-day values and wishes.
- Consider how changes in your personal life, such as new relationships or experiences, might influence your thoughts on treatments and interventions.

- Update your healthcare directive to capture any new desires, whether they pertain to life-sustaining measures, pain management, or other medical care priorities.

Updating Healthcare Proxy

The person you have appointed as your healthcare proxy or agent is responsible for making healthcare decisions on your behalf, and their ability to fulfill this role might change over time.

- Assess whether your chosen healthcare proxy is still the best representative for your healthcare decisions, considering their current circumstances, relationship with you, and ability to carry out your wishes.
- Select a new proxy better suited to advocate for your healthcare preferences if needed. This might be due to geographical proximity, changes in your relationship, or the proxy's health.
- Communicate any changes to your healthcare proxy to your family and healthcare providers to avoid confusion should the directive be enacted.

Reviewing and Updating Powers Granted

The power of attorney you have established provides someone you trust with authority over certain aspects of your life, from financial matters to legal decisions. As your situation changes, so might the scope of the authority you wish to grant.

- Take stock of the powers you have assigned through your power of attorney and adjust them to better fit your current requirements and comfort levels.

- If your power of attorney is springing—set to activate under certain conditions—ensure that the terms of activation are still relevant to your current health and circumstances.
- Provide your attorney-in-fact with updated instructions to reflect any changes in the scope of their authority and ensure they are prepared to act in accordance with your current wishes.

In adapting these crucial documents to the flow of life's currents, you maintain their integrity and capacity to function as intended—protecting your well-being and upholding your autonomy. Through these updates, you wield control over how you will be cared for and who will manage your affairs, reflecting the person you are today and the care you wish to receive.

Guided by the knowledge that life is neither static nor predictable, keeping your healthcare directive and power of attorney up to date is an ongoing task that underscores your commitment to personal autonomy and thoughtful care. The steps you take to ensure these documents remain relevant reflect your diligence and desire to provide clear instructions that can ease the burden on those you entrust with your care and your affairs.

With this chapter, we've navigated the essential updates to your healthcare directive and power of attorney, equipping you to control your personal and healthcare decisions. As we look ahead, remember that these updates are more than mere tasks on a checklist; they are affirmations of your life's narrative, ensuring it continues to be authored by you for every page that remains.

12

Adapting to the Digital Frontier in Estate Planning

In the ever-evolving landscape of our digital lives, estate planning has transcended the confines of paper and ink. We live in a time where our digital footprints are as substantial—and sometimes more intricate—than the physical trails we leave behind. The digital realm is vast, encompassing everything from the tweets we send to the online portfolios representing our financial acuity. This chapter is your guide through the digital thicket, illuminating how technology reshapes the way we plan for the future.

The fusion of technology and estate planning is not a wave of the future—it's the surf we're riding now. Digital assets, online wills, and virtual tax filings are the new normal. It's not just about being current; it's about being prepared in a world where digital assets can be as valuable as tangible ones. Let's peel back the layers of the digital onion to understand how technology weaves into the fabric of modern estate planning.

Digital Assets

Our lives are increasingly online, from social media accounts to cryptocurrency investments. Digital assets are unique because they often exist in a realm that's not entirely ours to control. Consider your social media profiles—repositories of memories and connections—or your online business, which might be your primary source of income. Even your digital music library has value. These assets require special consideration for several reasons:

- Access and Ownership: Unlike physical assets, digital ones are often governed by service agreements, not by simple ownership rules. Who can legally access your Facebook account after you pass away?
- Financial Worth: Online businesses or domain names can carry significant economic value. How do you ensure they fall into the right hands without exposing them to security risks?
- Sentimental Value: Photos stored in the cloud or an email history can hold immense sentimental value for loved ones. How do we pass on these new types of heirlooms?

Online Wills and Trusts

Creating legally binding documents online replaces the traditional image of signing a will in an attorney's office. The advantages here are convenience, speed, and often lower cost. But with these benefits come new considerations:

- Validity and Legality: Ensuring that an online will or trust is legally valid in your state is crucial. Are e-signatures accepted? What about witnesses?

- Security: The digital creation of such sensitive documents requires robust security measures. How do you protect your personal information from cyber threats?
- Updates: Online platforms can make updating your documents more manageable, but they also require vigilance to ensure that changes are legally sound.

Digital Estate Management

Managing a digital estate is a task for the tech-savvy. It involves understanding your digital assets and how to access and control them. Consider the potential complexity of managing:

- Cryptocurrency Holdings: The volatile nature of cryptocurrency means that the value of these assets can change drastically. Who manages it, and how can they access it?
- Digital Rights: Intellectual property, like a blog or a digital art collection, requires careful handling to maintain its value and legal standing.
- Online Accounts: Ensuring continuity or closure of various online accounts requires detailed knowledge of each platform's policies and procedures.

Online Tax Filing

Estate taxes don't escape the digital transition. Filing taxes online can streamline the process, offering real-time updates and electronic record-keeping. Here's what to consider:

- Electronic Records: Keeping digital records of tax filings and associated documents is efficient but requires careful organization and backup.

- Regulatory Compliance: To ensure compliance, online tax platforms must stay abreast of changing tax laws. How often are these updates, and how transparent is the platform about them?
- Digital Footprint: Your online tax filings leave a digital trail that needs protection. What measures are in place to secure your estate's financial data?

The digital realm has expanded the horizons of estate planning, but it also requires us to become adept navigators of this new world. The following sections will explore the tools and services to help you chart this territory, ensure your digital advisors are steering you right, and inform you of legal changes in the digital age.

Visual Element: Infographic
Understanding Your Digital Assets:

- Social Media: Accounts on Facebook, Instagram, Twitter, etc.
- Financial: Online banking, PayPal, Venmo, investment accounts.
- Cryptocurrency: Wallets, exchanges, portfolio trackers.
- Intellectual Property: Domain names, copyrighted materials, digital art.
- Personal: Email accounts, cloud storage, digital journal apps.

In the following sections, we'll further explore the tools and strategies that can aid you in managing these digital assets effectively and securely. We'll also consider how online legal services can simplify creating and updating your estate planning documents and how to stay informed in an age where the only constant is change.

Online Tools for Estate Planning

Estate Planning Software

In the quilt of estate planning, each patch—be it a will, trust, or healthcare directive—plays a crucial role in the final design. Estate planning software emerges as an invaluable needle, stitching together these elements precisely and efficiently. This software provides templates and guided workflows that simplify the creation of complex documents. They often feature:

- Interactive checklists that ensure no critical component is overlooked.
- Customizable templates that cater to individual needs and state-specific laws.
- Financial calculators that aid in assessing asset distribution and tax implications.

When used effectively, this software can simplify planning, allowing individuals to create legally binding documents without incurring high attorney fees. However, selecting a program that offers regular updates is vital to staying abreast of legal changes and ensuring your estate plan remains valid and enforceable.

Online Legal Services

The digital age has paved the way for many online legal services that democratize access to estate planning. These platforms offer a spectrum of services, from basic document generation to more comprehensive estate planning solutions. They typically feature:

- User-friendly interfaces that guide individuals through the process of document creation.
- Access to a network of legal professionals for personalized advice and document review.
- Secure cloud storage options for easy access and sharing of estate planning documents.

These services can be particularly advantageous for those with straightforward estates. They provide a cost-effective means to create essential estate planning documents while offering flexibility to consult with attorneys for more complex scenarios.

Digital Asset Management Tools

The digital realm is teeming with assets that require meticulous oversight. Digital asset management tools rise to the occasion, offering a centralized location to monitor everything from online accounts to digital currencies. These tools often provide:

- Secure inventories of digital assets, complete with login credentials and access instructions.
- Automated alerts for changes in asset values, especially pertinent for volatile investments like cryptocurrency.
- Encrypted protection for sensitive information, ensuring that details of digital assets are shielded from unauthorized access.

Adopting these tools into your estate planning ensures that digital assets are accounted for and managed with the same level of care as physical ones. They facilitate a seamless digital wealth and online presence transition to your designated beneficiaries.

Online Document Storage

Like a vault that safeguards treasured possessions, online document storage is the guardian for your estate planning documents. These digital repositories offer robust security and accessibility, ensuring critical information is safe and readily available. Features often include:

- Encryption and multi-factor authentication to protect against unauthorized access.
- Cloud-based platforms that allow for document access from anywhere at any time.
- Sharing capabilities that enable designated individuals, such as executors or family members, to access documents when necessary.

Incorporating online document storage into your estate planning creates an enduring archive of your most important documents. This digital vault becomes a cornerstone of your estate plan, ensuring that your carefully crafted documents are within reach for those who need them when the time comes.

Through the thoughtful application of these online tools, estate planning is no longer confined to dusty file cabinets and stoic lawyer's offices. Instead, it unfolds in a space where efficiency meets security, where the complexities of legal preparation meet the simplicity of modern technology. The result is an estate plan that reflects not only your earthly possessions but also your digital existence—a complete portrait of your life in the twenty-first century.

The Role of Digital Advisors and Online Legal Services

In an age where screens have become gateways to services once bound to the constraints of office hours and geography, the emergence of digital advisors and online legal services has redefined the estate planning landscape. This shift has broadened access and injected flexibility and personalization into a traditionally perceived rigid and daunting domain.

Virtual Consultations

In a world where face-to-face meetings are no longer a prerequisite for meaningful interaction, virtual consultations stand at the forefront of estate planning innovation. These digital meetings break down geographical barriers, enabling you to engage with legal experts regardless of location. This format is particularly advantageous for those who find mobility challenging or live in remote areas.

- Using secure video conferencing platforms ensures privacy and confidentiality, mirroring the sanctity of in-person attorney-client interactions.
- Scheduling flexibility allows discussions beyond traditional office hours, accommodating the busy lifestyles of today's clientele.
- The immediacy of virtual meetings can expedite decision-making processes, allowing for more dynamic estate planning.

The infusion of virtual consultations into estate planning is a testament to the adaptability of legal services, ensuring expert guidance is only a few clicks away.

Automated Document Preparation

The rise of automation in document preparation heralds a new era of efficiency. Automated systems can now generate complex legal documents with a precision that rivals seasoned professionals. This technology is reshaping the way estate plans are drafted:

- Algorithms tailor documents to individual needs by analyzing responses to targeted questions, ensuring a customized approach to each unique estate plan.
- Automating routine drafting tasks reduces the potential for human error, enhancing the accuracy of the final documents.
- The speed at which these automated systems operate significantly reduces the time traditionally required to draft estate planning documents.

Automated document preparation has emerged as a boon for those seeking to streamline the estate planning process, providing a fast and reliable alternative to manual drafting.

Online Legal Advice

The proliferation of online legal advice platforms has democratized access to legal expertise. These digital portals offer a wealth of information and direct counsel from qualified professionals, making legal advice more accessible than ever before.

- Interactive tools, such as chatbots and Q&A forums, provide immediate responses to pressing legal inquiries, offering guidance at the touch of a button.

- Subscription-based models allow for ongoing access to legal advice, creating a continuous support system throughout the estate planning process.
- The breadth of expertise available online ensures that you can find specialized advice tailored to the intricacies of your estate situation.

Online legal advice services have effectively opened the floodgates to legal knowledge, empowering individuals to make informed decisions about their estate plans confidently.

Digital Estate Planning Resources

The internet provides digital estate planning resources, from informative articles to comprehensive guides. These resources serve as a beacon for those navigating the complexities of estate planning.

- Online libraries collate a vast array of estate planning literature, offering insights into every facet of the process.
- Interactive estate planning checklists guide individuals through the preparatory steps, ensuring all critical components are addressed.
- Educational webinars and video tutorials provide visual and auditory learners with a dynamic approach to understanding estate planning concepts.

The wealth of digital resources available to individuals today supports a self-directed approach to estate planning. This empowerment through knowledge equips you with the understanding necessary to actively shape your legacy in the digital age.

The seamless integration of these digital services into the fabric of estate planning marks a pivotal shift in how we prepare for the future. They offer a blend of convenience, personalization, and accessibility that was once unfathomable. As we continue to embrace these digital tools and platforms, the scope of estate planning expands, transforming it into a process that is not only more efficient but also more attuned to the individual needs of each person. With the digital world at our fingertips, creating a comprehensive and personalized estate plan is no longer a distant possibility but an immediate reality.

Staying Updated with Law Changes in the Digital Age

Navigating the currents of legal change in estate planning can seem like charting a course through uncharted waters. Laws evolve, sometimes subtly, other times dramatically, impacting how estate plans are constructed and maintained. In the digital age, staying abreast of these changes is less about trawling through dense legal tomes and more about engaging with a flow of information that is as dynamic as it is pervasive.

Online Legal Updates

Legal websites serve as beacons, signaling shifts and trends in legislation that could affect your estate plan. A subtle alteration in tax law or a new ruling on digital asset inheritance could ripple through your arrangements, necessitating updates.

- Subscription services alert you to relevant legal changes, with experts translating legalese into actionable intelligence.

- Interactive forums allow for real-time discussions with professionals and peers, fostering a community approach to understanding and adapting to new laws.

Digital Newsletters and Blogs

In the vast expanse of the internet, newsletters and blogs act as compasses, guiding you towards relevant updates. Curated by legal experts, these periodic publications offer insights into the implications of recent changes and provide foresight into anticipated legal trends.

- Newsletters from esteemed law firms or legal thought leaders present condensed, insightful summaries of recent developments.
- Blogs often explore the practical application of legal changes, offering scenarios that could mirror your estate planning considerations.

Webinars and Online Courses

Webinars and online courses are the classrooms of the digital world. They offer structured learning from estate planning and law experts, often focusing on the latest legislative changes and their implications.

- Interactive webinars provide opportunities to pose questions directly to legal experts, gaining clarity on complex issues.
- Online courses on legal platforms offer in-depth explorations of specific topics, allowing for self-paced learning to deepen your understanding of changes that affect your estate plan.

Social Media Channels

Social media has become a vibrant tapestry of information sharing. Legal professionals, law firms, and industry organizations often broadcast updates and insights on these platforms.

- Following reputable legal entities on platforms like LinkedIn or Twitter can provide steady updates and professional interpretations.
- Engaging with content shared by legal professionals can lead to a deeper understanding of law changes and foster a network of resources for future inquiries.

The digital age has transformed staying informed from passively receiving information to an active pursuit. With tools and platforms designed to streamline knowledge acquisition, adapting your estate plan to the latest legal changes is a process marked by efficiency and engagement. The key lies in selecting the proper channels that resonate with your needs and preferences and integrating their use into your routine. Doing so ensures that your estate plan remains robust and responsive to the legal landscape, reflecting your wishes and the latest in legal compliance.

Staying informed is a perpetual endeavor, yet it need not be overwhelming. The digital age has provided us with many channels through which we can receive updates, engage with experts, and educate ourselves on the intricacies of estate planning law. This chapter has illuminated the resources available to keep your estate plan in harmony with the law's evolving tune. By embracing the digital tools at our disposal, we ensure that our planning remains current and relevant.

As we close this discussion, we focus on the horizon, where the principles of estate planning intersect with the practicalities of implementation. The journey continues as we apply the knowledge we've gained, crafting legally sound and deeply personal plans, reflecting our values and the legacies we aspire to leave behind.

Conclusion

As we draw the curtain on this journey through the intricacies of estate planning, you have traveled with me from the foundational aspects of wills and trusts to the nuances of healthcare directives and digital asset management. Together, we've charted a course through the sometimes turbulent, often complex, but always vital seas of securing your legacy.

Remember that estate planning involves much more than completing a simple checklist of tasks. By engaging with each chapter, you've empowered yourself with knowledge, turning what might once have seemed like a maze of legalese into a clear path forward.

The empowerment of informed estate planning cannot be overstated. It offers peace of mind, not just for you but also for those you hold dear. By taking the reins of your estate plan, you've stepped into a role that safeguards your future and honors your past. You've learned the significance of keeping your documents current, adapting to life's inevitable changes, embracing the digital revolution, and transforming how we think about our assets and legacies.

Now, I invite you to take the critical next step:

1. Secure your legacy.
2. Reflect on the strategies that resonate most with your life's narrative. Whether you're just starting or revisiting an existing plan, the moment to act is now.
3. Gather your documents, consult with professionals if needed, and ensure that your estate plan is a living, breathing reflection of your values and wishes.

The estate planning journey is unique for each of us, woven with individual threads of our experiences and dreams. Your estate plan is a testament to your life's work, a narrative crafted with intention and foresight. As you continue to write this story, remember that it's not just about the assets you leave behind but also the memories and the legacy that echo through generations.

In closing, I am grateful to you for allowing me to guide you through this process. Remember that estate planning is not a solitary endeavor but a bridge built on the pillars of community, guidance, and mutual support. As you move forward, know that you are not alone on this path. Your courage to face this essential aspect of life head-on is a profound act of responsibility and love.

Secure your legacy, embrace the future, and may your estate plan stand as a beacon of your dedication to those you love and the life you've lived.

References

What Is Estate Planning? Definition, Meaning, and Key ... https://www.investopedia.com/terms/e/estateplanning.asp#:

10 Risks or Consequences for Not Having an Estate Plan https://jackrobinson.com/10-risks-or-consequences-for-not-having-an-estate-plan/

Steps to Create an Estate Plan https://www.consumerreports.org/cro/2013/11/how-to-create-a-bulletproof-estate-plan/index.htm

How to Prepare for Upcoming Estate Tax Law Changes https://www.kiplinger.com/retirement/estate-tax-law-changes-how-to-prepare

Executor Of Estate: Definition And Duties https://www.quickenloans.com/learn/executor-of-estate

Power of Attorney (POA): Meaning, Types, and How and ... https://www.investopedia.com/terms/p/powerofattorney.asp

Glossary of Estate Planning Terms https://www.americanbar.org/groups/real_property_trust_estate/resources/estate_planning/glossary/

Probate: What It Is and How It Works With and Without a Will https://www.investopedia.com/terms/p/probate.asp

Wills — Legal Requirements & Limitations - Justia https://www.justia.com/estate-planning/wills/

Introduction to Wills https://www.americanbar.org/groups/real_property_trust_estate/resources/estate_planning/an_introduction_to_wills/

How to Write a Will: 7-Step Guide https://www.nerdwallet.com/article/investing/estate-planning/how-to-write-a-will

Intestate Succession: Dying Without a Will https://www.ramseysolutions.com/retirement/dying-without-a-will

5 potential benefits of a trust https://www.usbank.com/wealth-management/financial-perspectives/trust-and-estate-planning/benefits-of-setting-up-a-trust.html

Revocable Trust vs. Irrevocable Trust: What's the Difference? https://www.investopedia.com/ask/answers/071615/what-difference-between-revocable-trust-and-living-trust.asp

How to Set Up a Trust: An Easy 8-Step Guide https://copecorrales.com/articles/how-to-set-up-a-trust

Federal income tax and trust strategies | Trusts and taxes https://www.fidelity.com/viewpoints/wealth-management/insights/trusts-and-taxes

Four Powerful Estate Planning Strategies for Single People https://dworkenlaw.com/four-powerful-estate-planning-strategies-for-single-people/

Basic Estate Tax Planning For Married Couples https://www.wardandsmith.com/articles/basic-estate-tax-planning-married-couples-use-estate-tax-exemptions

Estate Planning For Blended Families (Complete Guide) https://www.trustworthy.com/blog/estate-planning-for-blended-families

Estate Planning for Unmarried Partners https://www.estateplanning.com/estate-planning-for-unmarried-couples

Digital Asset: Meaning, Types, and Importance - Investopedia https://www.investopedia.com/terms/d/digital-asset-framework.asp#:

Why You Must Put Digital Assets in Your Will or Estate Plan https://www.aarp.org/home-family/personal-technology/info-2021/remember-digital-assets-in-your-will.html

How To Properly Manage Digital Assets https://www.fastmetrics.com/blog/security/how-to-manage-digital-assets/

Estate planning for digital assets https://www.fidelity.com/viewpoints/wealth-management/estate-planning-for-digital-assets

Estate Tax | Internal Revenue Service https://www.irs.gov/businesses/small-businesses-self-employed/estate-tax

6 tips to help minimize estate taxes https://www.fidelity.com/learning-center/personal-finance/how-to-avoid-estate-taxes

The essential guide to estate planning and income taxes https://rsmus.com/insights/services/private-client/estate-planning-and-income-tax-key-considerations.html

Does Your State Have an Estate or Inheritance Tax? https://taxfoundation.org/data/all/state/state-estate-tax-inheritance-tax-2022/

Types of Advance Directives https://www.cancer.org/cancer/managing-cancer/making-treatment-decisions/advance-directives/types-of-advance-health-care-directives.html

If There is No Advance Directive or Guardian, Who Makes ... https://www.americanbar.org/groups/law_aging/publications/bifocal/vol_37/issue_1_october2015/hospitalist_focus_group/

5 types of power of attorney, explained https://www.freewill.com/learn/5-types-of-power-of-attorney

Advance Care Planning: Advance Directives for Health Care https://www.nia.nih.gov/health/advance-care-planning/advance-care-planning-advance-directives-health-care

An Executor's Legal Duties | Probate Law Center https://www.justia.com/probate/probate-administration/the-duties-of-an-executor-of-an-estate/

What is the difference between an estate executor and a ... https://www.legalzoom.com/articles/what-is-the-difference-between-an-estate-executor-and-a-trustee

Should You Choose Family or a Professional Trustee ... https://www.czepigalaw.com/blog/should-you-choose-family-or-a-professional-trustee-know-the-pros-and-cons/

Guidelines for Individual Executors & Trustees https://www.americanbar.org/groups/real_property_trust_estate/resources/estate_planning/guidelines_for_individual_executors_trustees/

The Importance of Open Communication in Estate Planning https://www.stoufferlegal.com/blog/the-importance-of-open-communication-in-estate-planning-balancing-transparency-and-discretion

Talking About Estate Planning - Tips from Fidelity https://www.fidelity.com/life-events/estate-planning/talking-estate-planning

Five tips for talking to loved ones about estate planning https://www.jsonline.com/story/news/solutions/2023/04/25/five-tips-for-talking-to-loved-ones-about-estate-planning/69791010007/

Estate Planning - How to Make a Family Meeting a Successful ... https://wilsonlawgroup.com/make-family-meeting-successful-part-estate-planning-process/

7 Reasons It's Time To Update Your Estate Plan https://www.forbes.com/sites/bobcarlson/2018/12/02/7-reasons-its-time-to-update-your-estate-plan/

6 life events that might impact your estate plan https://www.edwardjones.com/us-en/market-news-insights/guidance-perspective/events-impacting-estate-plan

What is the best way to update my will? https://www.nolo.com/legal-encyclopedia/what-the-best-update-will.html

Keep your health care directives up to date https://www.health.harvard.edu/staying-healthy/keep-your-health-care-directives-up-to-date

Digital Asset Management in Life and Death https://www.actec.org/resource-center/video/digital-asset-management-in-life-and-death/

Advantages and Disadvantages of Electronic Wills https://petronilaw.com/advantages-and-disadvantages-of-electronic-wills/

How RUFADAA Is Changing Digital Estate Planning https://www.kitces.com/blog/rufadaa-digital-estate-planning-rights-three-tiers-online-tool-fiduciary/

WealthCounsel Estate Planning Software, CLE and Legal ... https://www.wealthcounsel.com/

Nelson, Brett. 10 Inspirational Quotes About Estate Planning. Family Law, Divorce, Personal Injury in Texas. Last modified May 3, 2023. https://nelsonlawgrouppc.com/10-inspirational-quotes-about-estate-planning/

Retirement Planning for a More Rewarding Retirement

"I can't change the direction of the wind, but I can adjust my sails to always reach my destination."

Jimmy Dean

Retirement planning is something we all must do, but many people neglect to cover the whole spectrum of what should be included from the outset… and what that means is that either they're not properly prepared, or they suddenly realize they have yet to get all their affairs in order, and end up having to spend some of that well-earned retirement time worrying about estate planning.

Retirement is your reward after spending years in employment, and you should be able to enjoy it without worry. That means planning ahead and making sure you have full peace of mind when you finally walk out of your office for the last time. This complete retirement toolkit is designed to help you do just that – and we'd like to ask you to join us on our mission to bring this peace of mind to a wider audience.

Our goal is to make this easy for as many people as we can reach, and in order to reach further, we're going to need your help. Luckily, all that takes is for you to spend a few minutes writing a short review.

By leaving a review of this book on Amazon, you'll show new readers where they can find a one-stop shop for thorough retirement planning, and that's going to make a huge difference in their lives.

Reviews are how people discover the resources they're looking for and find out how they've helped others make up their minds that they've found the right thing. Your review will help them on their journey towards a rewarding and worry-free retirement – and taking a moment to do this will help you reflect on your own experience too.

Thank you so much for your support. We couldn't do this without you.

Retirement Planning Simplified

THE COMPLETE TOOLKIT FOR 401K, IRA, AND SMART TAX STRATEGIES TO MAXIMIZE YOUR WEALTH

RETIREWISE

Introduction

Welcome to a journey where the path to financial security and peace of mind in your golden years is demystified and made achievable. As we embark on this adventure together, I want you to know that this book is more than just a guide; it's a companion in navigating the often complex world of retirement planning. With a commitment to breaking down intricate financial concepts into understandable, actionable steps, I aim to empower you, the reader, to take control of your future confidently.

This isn't just another retirement planning guide. "Retirement Planning Simplified: The Complete Toolkit for 401K, IRA, and Smart Tax Strategies to Maximize Your Wealth" stands apart by offering a comprehensive approach that marries essential retirement planning tools with real-world applications. From the foundational principles of 401K and IRA accounts to advanced tax strategies and practical examples, each chapter is designed to build upon the last, equipping you with a well-rounded understanding of how to maximize your wealth for a comfortable retirement.

As the third installment in a series that has already explored Social Security, Medicare, Estate, Wills, and Trusts, this book expands upon those crucial topics while focusing on empowering you with the knowledge and tools to plan effectively for retirement. Whether you're familiar with the previous books or are joining us for the first time, you'll find invaluable insights and strategies catering to newcomers and seasoned planners alike.

This book is for you—adults aged 30 and over who may feel overwhelmed by the prospect of retirement planning or are seeking to refine their strategy with innovative, tax-efficient saving solutions. I understand the fears that come with the thought of not having enough saved up or the confusion that complex financial terms and concepts can evoke. That's why I promise to guide you through each step, offering clear, easy-to-follow strategies to help you overcome these hurdles.

Let me encourage you to take charge of your retirement planning journey. Regardless of where you stand today, there is always time to start. This book is designed to inspire, inform, and, most importantly, show you that planning for retirement can be an exciting opportunity to secure the future you envision for yourself and your loved ones.

As we move forward, I urge you to dive into each chapter with an open mind and a commitment to applying the strategies and insights shared. By the end of this book, you will possess a deep understanding of 401K, IRA, and smart tax strategies and a personalized toolkit designed to maximize your wealth for a fulfilling retirement.

The road to retirement planning may seem daunting, but together, we can navigate it with ease and optimism. Let's take this vital step towards securing your financial future.

Chapter 1

In the realm of retirement planning, the significance of having a clear and defined vision cannot be overstated. Often, the difference between a future approached with trepidation and one embraced with anticipation lies in the clarity of one's vision for retirement. This chapter delves into the foundational concept of crafting a retirement vision, elucidating why it's beneficial and crucial for effective financial planning.

A well-known adage states, "If you don't know where you're going, any road will get you there." This sentiment rings especially true when it comes to planning for retirement. Without a clear destination in mind, the path becomes ambiguous, and the steps to get there are uncertain. Visualizing your future serves as the compass that guides your retirement planning, ensuring every financial decision aligns with the future you aspire to create.

1.1 The Importance of a Retirement Vision

Visualizing Your Future

Visualizing your future is akin to setting the destination in your navigational app before starting a journey. It's about defining the endpoint or, in this case, picturing the life you wish to lead once you step away from the workforce. This visualization isn't merely about dreaming; it's a strategic step that lays the groundwork for your retirement planning. By painting a vivid picture of your retirement, including where you'll live, the activities you'll engage in, and the lifestyle you'll lead, you give substance to your goals, making them more tangible and attainable.

Motivation to Save

The direct correlation between having a vivid retirement vision and increased motivation to save and invest for the future is well-documented. Consider the process of saving for a vacation. The excitement of exploring a new destination or revisiting a cherished spot fuels your willingness to set aside funds regularly. Similarly, when you have a vibrant image of your retirement, the motivation to contribute to your retirement funds grows. You're no longer saving for an abstract concept called 'retirement'; you're investing in a future that promises joy, relaxation, and fulfillment.

Customized Planning

A one-size-fits-all approach falls short in retirement planning because each individual's vision of retirement is unique. Some envision a quiet life in a rural setting, surrounded by nature, while others dream of an urban retirement filled with cultural activities and social engagements. Recognizing that your retirement goals require tailored financial strategies is crucial. This realization prompts the customization of your savings and investment plans to suit the specific future you desire. It's about ensuring that your financial strategy is designed with your particular retirement vision in mind, accommodating your expected lifestyle, desired location, and personal aspirations.

Long-term Perspective

Adopting a long-term perspective is essential for making informed, beneficial financial decisions today. It involves looking beyond the immediate gratification of spending to consider the future benefits of saving and investing. This perspective is grounded in the understanding that your actions today significantly impact your future. With a clear retirement vision, it becomes easier to prioritize long-term financial health over short-term pleasures. Saving for retirement becomes a conscious choice to invest in your future self and the life you envisioned.

In essence, creating a retirement vision is not merely an exercise in daydreaming. It's a strategic step in retirement planning that aligns your financial decisions with the future you wish to realize. By clearly visualizing your retirement, you gain the motivation to save, the insight to customize your financial plan, and the wisdom to prioritize long-term gains over immediate satisfaction. This approach ensures that every financial decision is a step towards your envisioned retirement, imbuing your planning efforts with purpose and direction.

1.2 Crafting Your Retirement Vision

Creating a vision for your retirement is akin to sketching a blueprint for a dream home. Each stroke on the canvas is deliberate, aiming to bring your deepest desires to life. This process requires introspection and a genuine understanding of what happiness means to you in your later years. Here, we explore the facets of life that shape your retirement vision, from personal desires to the legacy you wish to leave behind.

Identifying Your Desires

The first step is to pinpoint what you truly want from your retirement. This part of the process is deeply personal and varies significantly from one individual to another. Some might dream of a quiet life surrounded by nature, while others might envision a retirement filled with adventure and travel. Begin by asking yourself a series of questions to uncover these desires:

- What have I always wanted to do but never had the time for?
- Where do I see myself living?
- How do I want to spend my days?

Your answers will serve as the foundation of your retirement vision and guide your financial planning process. Remember, there are no right or wrong answers here, only what feels true.

Consideration of Lifestyle

Your lifestyle choices, hobbies, and activities shape your retirement vision. These elements determine how you'll spend your time and have financial implications that must be considered. For instance, if you're passionate about travel, your retirement plan should account for the costs associated with your adventures. If you're keen on pursuing hobbies like golf or painting, consider the expenses tied to these interests. Reflect on the following to integrate your lifestyle into your retirement vision:

- The hobbies and activities you wish to pursue
- Any clubs or groups you want to join
- The pace of life you're looking for (e.g., active and busy vs. calm and relaxed)

This reflection ensures your retirement plan supports the lifestyle you aspire to, making your golden years genuinely fulfilling.

Impact of Health on Retirement

Health is a pivotal factor that influences your retirement planning, often dictating the activities you can partake in and the care you might require. It's essential to assess your current and potential future health considerations. This assessment helps create a retirement plan that accommodates healthcare costs, insurance, and any necessary adjustments to your living situation. Key considerations include:

- Your current health status and any ongoing medical needs
- Family health history and potential future health concerns
- Health insurance coverage and options for long-term care

By factoring in health considerations, you ensure your retirement plan is robust, adaptive, and capable of supporting you through various health scenarios.

Family and Legacy Aspirations

Finally, consider the role of family, community, and the legacy you wish to create in shaping your retirement vision. For many, retirement provides an opportunity to strengthen family bonds, contribute to the community, and leave a lasting impact. Reflect on the following to incorporate these aspects into your retirement vision:

- The kind of relationship you wish to have with your family and friends
- Any community service or philanthropic work you want to be involved in
- The legacy you hope to leave behind, whether through financial means, education, or other forms of support

This contemplation ensures your retirement plan caters to your personal and lifestyle needs and aligns with your broader aspirations for family and legacy.

In crafting your retirement vision, it's vital to weave together these diverse threads—from personal desires and lifestyle choices to health considerations and family aspirations. This holistic approach ensures your retirement plan is not just a financial strategy but a blueprint for a fulfilling and meaningful future.

1.3 Aligning Your Financial Goals with Your Vision

Once you have a vivid picture of your desired retirement, the next step is to translate this vision into concrete, achievable financial goals. This process is akin to charting a course on a map. You know your destination and must plot the waypoints to get there. Aligning your financial goals with your retirement vision requires specificity, prioritization, flexibility, and a commitment to regular reassessment.

Setting Measurable Goals

Setting specific, measurable goals is the first step in aligning your financial goals with your retirement vision. This specificity is what turns vague aspirations into actionable targets. For example, instead of the broad goal of "saving enough for retirement," a measurable goal would be "saving $1 million by age 65." This specificity provides clarity and a target to aim for.

- Break it down: Start by breaking down your retirement vision into aspects that require financial backing. Consider housing, daily living costs, healthcare, travel, hobbies, and family commitments.
- Quantify your needs: Estimate the financial resources needed for each aspect of your vision. Use online calculators or consult with a financial advisor to help quantify these needs.
- Set time frames: Assign a time frame to each goal. Knowing when you want to retire influences how much you need to save each year, adjusting for factors like investment growth and inflation.

Prioritizing Your Goals

With various components comprising your retirement vision, prioritizing your financial goals becomes crucial. It's about understanding that not all goals can simultaneously be pursued equally, especially when resources are limited.

- Essential vs. desirable: Categorize your goals into 'essential' and 'desirable.' Essentials are non-negotiable goals for retirement, such as healthcare funding and basic living expenses. Desirables might include travel or luxury items.
- Short-term vs. long-term: Some goals need immediate attention, while others are for the long term. Prioritizing helps in managing current financial pressures without losing sight of future objectives.
- Cost-benefit analysis: Assess the impact of each goal on your overall vision. Goals that significantly enhance your retirement happiness might take precedence over those with less impact.

Flexible Planning

Flexibility in planning acknowledges that life is unpredictable. Changes in health, economic conditions, or personal circumstances can affect your retirement vision and the financial goals aligned with it. Incorporating flexibility ensures your plan remains viable, no matter what life throws your way.

- Build in a buffer: When estimating the financial needs for your goals, consider adding a buffer to account for unforeseen expenses or economic changes. A buffer enhances your plan's resilience to shocks.
- Diversify your investments: A diversified portfolio can provide more stable returns and protect against market volatility. This stability supports your financial goals amidst changing economic landscapes.
- Adjustable goals: Be prepared to revise your goals based on life changes. For instance, a health setback might prioritize healthcare savings over leisure travel.

Review and Adjust

A critical aspect of aligning your financial goals with your retirement vision is the commitment to regularly review and adjust your goals. This process ensures that your plan evolves along with your life circumstances and retirement vision.

- Annual reviews: Set aside time each year to review your financial goals and the progress you've made towards them. This review should consider changes in your personal life, economic conditions, and any shifts in your retirement vision.
- Adjust contributions: Based on your annual review, you may need to increase or decrease your savings contributions. Adjusting contributions keeps you on track to meet your goals within the set time frames.
- Reassess risk tolerance: As you approach retirement, reassessing your risk tolerance is crucial. Shifting towards more conservative investments can protect your nest egg from market downturns as you near your retirement date.

Aligning your financial goals with your retirement vision is an ongoing process, not a one-time task. It's a dynamic strategy requiring regular attention and adjustments to ensure you continuously move toward your desired future. This approach not only keeps your retirement plans realistic and achievable but also provides peace of mind, knowing that you're actively steering your financial ship toward the retirement of your dreams.

Navigating this process requires dedication, foresight, and sometimes willingness to make tough decisions. However, the reward is a retirement that closely matches your vision, crafted through thoughtful planning and informed by a deep understanding of your personal aspirations and financial realities.

2

Demystifying Retirement Accounts: 401K and IRA Decoded

Imagine standing at the base of a mountain, gazing up at the peak. You're about to climb, not with gear and ropes, but with knowledge and strategies—your tools for scaling the financial heights of retirement planning. Now, think of 401K and IRA accounts as two distinct paths up the mountain. Both lead to the summit—your secure retirement—but each offers different views and challenges. This chapter aims to clear the fog around these paths, making your climb smoother.

2.1 Demystifying 401K and IRA: What You Need to Know

Understanding the basics

Before you set foot on either path, let's get familiar with the terrain. A 401K is often introduced through your workplace, offering a convenient way to save for retirement directly from your paycheck. Think of it as a savings account with a twist: the money you contribute is invested, allowing it to grow over time. On the other hand, an Individual Retirement Account (IRA) is something you set up on your own. It's like opening a personal savings account for retirement, with the freedom to invest in a broader range of options.

- 401K accounts typically come with an employer match, which is akin to free money towards your retirement. If your employer offers a match, try contributing at least enough to get the full match; it's an instant return on your investment.
- IRA accounts offer more investment choices than most 401K plans, allowing you to tailor your retirement savings more closely to your personal preferences and financial goals.

Contribution limits and rules

The IRS limits how much you can contribute to these accounts each year. For 2021, the limit for 401K contributions is $19,500, with an additional catch-up contribution of $6,500 if you're 50 or older. IRAs have lower limits: $6,000 per year, with an additional $1,000 for those 50 and up. These limits can change, so it's vital to stay updated.

- Tax treatment is a key difference between these accounts. Contributions to a traditional 401K or IRA can reduce your taxable income in the year you make them, potentially lowering your tax bill. However, you'll pay taxes on withdrawals in retirement.

Choosing between Roth and Traditional

Imagine you're at a fork in the road: one path is labeled "Traditional" and the other "Roth." With Traditional accounts, you get a tax break up front, leading to immediate savings. Roth accounts, however, flip the script. You pay taxes on your contributions now, but withdrawals in retirement are tax-free.

- For a Roth account, think about your current and future tax situation. If you expect to be in a higher tax bracket in retirement, paying taxes now might make more sense. The Roth option is like paying for all your mountain climbing gear upfront, knowing you won't have to worry about any costs when you reach the summit.
- For a Traditional account, it's beneficial if you anticipate being in a lower tax bracket in retirement than you are now. You defer taxes until retirement, potentially reducing your tax liability when your income may be lower.

Withdrawal rules and penalties

Understanding when and how you can access your money is crucial. For both 401K and IRA accounts, you're generally allowed to start making penalty-free withdrawals at age 59½. Withdraw too early, and you could face a 10% penalty on top of regular income taxes. However, some exceptions might allow you to tap into these funds early without penalty, such as certain medical expenses or a first-time home purchase.

- Required Minimum Distributions (RMDs) are another critical aspect. Once you reach age 72, the IRS requires you to take minimum withdrawals from your traditional 401K and IRA accounts. Roth IRAs are exempt from RMDs during the owner's lifetime, making them a flexible tool for managing your retirement income and tax situation.

- Visual Aid: Consider including a chart that compares Traditional and Roth accounts side by side, highlighting contribution limits, tax treatment, withdrawal rules, and RMD requirements. This visual could serve as a quick reference for readers to understand the differences at a glance.
- Interactive Element: A quiz titled "Which Retirement Account is Right for You?" could help readers assess their current financial situation, tax considerations, and retirement goals to guide them toward the type of account that might best suit their needs.

Both 401K and IRA accounts are powerful tools in your retirement planning toolkit. By understanding the basics, contribution limits and rules, and the differences between Roth and Traditional options, you're better equipped to make informed decisions that align with your retirement vision. Remember, choosing the right path depends on your goals, tax situation, and investment preferences. As you climb towards financial security in retirement, remember these insights to navigate the terrain confidently.

2.2 Roth vs. Traditional: Making Sense of Your Choices

In the landscape of retirement savings, selecting between Roth and Traditional accounts is akin to choosing the right gear for your climb. Both have distinct features and benefits, shaped mainly by tax implications, eligibility requirements, and their potential impact on long-term financial health. This section aims to demystify these options, providing insights to help you align your choice with your financial goals and circumstances.

Tax Implications

At the heart of the Roth versus Traditional debate lies their differing tax treatments. With Traditional accounts, your contributions are made pre-tax, reducing your annual taxable income. This immediate tax benefit can be particularly advantageous if you're in a higher tax bracket. However, when retirement comes, and you start withdrawing funds, those distributions are taxed as ordinary income. This deferred tax can be a double-edged sword, depending on your income level in retirement.

Roth accounts, conversely, offer a reverse tax scenario. Contributions are made with after-tax dollars, meaning there's no immediate tax deduction. The magic happens in retirement—withdrawals, including earnings, are tax-free, provided certain conditions are met. This can be a significant advantage, especially if you expect to be in a higher tax bracket in retirement or if tax rates rise across the board.

- Immediate vs. future tax benefits: Traditional accounts may offer a tax break today, while Roth accounts promise tax-free income in retirement.

Eligibility Requirements

Not everyone can freely choose between Roth and Traditional IRAs due to income eligibility requirements, particularly for Roth IRAs. For those with higher incomes, there may be limits to how much can be contributed to a Roth IRA, or they may not be eligible to contribute at all. Traditional IRAs, on the other hand, don't have these income restrictions for contributions. However, there are limits on the deductibility of contributions if a retirement plan at work covers you or your spouse.

- Roth IRA income limits: For individuals and couples exceeding certain income thresholds, Roth IRA contributions may be reduced or not allowed.
- Traditional IRA deductibility: If a workplace retirement plan covers you, your ability to deduct Traditional IRA contributions on your taxes may be limited based on your income.

Long-term Benefits

When evaluating Roth and Traditional accounts, consider the long-term implications of each choice. A Roth IRA can be particularly compelling if you anticipate needing flexibility with your withdrawals in retirement. Unlike Traditional IRAs, Roth IRAs do not require minimum distributions starting at age 72, allowing your savings to grow tax-free if you don't need to access them. This can significantly benefit estate planning, enabling you to leave tax-free money to your heirs.

Traditional IRA funds are taxed at your income tax rate when withdrawn in retirement. If your tax rate is lower in retirement than during your working years, this can work in your favor. However, required minimum distributions (RMDs) from these accounts can push you into a higher tax bracket, affecting your overall tax situation.

- Withdrawal flexibility: Roth IRAs offer more flexibility, with tax-free withdrawals and no RMDs, which can benefit estate planning.
- Tax rate considerations: If you anticipate a lower tax rate in retirement, Traditional accounts could offer more benefits in the long run.

Case Studies

To illustrate the impact of choosing between Roth and Traditional accounts, consider two hypothetical case studies:

- Case Study 1: Alex, age 30, expects her career trajectory to significantly increase her income over time. She opts for a Roth IRA, contributing $6,000 annually. By retirement at 65, assuming a 7% annual return, her account grows to over $1 million, with all withdrawals tax-free, offering a substantial benefit given her higher expected tax bracket in retirement.
- Case Study 2: Jordan, also 30, is currently in a high tax bracket but expects a more modest income in retirement. He chooses a Traditional IRA for the immediate tax deduction, contributing $6,000 annually. At a 7% return, his account also grows to over $1 million by age 65. However, his withdrawals are taxed as ordinary income. Assuming a lower tax bracket in retirement, Jordan still benefits from significant tax savings.

These case studies underscore the importance of aligning your retirement account choice with your financial situation and expectations for the future. While Roth IRAs offer tax-free growth and withdrawals, their benefits are maximized when you expect to be in a higher tax bracket in retirement. With their tax-deferred growth and contributions, traditional IRAs can be advantageous if you anticipate being in a lower tax bracket when you retire.

2.3 Understanding Asset Allocation and Diversification

Asset allocation and diversification play pivotal roles in retirement savings. When applied thoughtfully, these strategies are the backbone of effective risk management and instrumental in steering you toward your retirement objectives. This section will illuminate how these strategies mitigate investment risk and ensure your portfolio aligns with your evolving retirement vision.

Risk Management

Asset allocation involves dividing your investment portfolio among different asset categories—stocks, bonds, and cash being the most common. This strategy is fundamental for managing investment risk because different asset classes respond differently to market conditions. While stocks offer high growth potential, they come with increased volatility. Bonds, on the other hand, typically provide more stable returns. Cash, or cash equivalents like money market funds, offer the lowest risk and potential returns.

Balancing these asset categories to reflect your risk tolerance and investment timeline is key to effective risk management. For instance, if market fluctuations keep you awake at night, you might lean towards a higher allocation in bonds and cash. Conversely, if you're comfortable with short-term market swings in exchange for potential long-term growth, a higher stock allocation could be more your speed.

Achieving Your Retirement Vision

Diversification, or spreading your investments across various assets, further refines the concept of asset allocation. It's about not putting all your eggs in one basket. Within each asset category, you can diversify further—by investing in a mix of sectors, industries, and geographies. This approach can cushion your portfolio against significant losses if one investment or market segment underperforms.

Proper diversification is aligned closely with achieving your retirement goals. It allows for the potential growth needed to reach your objectives while mitigating risk to a comfortable level. For example, if part of your vision involves traveling extensively, ensuring your portfolio has growth potential through diversified equity investments can help fund those dreams. At the same time, maintaining a portion of your portfolio in more stable investments provides a safety net.

Balancing Your Portfolio

Maintaining balance in your investment portfolio is an ongoing process. Over time, market movements can cause your initial asset allocation to shift, potentially exposing you to more risk than intended or skewing your investments away from your retirement goals. Regularly reviewing and rebalancing your portfolio ensures it stays aligned with your strategic asset allocation.

The rebalancing process might involve selling investments that have grown to constitute a more significant portion of your portfolio than desired and buying more of those that now make up less. This disciplined approach forces you to "buy low and sell high," contributing to the potential for solid long-term returns.

Age-Based Allocation Strategies

As you approach retirement, adjusting your asset allocation becomes increasingly important. In your early working years, a higher proportion of stocks might be appropriate, capitalizing on their growth potential over a longer period. However, as retirement approaches, gradually shifting towards bonds and cash equivalents can help preserve your accumulated wealth.

This doesn't mean shifting entirely out of stocks. Maintaining a portion of your portfolio in equities can still be beneficial, providing growth potential to counteract inflation and extend the longevity of your savings. Age-based allocation strategies offer a structured approach to gradually decrease investment risk as you age, keeping your portfolio in tune with your changing risk tolerance and time horizon.

By embracing asset allocation and diversification, you create a robust framework for your retirement savings. This strategic approach manages risk and propels you towards your retirement aspirations. It's about finding the right balance that matches your risk tolerance with your long-term goals, ensuring your investment strategy evolves alongside your life's journey.

Remember what we've discussed as we wrap up this exploration of asset allocation and diversification. These strategies are about more than just numbers and allocations; they're about crafting a pathway that leads to the retirement you envision. Balancing risk and growth, ensuring your investments reflect your goals, and adjusting your approach as you age are all critical steps.

Looking ahead, staying informed, and making educated decisions about your retirement planning cannot be overstated. Our journey continues as we delve deeper into the intricacies of retirement planning, equipping you with the knowledge and tools needed to navigate the complexities of this critical life stage. Your proactive engagement with these concepts lays the groundwork for a retirement filled with the fulfillment of your dreams and goals.

3

Laying the Financial Foundation for Retirement

Imagine you're setting out to build your dream home. Before the first brick is laid, you need a clear blueprint and a solid foundation. Similarly, a secure retirement rests on understanding your current financial situation. This chapter is your guide to conducting a personal financial audit, an essential step to ensure your retirement planning is built on solid ground.

A personal financial audit provides a snapshot of where you stand financially. It's like a financial health check-up, highlighting areas of strength and those needing attention. This process is critical for anyone looking to make informed decisions about their retirement planning. Let's dive into how you can conduct your own financial audit, starting with listing your assets and liabilities, understanding your cash flow, identifying your financial strengths and weaknesses, and setting the stage for improvement.

Listing Assets and Liabilities

The first step in a financial audit is to list all your assets (what you own) and liabilities (what you owe). This might sound straightforward, but it's essential to be thorough.

Assets include:

- Savings and checking accounts
- Retirement accounts (401K, IRA)
- Real estate
- Investments (stocks, bonds, mutual funds)
- Personal property (vehicles, jewelry)

Liabilities include:

- Mortgage
- Car loans
- Credit card debt
- Student loans
- Other personal loans

Creating a detailed list gives you a clear picture of your net worth. It's like taking inventory before a big move; you need to know what you have and what's weighing you down.

Understanding Your Cash Flow

Next, it's time to analyze your income and expenses. This step tracks how much money comes in and where it goes each month.

Start by listing all sources of income, including:

- Salary
- Rental income
- Interest and dividends
- Any other earnings

Then, categorize your expenses. Common categories include:

- Housing (rent or mortgage)
- Utilities
- Groceries
- Transportation
- Insurance premiums
- Entertainment
- Savings and investments

This exercise helps you identify spending patterns and areas to cut back. It's akin to reviewing your grocery list to see where you can save money without compromising quality.

Identifying Financial Strengths and Weaknesses

With a clear understanding of your assets, liabilities, and cash flow, you can now identify your financial strengths and areas for improvement. Strengths might include a robust emergency fund or a well-diversified investment portfolio. Weaknesses could be high levels of debt or insufficient savings for future goals.

This process is like a coach reviewing game footage. It's about understanding what strategies are working and where adjustments are needed to improve performance.

Setting the Stage for Improvement

With this knowledge, you can start making impactful changes toward your retirement goals. This might involve increasing your savings rate, paying down debt, or reallocating your investments. The key is to create a plan of action that moves you closer to your ideal retirement.

Consider setting SMART goals (Specific, Measurable, Achievable, Relevant, Time-bound) for each area you'd like to improve. For example, rather than a vague goal like "save more money," a SMART goal would be "increase monthly savings by $200 for the next 12 months."

3.1 Tools and Resources to Assist Your Audit

- Budgeting apps can automate much of the work involved in tracking income and expenses. Many apps link directly to your financial accounts, categorizing transactions in real time.
- Net worth trackers help you monitor your assets and liabilities, giving you an instant view of your financial health.
- Debt repayment calculators offer strategies for efficiently paying down liabilities, showing how changing payment amounts or frequencies can impact your overall interest paid.

Interactive Element: Financial Audit Checklist

A comprehensive checklist can ensure you recognize all assets and liabilities during your audit. This tool simplifies the process, guiding you through each step and helping you organize your financial information effectively.

- Assets: List all checking and savings accounts, retirement accounts, other investments, real estate, and valuable personal property.
- Liabilities: Detail all mortgages, car loans, student loans, credit card debt, and other personal loans.
- Income: Record all sources of monthly income, including salary, rental income, and any other earnings.
- Expenses: Categorize monthly expenses, including housing, utilities, groceries, transportation, insurance, entertainment, and savings.

This checklist serves as a roadmap for your financial audit, ensuring a thorough examination of your current financial situation. By completing each section, you lay the groundwork for informed, strategic retirement planning.

Setting the stage for improvement involves taking proactive steps based on the insights gained from your financial audit. It's about making choices today that align with your long-term retirement vision, ensuring that when the time comes, you're ready to build your dream retirement brick by brick.

3.2 Calculating Your Net Worth for Retirement Planning

Understanding your net worth is like having a financial compass that points you toward your retirement goals. It's a measure of what you own minus what you owe, providing a clear snapshot of your financial health at any given time. This clarity is indispensable for making informed decisions about your retirement planning.

Defining Net Worth

At its core, net worth encapsulates the value of all your assets after subtracting your liabilities. Assets can be anything from savings accounts, retirement funds, investments, and personal property like your home or car. Liabilities include mortgages, loans, and any other debts. The equation is straightforward: Assets - Liabilities = Net Worth. Yet, its implications for your financial strategy are profound, serving as a litmus test for your fiscal well-being.

Importance of Knowing Your Net Worth

Pinpointing your net worth is not merely about crunching numbers; it's about laying the groundwork for a secure future. This figure acts as a benchmark, helping you assess whether you're on track to meet your retirement objectives or if adjustments are needed. A positive and growing net worth indicates financial stability and progress toward your goals. At the same time, a stagnant or negative figure might signal the need for a strategic pivot in your financial planning.

Steps to Calculate Net Worth

Calculating your net worth involves a few straightforward steps:

1. List all assets: Start by making a comprehensive list of your assets. Include everything from liquid assets like cash in checking and savings accounts to retirement accounts (401K, IRA), other investments, and valuable personal property. Remember to appraise items like your home or vehicles at market value.
2. Tally up liabilities: Next, list all your liabilities. This includes the remaining balance on your mortgage, car

loans, student loans, credit card debt, and any other money you owe.
3. Subtract liabilities from assets: With both totals in hand, subtract your total liabilities from your total assets. The result is your net worth.
4. Review and adjust: This calculation isn't a one-time task; it's something you should do regularly. As your financial situation evolves, so too will your net worth. Regular reviews help you stay aligned with your retirement goals.

Using Net Worth as a Planning Tool

Your net worth isn't just a number; it's a tool that can guide your financial strategy. Here's how you can use it effectively:

- Set benchmarks: Use your net worth as a benchmark to gauge your financial progress over time. Regularly tracking this figure can motivate you to increase your assets and decrease your liabilities, pushing you closer to your retirement goals.
- Assess financial health: A comprehensive view of your net worth allows you to evaluate your financial health. It shows where you stand today and helps identify areas needing more attention, whether boosting your savings, investing more aggressively, or paying down debt.
- Inform decision-making: When faced with financial decisions, your net worth provides a clear reference point. It can help determine if you're in a position to make significant financial moves, such as purchasing a home, investing in property, or even retiring early.
- Strategic adjustments: If your net worth isn't where you want it to be, knowing your exact financial position allows you to make strategic adjustments to your savings and

investment plans. This might mean reallocating assets to more productive investments, finding ways to increase income, or implementing a more aggressive debt reduction strategy.

Calculating and understanding your net worth is a vital step in retirement planning. It offers a precise, quantitative measure of your financial health, guiding your journey towards a secure and fulfilling retirement. By regularly assessing your net worth, you can make informed decisions that bring you closer to achieving your financial and retirement goals.

3.3 Setting Up Your Emergency Fund: A Pre-Retirement Must

An emergency fund is a financial safety net designed to cover unexpected expenses without derailing your long-term financial plans. In retirement planning, this fund takes on an even greater significance. It serves as a buffer against unforeseen costs and ensures that your retirement savings continue to grow, uninterrupted by life's unpredictable events.

Why You Need an Emergency Fund

Life is full of surprises, some less welcome than others. Medical emergencies, sudden home repairs, or unexpected job loss can stress your finances. Without an emergency fund, you might be forced to dip into your retirement savings or take on high-interest debt to cover these costs. This fund acts as a protective barrier, safeguarding your retirement plans from short-term upheavals.

Determining the Size of Your Fund

The size of your emergency fund should reflect your unique circumstances, considering your monthly expenses, job stability, and the number of income earners in your household. A general guideline is to have three to six months' worth of living expenses saved. However, if your job situation is less stable or you're the sole income provider, aiming for a larger fund—perhaps up to a year's worth of expenses—might be prudent.

To calculate the size of your fund:

- Tally your monthly essential expenses, including housing, utilities, groceries, and insurance.
- Multiply this total by the number of months you aim to cover (between three and twelve, depending on your situation).
- Consider adding a buffer for additional peace of mind.

Best Practices for Managing Your Fund

Where and how you store your emergency fund can significantly impact its effectiveness. The fund should be easily accessible but not so easy that you're tempted to use it for non-emergencies. High-yield savings accounts or money market accounts are excellent choices. They offer better interest rates than traditional savings accounts while providing the liquidity you need to withdraw funds quickly in an emergency.

When managing your emergency fund:

- Keep it separate from your daily checking account to avoid the temptation to dip into it for everyday expenses.

- Regularly review and adjust the fund size as your living expenses or income changes.
- Automate contributions to your emergency fund to ensure it continues to grow.

Integrating Your Fund with Your Overall Retirement Plan

An emergency fund is not just another account; it's an integral component of your broader retirement planning strategy. It supports your long-term goals by providing a financial cushion, allowing your investments to remain untouched and continue compounding. Additionally, this fund can give you the confidence to invest more aggressively in your retirement accounts, knowing you have a safety net for short-term needs.

Incorporating your emergency fund into your retirement strategy involves:

- Regularly reassess your fund size in the context of your overall retirement plan to ensure it remains aligned with your changing financial landscape.
- Considering the role of your emergency fund in your asset allocation, particularly as you approach retirement, your risk tolerance may decrease.
- Using your emergency fund as a buffer to avoid premature withdrawals from retirement accounts, which can incur penalties and set back your retirement progress.

A well-planned emergency fund is more than just a financial safeguard; it's a cornerstone of a resilient retirement strategy. It ensures that when faced with life's inevitable surprises, you have the resources to manage without compromising your long-term financial well-being. By carefully determining the size of your fund, choosing the right place to keep it, and seamlessly integrating it with your retirement planning, you create a comprehensive approach that supports both your present and future financial security.

As this chapter concludes, remember that an emergency fund is not optional but a fundamental element of your retirement planning. It acts as your first line of defense against life's unpredictability, ensuring that your plans for a secure, comfortable retirement remain on track regardless of what comes your way. Moving forward, the insights you've gained here will serve as a solid foundation for building a comprehensive retirement strategy that not only withstands life's storms but thrives in anticipation of the sunny days ahead.

4

Maximizing Your Retirement Potential

In the tapestry of retirement planning, few threads are as vibrant and crucial as understanding the power of compounding. It's a simple concept with profound implications, yet it often flies under the radar, overshadowed by more immediate financial concerns. This chapter sheds light on this financial phenomenon, revealing how it can significantly amplify your retirement savings.

4.1 The Power of Compounding in Your Retirement Accounts

Understanding Compounding

Compounding is about earning interest on your interest, creating a snowball effect that can substantially grow your retirement savings over time. It's akin to planting a tree. Initially, the growth seems slow, but given time, that same tree sprawls out, providing shade far beyond its original size. Similarly, even modest contributions to your retirement accounts can expand exponentially through compounding, provided they have sufficient time to grow.

Start Saving Early

The secret to harnessing the full potential of compounding lies in starting early. The sooner you begin saving, the more time your money has to work for you. Consider two savers: one starts contributing to their retirement account at 25, while the other waits until 35. Even if the latter saves more money overall, the early starter often comes out ahead by retirement, thanks to the extra decade of compounding growth. This emphasizes the importance of saving and starting as soon as possible.

Reinvesting Dividends and Interest

For compounding to truly take effect, reinvesting dividends and interest is crucial. Instead of pocketing these earnings, funneling them back into your retirement account allows them to contribute to the compounding process. It's like adding more snow to your snowball; the more you add, the bigger it grows. This strategy requires discipline but can significantly increase the size of your retirement nest egg over time.

Real-Life Examples

To illustrate the power of compounding, let's look at an actual scenario involving a retirement savings account. Imagine starting with a $5,000 investment and contributing an additional $200 monthly. With an average annual return of 7%, your investment would grow to over $263,000 in 30 years. Without adding to the initial investment, that $5,000 alone would grow to nearly $40,000 in the same timeframe, showcasing compounding's ability to multiply your savings.

Visual Element: Infographics on Compounding

An infographic titled "The Magic of Compounding" could visually show how a consistent, modest investment can grow over different periods, highlighting the impact of early and continued contributions versus starting later in life.

Interactive Element: Compounding Calculator Exercise

A compounding calculator exercise could engage readers by allowing them to input their savings information—starting balance, monthly contribution, expected annual return, and time frame—to see firsthand how their retirement savings could grow. This real-time interaction makes the concept of compounding more tangible. It personalizes it, showing the potential growth of their specific investments.

Textual Element: Reflection Section on Financial Habits

A reflection section could invite readers to assess their current savings habits and consider adjustments to better leverage compounding. Questions might include:

- How early did I start saving for retirement?
- Do I regularly reinvest dividends and interest?
- What changes can I make to maximize the benefits of compounding in my retirement planning?

By directly engaging with these concepts, readers can better understand the importance of early and consistent saving, the benefits of reinvesting earnings, and the tangible impact these strategies can have on their retirement savings. Through real-life examples, interactive exercises, and personal reflection, this chapter aims to transform the abstract concept of compounding into a concrete, actionable strategy for maximizing retirement potential.

4.2 Catch-Up Contributions: It's Never Too Late to Start

In retirement savings, a provision exists that acts like a second wind for those who find themselves behind in their journey toward financial security. This provision, known as catch-up contributions, addresses the concerns of individuals 50 or older, offering them an opportunity to accelerate their savings as they approach retirement. This section highlights what catch-up contributions entail, who is eligible, and how they can significantly bolster your retirement savings.

Defining Catch-Up Contributions and Eligibility

Catch-up contributions allow individuals aged 50 and above to contribute additional funds beyond the standard limits to their retirement accounts, such as 401Ks and IRAs. This is particularly beneficial for those who might not have saved enough in their earlier years or wish to maximize their savings in the final stretch before retirement. The government updates these contribution limits annually, so staying informed on the latest figures is crucial.

Strategies for Making Catch-Up Contributions

Several strategies can enhance the impact of catch-up contributions on retirement savings for those eligible.

- Maximize Contributions: First and foremost, if financially feasible, maximize your catch-up contributions each year. This might mean adjusting your budget to allocate more to

your retirement accounts. Still, the potential payoff in terms of additional savings can be substantial.
- Focus on High-Interest Accounts: Consider directing your catch-up contributions to accounts with higher growth potential. While this might involve a higher risk, the potential for increased returns can significantly improve your retirement savings over time.
- Tax Considerations: Evaluate the tax implications of contributing to different types of retirement accounts. For example, contributions to a traditional IRA might offer immediate tax deductions, whereas contributions to a Roth IRA provide tax-free withdrawals in retirement.
- Professional Advice: Consult with a financial advisor to tailor a catch-up contribution strategy that aligns with your retirement plan and financial situation. A personalized approach can help identify the most effective way to leverage catch-up contributions for your specific needs.

Impact on Retirement Savings

The effect of catch-up contributions on your retirement savings can be profound. By taking advantage of this opportunity, you can significantly close the savings gap if you started saving later in life or enhance your existing nest egg. The additional contributions compound over time, potentially increasing your retirement savings by tens or even hundreds of thousands of dollars, depending on how much and how long you contribute.

Motivational Success Stories

Consider the stories of individuals who have successfully utilized catch-up contributions to enhance their retirement savings to illustrate the real-world impact.

- Case Study 1: Sarah began focusing on her retirement savings at 50, feeling concerned that she hadn't saved enough. By maximizing her catch-up contributions annually and focusing on high-growth investment options, she was able to significantly increase her retirement fund, giving her the financial security she sought for her retirement years.
- Case Study 2: Mark, at 55, realized he was not on track to retire comfortably. He consulted with a financial advisor and adjusted his budget to maximize his catch-up contributions to both his 401K and IRA. By the time he retired at 67, these strategic contributions had added over $150,000 to his retirement savings, significantly improving his retirement lifestyle.

These stories underscore that enhancing your retirement savings is never too late. With the right strategy and a commitment to maximizing catch-up contributions, you can make meaningful progress toward your retirement goals, regardless of when you started saving.

Catch-up contributions are a powerful tool for those looking to boost their retirement savings later in life. Whether you're playing catch-up or simply aiming to fortify your nest egg, taking full advantage of these contributions can have a lasting impact on your financial well-being in retirement. By understanding and strategically employing catch-up contributions, you allow yourself to secure the retirement you envision, filled with the freedom and peace of mind that financial stability brings.

4.3 Employer Match: Maximizing Free Money

Grasping Employer Match Programs

In the landscape of retirement savings, employer match programs stand out as pivotal benefits that can significantly enhance your financial readiness for retirement. These programs, offered with 401(k) plans and sometimes other retirement accounts, involve your employer contributing a certain amount to your retirement savings plan based on the amount you contribute, up to a certain percentage of your salary. It's akin to receiving a bonus that grows over time, a reward for your foresight in saving for the future.

Pinpointing Optimal Contribution Rates

To fully benefit from an employer match program, you must contribute enough from your paycheck to trigger the maximum match from your employer. This optimal rate varies but is often expressed as a percentage of your salary. For instance, if your employer offers a 100% match on the first 3% of your salary that you contribute, you should aim to contribute at least that 3%. Failing to do so leaves money on the table. A straightforward approach to calculating this is to review your pay stubs and employer's plan documentation to understand the match formula and adjust your contribution rate accordingly.

Sidestepping Common Pitfalls

While employer match programs are lucrative, employees often commit several avoidable mistakes. Not contributing enough to get the full match, delaying participation in the plan, or not increasing contributions as salaries rise can all diminish the potential benefits.

Another common oversight is not comprehensively understanding the vesting schedule, which dictates when the employer-matched funds become entirely yours. Staying informed and proactive can help you navigate these pitfalls, maximizing the benefit.

Advocating for Enhanced Benefits

Negotiating better retirement benefits, including improved employer match rates, is seldom approached by employees but can be a fruitful discussion. Preparation is key; arm yourself with knowledge of standard practices in your industry and present a reasoned case to your HR department or management. Highlighting the mutual benefits of enhanced retirement contributions, such as increased employee retention and satisfaction, can bolster your argument. Remember, negotiations should be approached with tact and an understanding of your employer's perspective.

As we conclude this section, it's crucial to remember the value of employer match programs as part of your retirement planning strategy. By understanding how these programs work, calculating the optimal contribution rates, avoiding common mistakes, and even negotiating for better terms, you're positioning yourself for a more secure financial future. Each step you take strengthens the foundation of your retirement savings, bringing you closer to realizing your goals for a comfortable and fulfilling retirement.

Moving forward, the insights gained here serve as building blocks for more advanced strategies in retirement planning. Each decision you make, from how much to contribute to your retirement accounts to how you negotiate your benefits, is critical in shaping your financial landscape for the years to come.

5

Smart Investment Choices for Retirement

Imagine walking into an art gallery where the walls are adorned with a myriad of paintings. Each artwork's distinct style and color palette contributes to the gallery's overall appeal. This variety isn't just visually pleasing; it's essential, ensuring that every visitor finds something that resonates. Similarly, building a diversified retirement portfolio involves mixing various investment types to meet your financial goals. This chapter will guide you through this process, akin to curating your financial gallery, ensuring it reflects your unique needs and aspirations.

5.1 Building a Diversified Portfolio: A Beginner's Guide

Principles of diversification

Diversification is a strategy that involves spreading your investments across various assets to reduce risk. Think of it as not putting all your eggs in one basket. If one investment performs poorly, you're less likely to see a significant impact on your entire portfolio because other investments might perform well, balancing out the overall performance. This principle is crucial for retirement investing because it aims to achieve a smoother ride over the long term, mitigating the ups and downs of the market.

Asset classes overview

A well-diversified portfolio includes a mix of asset classes. Here's a brief overview:

- Stocks: Represent shares in companies. While they can be volatile, they also offer high growth potential over the long term.
- Bonds: Loans made to corporations or governments that pay back with interest. They are generally less risky than stocks and offer regular income.
- Cash and cash equivalents: These include savings accounts and money market funds. They are the least risky assets but provide lower returns.
- Real estate: These can be direct investments in property or through real estate investment trusts (REITs). Real estate can provide income and potential appreciation.
- Commodities: Such as gold, oil, and agricultural products. They can be a hedge against inflation but are subject to market fluctuations.

Diversification strategies

To create a diversified portfolio, consider the following strategies:

- Spread your investments across asset classes: This reduces the risk that poor performance in one area will drag down your entire portfolio.

- Diversify within asset classes: Don't just invest in one stock or bond. Consider a range of sectors, industries, and geographies.
- Adjust over time: As you approach retirement, you might want to shift towards more conservative investments to protect what you've accumulated.

Monitoring and rebalancing

Regularly checking in on your portfolio is vital. Over time, some investments may grow faster than others, skewing your original asset allocation. Here's how to keep your portfolio in line with your goals:

- Review your portfolio at least annually: This will help you determine whether your investments are still aligned with your retirement objectives.
- Rebalance when necessary: If your asset allocation drifts from your target, sell off some overperforming assets and buy more underperforming ones to get back on track.

Visual Element: Infographics on Portfolio Diversification

An infographic could visually break down the components of a diversified portfolio, showing examples of asset classes and how they might be combined based on different risk tolerances.

Interactive Element: Portfolio Builder Exercise

This is an online exercise where you input your retirement goals, risk tolerance, and investment preferences to receive suggestions for building a diversified portfolio. This tool can offer immediate, personalized insights into how diversification can work for you.

Textual Element: Real-life Diversification Strategies

This section offers insights from financial experts on diversifying investments. It can include quotes and advice on building a portfolio that withstands market volatility. It might cover topics like the importance of international investments or how emerging technologies create new investment opportunities.

By understanding and applying the principles of diversification, you're not just protecting your investments from the unpredictable nature of markets but also positioning yourself to take advantage of a range of opportunities. Like a well-curated art gallery, your portfolio should be a reflection of diverse and strategic choices that come together to create a cohesive and resilient financial future.

5.2 Understanding Risk Tolerance and Time Horizon

Defining Risk Tolerance

Risk tolerance is an investor's capacity to endure market volatility and the possibility of losing money on investments in the short term. It is a fundamental aspect that influences not just the selection of investments but also the ability to maintain a calm demeanor during market downturns. Individuals have varying levels of comfort with risk, shaped by their financial situation, investment experience, and even psychological disposition towards loss. Recognizing and accepting your risk tolerance is pivotal in creating an investment strategy you can stick with, avoiding panic-driven decisions during market fluctuations.

Assessing Your Risk Tolerance

Determining your personal risk tolerance involves introspection and, sometimes, complex evaluations. Here are steps to guide you through this essential process:

- Financial assessment: Examine your financial situation, including emergency funds, debts, and income stability. A solid monetary base can offer the leeway to take on more risk.
- Experience and knowledge: Reflect on your investment experience and understanding of financial markets. Familiarity can sometimes mitigate discomfort with volatility.
- Psychological comfort: Consider how you've reacted to past market downturns. Did you lose sleep over temporary losses, or could you see beyond the volatility toward long-term gains?
- Use tools and quizzes: Numerous online assessments can provide a rough estimate of your risk tolerance, combining various factors into a comprehensive analysis. While not definitive, these tools can offer a starting point for understanding your disposition toward investment risk.

Matching Investments to Your Risk Tolerance

Once you've gauged your risk tolerance, the next step is aligning your investment choices accordingly. This ensures your portfolio matches your comfort level, preventing rash decisions during market lows. Here's how to approach this alignment:

- Conservative investors might choose bonds, fixed-income funds, and high-quality dividend-paying stocks. These options offer stability and regular income, which is suitable for those with low-risk tolerance.
- Moderate investors could consider a balanced mix of stocks and bonds, providing a blend of growth potential and income. This middle ground suits those comfortable with some level of volatility but cautious of significant risks.
- Aggressive investors, comfortable with high volatility for the chance of higher returns, might focus on stocks, particularly in high-growth sectors, or explore options like venture capital for part of their portfolio. Their higher risk tolerance allows them to weather market swings in pursuit of substantial gains.

Adjusting for Changes in Risk Tolerance

Risk tolerance is not static; it can evolve due to changes in your financial situation, nearing retirement, or shifts in market conditions. Hence, adjusting your investment strategy over time is crucial. Here are considerations for making these adjustments:

- Regular reviews: Periodically reassess your risk tolerance, especially after major life events such as marriage, the birth of a child, or receiving an inheritance. These changes can impact your financial goals and, by extension, how much risk you're willing to take.
- Gradual shifts in asset allocation: As you approach retirement, gradually reducing exposure to high-risk investments can help protect your savings. This doesn't mean a sudden switch but a thoughtful reallocation over time.

- Stay informed: Keeping abreast of financial news and market trends can help you make informed decisions about adjusting your portfolio in response to changing economic landscapes.

You can create a resilient strategy that supports your financial goals through careful assessment and alignment of your investments with your risk tolerance, coupled with adjustments as your situation and the markets change. This approach allows for a smoother investment experience tailored to your unique profile and life journey.

5.3 Index Funds and ETFs: Investing Made Simple

Two investment vehicles stand out in retirement savings for their simplicity and effectiveness: index funds and exchange-traded funds (ETFs). These options provide a straightforward path for individuals looking to grow their retirement savings without becoming stock market experts. The allure of these investment types lies in their ability to offer broad market exposure, which is critical for building a resilient retirement portfolio.

Benefits of Index Funds and ETFs

Index funds and ETFs have gained popularity among investors for several reasons, paramount among them being their ability to mirror the performance of a market index. This could be a broad market index like the S&P 500 or a more specialized one focusing on a particular sector or region. This mirroring effect ensures that investors can participate in the collective performance of many companies, spreading out their risk and potential for returns. Another advantage is the transparency these funds offer, as their holdings reflect those of the indexes they track, allowing investors to know exactly where their money is at all times.

Cost-effectiveness

One of the most compelling arguments for choosing index funds and ETFs is their cost-effectiveness. These funds typically have lower management fees than actively managed funds because they follow a passive investment strategy. This means they do not require a team of analysts and portfolio managers to pick stocks, which can significantly reduce expenses. Lower fees mean more of your investment goes towards growing your retirement savings rather than covering administrative costs. Additionally, the tax efficiency of these funds, particularly ETFs, which often have lower capital gains distributions, can further enhance their attractiveness to investors focused on maximizing their retirement savings.

Selecting the Right Funds

With many options available, selecting suitable index funds and ETFs for your retirement portfolio can seem daunting. However, a few key considerations can guide your selection process:

- Match your risk tolerance and investment goals: Choose funds that align with your comfort with risk and long-term objectives. Consider bond index funds for a more conservative approach; for growth, look towards stock index funds.
- Consider the expense ratio: While these funds are known for cost-effectiveness, some still have higher fees than others. Opt for funds with a low expense ratio to maximize your investment returns.

- Diversification: Ensure the funds you select offer the diversification needed to protect your portfolio from volatility. This might mean choosing a mix of stock and bond funds and considering funds that provide exposure to international markets.

Passive vs. Active Management

The debate between passive and active management is central to investing in index funds and ETFs. Passive management, the strategy behind these funds, is predicated on the belief that it is difficult, if not impossible, for fund managers to consistently outperform the market over the long term. Therefore, passive funds can capture the market's returns by following a market index. This approach contrasts with active management, where fund managers attempt to beat the market through stock selection and timing. However, the higher fees associated with active management and the inconsistency in outperforming the market make passive index funds and ETFs a more attractive option for many retirement savers. Their simplicity, the potential for solid returns, and low costs make them essential to a retirement investment strategy.

In closing, index funds and ETFs represent a streamlined path to achieving a diversified and robust retirement portfolio. Their broad market exposure, combined with low costs and the efficiency of passive management, positions them as wise choices for investors aiming to grow their retirement savings. These investment vehicles demystify the retirement savings process, making it accessible to all, regardless of financial acumen. As we move forward, remember that the key to a successful retirement strategy lies in making informed choices that align with your goals, risk tolerance, and the changing landscape of the financial markets.

6

Tax-Savvy Strategies for Retirement Savings

Imagine you've found an old map leading to hidden treasure. The map is complex, filled with symbols and paths. Navigating the tax implications of retirement savings can feel just as intricate, yet mastering this map can lead to substantial rewards—maximizing your wealth and minimizing your tax liabilities. This chapter is your guide, helping you decode the symbols and choose the best paths to ensure your retirement savings work as efficiently as possible, keeping more money in your pocket.

Tax Advantages of Retirement Accounts

Let's start with the basics. Different retirement accounts offer unique tax advantages that, when used strategically, can significantly enhance your savings. For instance, traditional IRAs and 401(k)s provide tax deductions on contributions, lowering your taxable income for the year you contribute. On the flip side, Roth IRAs and Roth 401(k)s, funded with after-tax dollars, promise tax-free withdrawals in retirement.

Consider this when planning contributions:

- If you're currently in a high tax bracket and expect to be in a lower one in retirement, traditional accounts might be more beneficial due to the immediate tax break.
- Conversely, if you're in a lower tax bracket now but expect to be in a higher one upon retirement, Roth accounts could save you on taxes in the long run.

Withdrawal Strategies to Minimize Taxes

When it comes time to withdraw your savings, having a smart strategy is crucial. Withdrawing from different types of accounts in a specific order can keep you in a lower tax bracket, reducing the tax impact.

- Start with withdrawals from your taxable accounts, such as brokerage accounts, as these can have a lower tax rate, especially if you're selling assets that qualify for long-term capital gains.
- Next, turn to your tax-deferred accounts like traditional IRAs and 401(k)s. Since these withdrawals are taxed as regular income, timing them to keep you within favorable tax brackets can be a game-changer.
- Save your Roth IRA and Roth 401(k) withdrawals for last. Since these are tax-free, they won't bump you into a higher tax bracket.

Understanding Tax Brackets

Getting a grip on how tax brackets work is like having a decoder ring for your financial map. In the U.S., the tax system is progressive, meaning the rate increases as your income does. Planning your retirement withdrawals to stay within the lower brackets can save you a significant amount in taxes.

- Monitor how your retirement accounts' required minimum distributions (RMDs) might impact your taxable income. Starting at age 72, these mandatory withdrawals could push you into a higher bracket if not carefully managed.
- Consider consolidating smaller accounts to simplify your RMDs and potentially keep you in a lower tax bracket.

Tax Implications of Social Security and Other Income

Social Security benefits can also play a role in your tax situation. Depending on your overall income, some of your benefits may be taxable. Here's what to keep in mind:

- If Social Security is your only source of income, your benefits likely won't be taxed.
- However, if you have other substantial income, up to 85% of your Social Security benefits could be subject to tax.
- Strategies like Roth conversions or tapping into your Roth accounts can help manage this, potentially reducing the tax on your Social Security benefits.

Visual Element: "Your Retirement Tax Map"

An infographic titled "Your Retirement Tax Map" could visually depict:

- The different retirement accounts and their tax treatments
- A suggested order of withdrawals to minimize taxes
- How tax brackets work and tips for staying in lower brackets

Interactive Element: "Tax Impact Calculator"

An online calculator where you input details about your retirement accounts, expected income, and age to see:

- How different withdrawal strategies could impact your taxes
- A visualization of potential tax savings over time

Textual Element: Real-life Tax Planning Strategies

A section dedicated to strategies people have used to navigate the tax landscape in retirement effectively, including:

- How timing withdrawals from various accounts helped them stay in a lower tax bracket.
- The impact of Roth conversions during lower-income years to minimize taxes long-term.

Navigating the tax implications of retirement savings can be manageable. With the proper knowledge and strategies, you can make informed decisions that protect your hard-earned savings from unnecessary taxes. This chapter has laid out the basics, giving you the tools to plot your course. As you move forward, remember that staying informed, flexible, and proactive in your tax planning can make all the difference in securing the retirement you envision.

6.1 Roth Conversions: Timing and Strategy

A Roth conversion is a strategic move that involves transferring funds from a traditional IRA or 401(k) into a Roth IRA. This financial maneuver can be an advantageous part of your tax planning arsenal, especially if you anticipate being in a higher tax bracket in retirement than you are currently. Understanding when and how to execute a Roth conversion can significantly optimize your retirement savings and tax situation.

What is a Roth Conversion?

In essence, a Roth conversion shifts your savings from a tax-deferred account, where taxes are paid upon withdrawal, to a Roth account, which allows for tax-free growth and withdrawals in retirement. This process requires paying taxes on the converted amount in the year of the conversion. While the upfront tax bill may seem daunting, the long-term benefits of tax-free growth can outweigh the initial cost for many investors. This strategy is particularly appealing if you expect your tax rate to increase in the future, as it locks in the current lower tax rate on the converted funds.

Analyzing the Timing for a Roth Conversion

Timing is everything when it comes to a Roth conversion. The goal is to convert when it will result in the lowest tax burden, both now and in the future. Factors to consider include:

- Current and future tax rates: If you believe your tax rate will be higher in retirement, converting at today's lower rate can result in significant tax savings.
- Market conditions: A market downturn can be an opportune time to convert, as the reduced value of your investments will result in a lower tax bill on the conversion.
- Income fluctuations: Periods of lower income, such as a gap year between jobs, can also be an ideal time to convert since your overall tax rate may be lower.

Calculating the Cost and Benefits

A meticulous calculation is vital to weigh the pros and cons of a Roth conversion. Start by estimating the tax due on the amount you plan to convert, considering your current tax bracket and state taxes, if applicable. Next, project the potential growth of these funds in a Roth IRA, factoring in tax-free withdrawals in retirement. Compare this to the projected growth in a traditional IRA, considering future tax liabilities. Tools and calculators available online can assist in these projections, but consulting with a financial advisor for a personalized analysis is recommended.

Considerations include:

- Immediate tax implications: The added income from the conversion could push you into a higher tax bracket.
- Long-term tax savings: Compare the value of tax-free withdrawals from a Roth IRA against the deferred tax benefits of a traditional IRA.
- Required Minimum Distributions (RMDs): Traditional IRAs require RMDs starting at age 72, which can increase your taxable income in retirement. Roth IRAs do not have RMDs, potentially offering a more flexible retirement income strategy.

Case Studies

To illustrate the impact of Roth conversions, let's examine two scenarios:

- Case Study 1: Early Career Conversion John, in his early 30s, expects his income to grow significantly throughout his career. He converts $50,000 from his traditional IRA to a

Roth IRA during a year when his income is lower due to a sabbatical. Despite the upfront tax payment, the conversion allows his investment to grow tax-free for over 30 years. By retirement, the tax-free withdrawals from his Roth IRA significantly outweigh the initial tax cost of the conversion.
- Case Study 2: Pre-Retirement Conversion Linda, in her late 50s, plans to retire in a high-tax state and expects her tax rate to increase. She strategically converts portions of her 401(k) to a Roth IRA over several years, staying within her current lower tax bracket. This staggered approach minimizes her tax liability and sets her up for tax-free income in retirement, aligning perfectly with her financial goals.

These examples underscore the importance of strategic planning when considering a Roth conversion. The right timing and circumstances can lead to substantial tax savings and a more flexible retirement income strategy. However, every investor's situation is unique, and the decision to convert should be made with a thorough understanding of the potential costs and benefits.

6.2 Harvesting Tax Losses to Optimize Retirement Income

Tax loss harvesting stands out for its elegance and effectiveness in the tapestry of seasoned investors' financial strategies to optimize their retirement income. While less familiar to some, this strategy is a powerful tool in the savvy investor's kit, offering a way to mitigate the impact of taxes on investment returns. Here, we explore the nuances of tax loss harvesting, from its basic definition to the strategies, limits, and integration into broader tax planning efforts to enhance retirement income.

Introduction to Tax Loss Harvesting

Tax loss harvesting involves selling investments that have declined in value to realize losses, which can be used to offset taxes on both gains and income. The idea is to turn the lemons of investment losses into the lemonade of tax reduction. It's a proactive approach that requires monitoring your portfolio for opportunities to realize losses without derailing your long-term investment goals.

Strategies for Effective Tax Loss Harvesting

Implementing tax loss harvesting within your retirement portfolio requires both timing and strategy. Here are some actionable steps:

- Regular Portfolio Review: Keep an eye on the performance of your investments, looking for positions that have lost value and might be candidates for selling.
- Matching Losses with Gains: If you have realized gains, look for losses that can offset these gains. This balancing act can effectively reduce your capital gains tax.
- Beware of the Wash Sale Rule: The IRS prohibits claiming a tax deduction for a security sold in a wash sale. This rule prevents investors from selling a security at a loss and repurchasing the same or substantially identical security within 30 days before or after the sale. To comply, consider replacing the sold asset with a different investment that meets your portfolio's diversification and asset allocation needs.
- Consider the Timing: While tax loss harvesting can be done anytime during the year, many investors look to implement this strategy towards the end of the year to offset realized capital gains. However, being too focused on a specific time can lead to missed opportunities or rushed decisions.

Flexibility and attention throughout the year can yield better results.

Limits and Rules

The IRS has set clear guidelines and limits for tax loss harvesting to ensure compliance:

- $3,000 Limit: Investors can use capital losses to offset a maximum of $3,000 ($1,500 if married filing separately) of other income, such as wages or salaries, annually. Any excess losses can be carried forward to future years.
- Long-term vs. Short-term: The IRS distinguishes between long-term and short-term capital gains and losses. Short-term losses must offset short-term gains, and long-term losses must offset long-term gains. If additional losses remain, they can be applied to the opposite type of gain.

Integrating Tax Loss Harvesting with Overall Tax Planning

For those navigating the complexities of retirement income planning, integrating tax loss harvesting into your broader tax strategy can create a more cohesive approach to managing your finances. This integration involves several considerations:

- Holistic View: Look at your financial picture through a wide lens, considering all sources of income, including retirement accounts, Social Security benefits, and any part-time work, and how tax loss harvesting fits into this mix.
- Coordination with Financial Advisors: Work closely with your financial advisor or tax professional to ensure that tax loss harvesting aligns with your financial goals and tax planning strategies. This collaboration is critical to

making informed decisions that benefit your financial well-being.
- Flexibility and Adaptation: The financial landscape and tax laws are ever-changing. It is crucial to stay informed and ready to adapt your strategies in response to new information and changes in your life circumstances.

Tax loss harvesting is more than just a tactical move in investment management; it reflects a thoughtful and adaptive approach to building your financial future. By acknowledging the inevitability of market fluctuations and positioning yourself to navigate these with an eye toward tax efficiency, you set the stage for a retirement income strategy that reflects both wisdom and foresight.

In closing, the journey through tax loss harvesting reveals it as a nuanced strategy that, when executed with care, enhances the fabric of your retirement savings plan. It underscores the importance of vigilance, strategic action, and the integration of investment decisions within the broader context of your financial life. As we move forward, the insights gleaned from this exploration of tax loss harvesting serve as a valuable companion, guiding you toward a future where your retirement savings are preserved and optimized for the long road ahead.

7

Navigating Healthcare Costs in Retirement

Imagine for a moment you're planning a cross-country road trip. Your route is mapped out, the car's tank is full, and you're ready to hit the road. But have you considered the pit stops for fuel, the occasional roadside diner for meals, or even potential detours due to unforeseen roadblocks? Much like this journey, planning for healthcare costs in retirement involves anticipating not just the predictable expenses but also preparing for the unexpected ones that might arise.

Healthcare is a critical aspect of retirement planning, often underestimated in its complexity and impact on retirement savings. Understanding how to project your healthcare needs, the role of Medicare, considerations for long-term care, and creating a healthcare budget are pivotal. Together, these elements shape a strategy that safeguards your retirement savings against potentially high healthcare costs.

Projecting Your Healthcare Needs

Estimating future healthcare needs involves examining your current health status, lifestyle, and family medical history. While it's impossible to predict every medical issue you might encounter, a realistic appraisal of these factors can offer valuable insights into potential healthcare needs and costs. For instance, if chronic conditions such as diabetes or heart disease run in your family, you might face similar issues, which could significantly impact your healthcare budget.

Here are steps to project your healthcare needs more accurately:

- Document your current health status: Track any existing conditions, medications, and regular healthcare services you use.
- Review your family medical history: This can give clues about what conditions you might be predisposed to.
- Consult healthcare providers: They can offer professional insights into how your current health might evolve and impact your future healthcare needs.

The Role of Medicare

Medicare is central to retirement healthcare planning but doesn't cover everything. Understanding what Medicare covers and what you'll need to budget for out-of-pocket is crucial. Generally, Medicare covers a portion of hospital stays, doctor visits, and some preventive services. However, it doesn't cover long-term care, most dental care, eye exams related to prescribing glasses, or hearing aids.

7

Navigating Healthcare Costs in Retirement

Imagine for a moment you're planning a cross-country road trip. Your route is mapped out, the car's tank is full, and you're ready to hit the road. But have you considered the pit stops for fuel, the occasional roadside diner for meals, or even potential detours due to unforeseen roadblocks? Much like this journey, planning for healthcare costs in retirement involves anticipating not just the predictable expenses but also preparing for the unexpected ones that might arise.

Healthcare is a critical aspect of retirement planning, often underestimated in its complexity and impact on retirement savings. Understanding how to project your healthcare needs, the role of Medicare, considerations for long-term care, and creating a healthcare budget are pivotal. Together, these elements shape a strategy that safeguards your retirement savings against potentially high healthcare costs.

Projecting Your Healthcare Needs

Estimating future healthcare needs involves examining your current health status, lifestyle, and family medical history. While it's impossible to predict every medical issue you might encounter, a realistic appraisal of these factors can offer valuable insights into potential healthcare needs and costs. For instance, if chronic conditions such as diabetes or heart disease run in your family, you might face similar issues, which could significantly impact your healthcare budget.

Here are steps to project your healthcare needs more accurately:

- Document your current health status: Track any existing conditions, medications, and regular healthcare services you use.
- Review your family medical history: This can give clues about what conditions you might be predisposed to.
- Consult healthcare providers: They can offer professional insights into how your current health might evolve and impact your future healthcare needs.

The Role of Medicare

Medicare is central to retirement healthcare planning but doesn't cover everything. Understanding what Medicare covers and what you'll need to budget for out-of-pocket is crucial. Generally, Medicare covers a portion of hospital stays, doctor visits, and some preventive services. However, it doesn't cover long-term care, most dental care, eye exams related to prescribing glasses, or hearing aids.

To navigate Medicare effectively:

- Educate yourself on the different parts of Medicare: Part A covers hospital insurance, Part B covers medical insurance, Part D covers prescription drugs, and Medicare Advantage Plans (Part C) offer an alternative way to receive your Medicare benefits.
- Consider a Medicare Supplement Insurance (Medigap) policy: This can help pay some of the healthcare costs that Original Medicare doesn't cover, like copayments, coinsurance, and deductibles.

Long-Term Care Considerations

Long-term care could become necessary if you're unable to perform basic self-care tasks due to aging or illness. The cost of long-term care, whether provided at home or in a facility, can be substantial and is not covered by Medicare. Planning for this possibility is critical to a comprehensive retirement healthcare strategy.

Effective long-term care planning might involve:

- Researching long-term care insurance: While premiums can be high, especially if you purchase a policy later in life, the benefits can significantly offset the cost of long-term care services.
- Exploring other funding options: Depending on your financial situation, these might include savings, retirement income, or even reverse mortgages.

Creating a Healthcare Budget

A healthcare budget for retirement should account for premiums, out-of-pocket costs, and potential long-term care expenses. This budget is not static; it should be reviewed and adjusted as you age and as healthcare costs evolve.

Steps to create a healthcare budget include:

- Estimating annual healthcare expenses: Include Medicare premiums, out-of-pocket costs for services and medications not covered by Medicare, and Medigap premiums if applicable.
- Planning for inflation: Healthcare costs historically rise faster than general inflation, so it's wise to factor in higher costs yearly.
- Considering long-term care costs: Even if you're healthy now, including long-term care costs in your budget ensures you're prepared for any eventuality.

Visual Element: Healthcare Costs Infographic

An infographic titled "Breaking Down Retirement Healthcare Costs" could visually represent:

- The average costs associated with Medicare premiums and out-of-pocket expenses.
- The percentage of retirees likely to need long-term care and the average cost of care.
- A pie chart showing the typical distribution of healthcare expenses in retirement.

Interactive Element: Healthcare Budget Calculator

An online calculator that allows you to input details such as current age, health status, and lifestyle factors could generate an estimated healthcare budget for retirement. This tool can help you visualize potential costs and adjust your retirement planning accordingly.

Healthcare planning in retirement is about more than just understanding Medicare; it's about anticipating your needs, knowing your options, and creating a budget that ensures your retirement savings can support your lifestyle and well-being. Like making those necessary pit stops on a long road trip, addressing healthcare costs in retirement ensures you can enjoy the journey without unexpected financial detours.

7.1 Navigating Medicare: What You Need to Know

Medicare is a cornerstone for retirees' healthcare in the United States, yet its various components can seem like a maze. A clear understanding of what Medicare entails and how its parts differ is necessary to make informed decisions. Knowing when to enroll and how to choose between additional coverage options can also significantly influence your healthcare experience and expenses in retirement.

Medicare Basics

Medicare is divided into distinct sections, each designed to cover different aspects of healthcare:

- Part A covers hospital stays, skilled nursing facility care, hospice, and home health care services. For most people,

Part A comes without a monthly premium if they or their spouse paid Medicare taxes while working.
- Part B pays for doctor visits, outpatient care, medical supplies, and preventive services. Unlike Part A, Part B requires a monthly premium that varies based on your income.
- Part C, also known as Medicare Advantage, is an alternative to Original Medicare offered by private companies approved by Medicare. These plans include all benefits and services covered under Parts A and B, often providing additional coverage like vision, hearing, and dental.
- Part D adds prescription drug coverage to Original Medicare, some Medicare Cost Plans, some Medicare Private-Fee-for-Service Plans, and Medicare Medical Savings Account Plans. These plans are offered by insurance companies and other private companies approved by Medicare.

Understanding these parts is the first step in navigating Medicare effectively. Each plays a role in covering the spectrum of healthcare services you might need, yet they operate under different rules and costs.

Enrollment Timelines and Penalties

Timing is crucial when enrolling in Medicare. To sign up, you have a 7-month Initial Enrollment Period around your 65th birthday—3 months before, the month of, and 3 months after. Missing this window can lead to lifetime penalties and a gap in your healthcare coverage. For example, if you delay Part B enrollment, your monthly premium may go up 10% for each full 12-month period you were eligible but didn't enroll.

Special Enrollment Periods allow you to sign up for Part A and/or Part B during certain life events, like losing job-based coverage, without facing late penalties. Understanding these timelines ensures you avoid unnecessary costs and maintain continuous coverage.

Medigap and Medicare Advantage Plans

Deciding between Medigap and Medicare Advantage requires weighing their benefits against your healthcare needs and budget.

- Medigap policies supplement Original Medicare benefits by covering costs like deductibles, copayments, and coinsurance. These policies are standardized across most states, offering predictable coverage but not services like dental or vision. You cannot have both a Medigap policy and Medicare Advantage; it's one or the other.
- Medicare Advantage Plans bundle Medicare Parts A and B, and usually D, into one plan. They often include benefits not covered by Original Medicare, such as dental, vision, and hearing, sometimes at no extra cost. However, they come with network restrictions, meaning you may have to see providers within the plan's network for care.

Your choice impacts your out-of-pocket costs, and where you can receive care, so it's important to consider your health needs and preferences when making a decision.

Managing Costs with Medicare

Strategies to keep your healthcare expenses manageable with Medicare include:

- Review your coverage annually during the Open Enrollment Period. This is your chance to switch plans if you find another that better meets your needs or offers a better value.
- Understand your plan's out-of-pocket costs, including deductibles, copayments, and coinsurance. This knowledge helps budget for healthcare expenses throughout the year.
- If you take prescription drugs, consider a Part D plan. Review the plan's formulary to ensure it covers your medications and compare costs across plans.
- Use preventive services that Medicare covers, like flu shots and screening tests. These can help catch health issues early when they're more manageable and less costly.

Navigating Medicare effectively means staying informed about your options and how they align with your healthcare needs. By understanding its components, enrollment rules, and how to manage costs, you can make choices that support your health and financial well-being in retirement.

7.2 Long-Term Care Insurance: Is It Right for You?

When considering the later stages of life, it's natural to consider the support you might need. Long-term care insurance emerges as a beacon for those who wish to prepare for the possibility of requiring extended medical or personal assistance. This form of insurance is designed to cover services not typically included in regular health insurance, Medicare, or Medicaid, such as in-home care, nursing home stays, or assisted living facilities.

The initial step involves a clear-eyed evaluation of what long-term care insurance entails. It's a policy you purchase to provide for the cost of long-term care beyond a predetermined period. Unlike traditional health insurance, it covers the cost of help with daily activities, like bathing and dressing, when you have a chronic medical condition, a disability, or a disorder such as Alzheimer's disease.

Evaluating the Need for Long-Term Care Insurance

Understanding your risk and the financial implications is crucial. Consider these factors:

- Personal and family health history can provide clues about your future needs. Genetics play a role in many conditions that require long-term care.
- Age and current health status: The younger and healthier you are when you buy the policy, the lower your premiums will be. However, buying too early could mean paying premiums for a more extended period.
- Financial resources: Assess whether you have the financial means to pay for care without insurance. Long-term care costs can quickly deplete savings, impacting the quality of life and inheritance of heirs.

Choosing the Right Policy

Not all long-term care insurance policies are created equal. When shopping for a policy, pay attention to these details:

- Coverage options: Policies can differ greatly in what they cover. Look for one that provides the flexibility to use your

benefits in various settings, including your home, community organizations, or specialized facilities.
- Benefit period: The length of time a policy will pay out benefits can vary. Some may offer a few years of coverage, while others cover you for life.
- Elimination period: This refers to the time between when an injury or illness begins and when you start receiving benefits. Shorter elimination periods mean higher premiums.
- Inflation protection: With the cost of care rising, this feature adjusts your benefits over time to keep pace with inflation.

Alternatives to Traditional Long-Term Care Insurance

For those unsure about traditional long-term care insurance, alternatives exist:

- Hybrid insurance policies: These combine life insurance with long-term care coverage. You can access some of the death benefit early for long-term care, with the remainder paid out as a death benefit.
- Self-insurance: This strategy involves setting aside funds specifically for long-term care. It requires discipline and a solid investment plan but offers flexibility.
- Government programs: While Medicare's coverage is limited, Medicaid may provide for long-term care, primarily for those with low income and few assets.

Choosing the best way to plan for long-term care is a deeply personal decision. It hinges on your health outlook, financial situation, and individual preferences regarding the care you envision receiving. Taking the time to understand the nuances of long-term care insurance and its alternatives allows you to make an informed choice, one that aligns with your aspirations for your later years.

As we wrap up this exploration of long-term care insurance, remember that planning for the future extends beyond mere financial calculations. It's about ensuring peace of mind for yourself and your loved ones, knowing that you've taken steps to maintain your dignity and independence in later life. This thoughtful approach to planning illuminates the path forward, guiding you toward decisions that resonate with your values and long-term aspirations. With a clear strategy for managing healthcare costs, including the potential need for long-term care, you can confidently face the future.

As we transition from focusing on healthcare and long-term care planning, the next chapter shifts our attention to another vital aspect of retirement planning: ensuring your estate is in order. This progression from safeguarding your health to securing your legacy is a natural step in crafting a comprehensive retirement plan that reflects your desires for a vibrant retirement and your wishes for the impact you'll leave behind.

8

Maximizing Your Social Security

Picture this: every paycheck you've earned over the years is a brick. Some bricks are bigger, some smaller, but together, they've built the foundation for your retirement in the form of Social Security benefits. Unlike the straightforward process of piecing together a physical structure brick by brick, understanding how these financial building blocks translate into Social Security benefits can feel like deciphering an intricate puzzle. This chapter aims to simplify that puzzle, turning confusion into clarity.

8.1 Understanding Your Social Security Benefits

How Benefits Are Calculated

Social Security benefits are not pulled from thin air; they're meticulously calculated based on your earnings history. The formula considers your highest 35 years of earnings, adjusting for inflation. The aim is to provide a benefit that reflects your career's earning pattern. It's like looking back at the tapestry of your working life, highlighting the years that contributed most to your financial well-being.

- Average Indexed Monthly Earnings (AIME): This is where your 35 highest-earning years come into play, adjusted for inflation.
- Primary Insurance Amount (PIA): This is the base figure used to determine your benefit at full retirement age (FRA), calculated from your AIME using a progressive formula designed to benefit lower-income workers proportionately more.

The Impact of Work History

Your paycheck's size and the length of your career significantly impact your Social Security benefits. If you have yet to hit 35 years of work, zeros get factored into the calculation, which can pull down your benefit amount. On the other hand, higher-earning years can replace lower-earning ones in the formula, potentially increasing your benefit. It's akin to upgrading the bricks in your foundation with more substantial, more valuable materials as your career progresses.

- Years of work: Less than 35 years means zeros are included in your calculation, reducing your benefit.
- Earnings Record: Higher recent earnings can replace lower earnings from earlier in your work history, potentially increasing your benefit.

Spousal and Survivor Benefits

Social Security doesn't just look after you; it extends its support to your spouse and potentially other family members. Spousal benefits allow your husband or wife to receive up to 50% of your benefit at FRA, depending on their own Social Security record. Survivor benefits go a step further, providing your spouse up to 100% of your benefit in the event of your passing. It's a way of ensuring that the financial structure you've built offers shelter not just to you but to your loved ones as well.

- Spousal benefits: Up to 50% of the worker's FRA benefit is reduced if the spouse takes it before their own FRA.
- Survivor benefits: Up to 100% of the deceased worker's benefit is available to the spouse at their FRA.

Benefit Statements and Estimates

Understanding what you're projected to receive from Social Security is crucial for planning your retirement finances. Thankfully, the Social Security Administration (SSA) sends annual statements (now primarily online) that lay out your estimated benefits at various ages. These statements also provide a detailed record of your earnings history, allowing you to ensure all your bricks are accounted for accurately.

- Online: Create a "my Social Security" account on the SSA's website to access your statement and keep track of your estimated benefits.
- Accuracy Check: Use your annual statement to verify your earnings history and ensure your future benefits are calculated correctly.

Visual Element: Infographic on Social Security Calculation

An infographic titled "Decoding Your Social Security Benefits" could visually break down:

- The formula for calculating AIME and PIA.
- A comparison of benefits for different career lengths.
- How spousal and survivor benefits are determined.

Interactive Element: Social Security Benefit Calculator

An online calculator provided by the SSA allows you to input your earnings information and project your future benefits based on various retirement ages. This tool demystifies the calculation process, offering personalized insights into how your work history translates into retirement income.

Textual Element: Navigating Spousal Benefits

A detailed guide on optimizing spousal benefits could cover the following:

- Strategies for couples to consider when claiming benefits to maximize their total income.
- Real-life scenarios where one spouse's work history significantly influences the couple's Social Security planning.
- Tips for ensuring your spouse is positioned to receive the maximum possible survivor benefits.

Understanding your Social Security benefits is akin to reading a map of your financial future. With the proper knowledge and tools, you can confidently navigate this landscape, making informed decisions that ensure your retirement is as robust and rewarding as the career that paved the way for it.

8.2 The Best Time to Start Taking Social Security

Navigating when to begin claiming Social Security benefits involves weighing various factors, each with its financial implications. This strategic choice can significantly influence your retirement income and demands careful consideration.

Early vs. Full Retirement Age

The age at which you choose to start receiving Social Security benefits impacts the monthly amount you will receive. Opting to take benefits before reaching your full retirement age (FRA), which ranges from 66 to 67 depending on your birth year, reduces benefits. On the other hand, delaying benefits beyond your FRA can increase your monthly amount by a certain percentage until you reach 70.

- Early Claiming: Starting benefits between the ages of 62 and your FRA reduces your monthly benefit. This reduction is permanent and can range from a 25% to 30% decrease, depending on your FRA.
- At Full Retirement Age: Claiming at your FRA entitles you to your full benefit amount, calculated based on your lifetime earnings.
- Delaying Benefits: For each year you delay past your FRA, your benefit increases by about 8% until you reach 70. This increase creates an incentive to wait, but it's not the best choice for everyone.

Breakeven Analysis

A breakeven analysis can illuminate when the total value of starting benefits early equals the total value of waiting until later. This calculation considers your cumulative benefits over time, comparing different start ages.

- To perform this analysis, you'll need to estimate the monthly benefit amounts you'd receive at different claiming ages.
- Factor in how long you would need to receive the higher delayed benefits to compensate for the years you didn't receive benefits by waiting.

This analysis can help clarify how long it would take for the decision to delay benefits to financially "pay off," considering the foregone benefits in the earlier years.

Personal Factors Affecting Your Decision

Several personal considerations can influence the optimal time for you to start receiving Social Security:

- Health and Life Expectancy: If you're in good health and have a family history of longevity, delaying benefits could result in a higher lifetime income. Conversely, claiming earlier might make more sense if you have health concerns or a shorter life expectancy.
- Financial Needs: Immediate financial needs may necessitate claiming benefits earlier. If you can comfortably cover your expenses without Social Security, waiting for an increased benefit could be advantageous.
- Employment Status: Working while receiving benefits before your FRA can temporarily reduce your benefits if your earnings exceed certain limits. This might encourage some to delay claiming.

Strategies for Married Couples

Married couples have unique opportunities to optimize their combined Social Security benefits. Coordinating when and how you each claim benefits can maximize your lifetime income.

- Consider Both Lifespans: When one spouse has a significantly higher benefit, it may be beneficial for that spouse to delay claiming. This strategy ensures the surviving spouse receives the highest possible survivor benefit.
- Claim and Suspend: While recent rule changes have limited the effectiveness of some strategies, a version of "claim and suspend" can still be beneficial in specific situations. For example, if the higher-earning spouse delays their benefit to increase it but the other spouse needs to claim their spousal benefit, navigating these rules effectively can optimize your combined benefits.
- Minimize Taxes: The timing of your claims can also impact your tax situation, especially if you have other sources of income. Coordinating your Social Security benefits with withdrawals from retirement accounts can help minimize your tax liability.

For married couples, these strategies underscore the importance of viewing your Social Security decisions as part of a broader financial plan that considers your individual and joint needs and goals.

In summary, the decision of when to start taking Social Security benefits is multifaceted, influenced by a range of personal and financial factors. Whether navigating this decision solo or with a spouse, understanding the implications of early versus delayed claiming, performing a breakeven analysis, and considering your unique circumstances can guide you to a choice that supports your financial security in retirement.

8.3 Strategies for Married Couples to Maximize Benefits

Navigating Social Security can be notably more intricate for married couples, presenting both opportunities and challenges in optimizing benefits. A well-coordinated approach enhances household income and ensures financial stability for the surviving spouse. Here, we explore specific strategies couples may employ, mindful of the nuances that could influence their decisions.

File and Suspend Strategy

The file-and-suspend strategy was a popular method, allowing one spouse to claim benefits based on the other's record while the latter's benefits continued to grow. However, significant changes to Social Security rules in 2015 have largely phased out this option. Previously, a higher-earning spouse could file for benefits at full retirement age and immediately suspend them. This action allowed the lower-earning spouse to claim a spousal benefit while the higher earner's benefits accrued delayed retirement credits. Under current regulations, if you suspend your benefits, no benefits can be paid to others based on your record during the suspension. This change underscores the importance of staying current with Social Security regulations, as evolving rules can impact planning strategies.

Restricted Application Strategy

The restricted application strategy remains a viable option for some couples. This tactic permits one spouse who has reached full retirement age to claim only spousal benefits while deferring their own benefits to accumulate delayed retirement credits. It's key to note that this strategy is only available to individuals born before January 2, 1954. For those eligible, it offers a way to boost household income in retirement without compromising the growth of their retirement benefits. This approach requires careful timing and understanding of eligibility criteria to ensure it aligns with your broader retirement planning goals.

Coordinating Retirement and Benefits

Effectively coordinating retirement dates and Social Security claiming strategies can significantly impact a couple's financial landscape in retirement. Couples should consider various factors, including age differences, health status, and whether both spouses have similar earnings histories or if one has notably higher earnings. For instance, in scenarios where one spouse has a much lower earnings record, it might make sense for the higher earner to delay claiming benefits to maximize the survivor benefit. Simultaneously, the lower earner could claim benefits earlier, providing additional income in the short term. This coordinated approach ensures a balanced income stream throughout retirement while safeguarding the financial security of the surviving spouse.

Impact of Divorce and Widowhood

Social Security benefits also extend protections to divorced spouses and widows or widowers, offering avenues for them to claim benefits based on their former spouse's earning record. Divorced individuals may qualify for benefits on their ex-spouse's record if the marriage lasted at least ten years. They must also remain unmarried and be at least 62 years old. Similarly, widows and widowers can receive survivor benefits as early as 60. Understanding these provisions is crucial for individuals navigating the complexities of divorce or widowhood, as these benefits can provide a critical source of income in the absence of their spouse's earnings.

In the intricate dance of planning for retirement, married couples possess several moves at their disposal to maximize their Social Security benefits. From considering the implications of recent rule changes to employing strategies like restricted application and thoughtful coordination of benefits, couples are equipped with tools to enhance their financial well-being in retirement. However, it's essential to approach these strategies with a clear understanding of the rules and an eye toward how they fit into your overall retirement plan. This careful planning and coordination ensure that both spouses, and eventually the surviving spouse, are supported by the most robust financial framework.

As we close this chapter on Social Security strategies for married couples, the key takeaways center on the importance of informed decision-making and strategic planning. These approaches optimize your benefits and secure a stable financial foundation for the years ahead. With a thorough grasp of your options and the implications of your choices, you're better positioned to navigate the complexities of retirement planning. Now, as we transition from the specifics of Social Security to exploring estate and legacy planning, we continue to build on the foundation laid here, focusing next on securing and managing your assets for the future.

9

Estate Planning Made Clear

Imagine a scenario where you've spent a lifetime gathering pieces to an intricate puzzle: your estate. When put together correctly, this puzzle represents a clear picture of your wishes for your assets and legacy. Now, consider the challenge of ensuring this puzzle gets solved precisely as you envisioned after you're gone. That's where estate planning steps in, acting as the blueprint for assembling the pieces in your absence. It's not simply about wealth distribution; it's about making heartfelt decisions today that affect your loved ones tomorrow.

Estate planning often brings to mind complex legal documents and difficult conversations, leading many to put it off indefinitely. However, breaking down the process into understandable components can turn a daunting task into a manageable one. This chapter aims to shed light on the basics of wills and trusts, guide you in choosing the right executor or trustee, explain the probate process, and highlight common mistakes to avoid, all to ensure your estate plan stands on a solid foundation.

The Basics of Wills and Trusts

A will is a legal document detailing how you want your assets distributed after death. It's like leaving behind detailed instructions for a trusted friend on how to care for your prized possessions. Meanwhile, trusts offer a way to manage your assets both during your lifetime and after, with the benefit of potentially avoiding the lengthy probate process. Think of a trust as a secure box where you can place your assets, which a chosen individual, the trustee, holds the key to for the benefit of your chosen beneficiaries.

Choosing between a will and a trust, or deciding to use both, depends on various factors, including the size of your estate, your privacy concerns, and your goals for asset distribution. While a will might suffice for straightforward estates, a trust can offer more control over when and how your assets are distributed.

Choosing an Executor or Trustee

Selecting the right person to manage your estate or trust is akin to choosing the captain of a ship who will navigate your financial legacy through potentially choppy waters. This role requires someone trustworthy and capable of handling financial matters and the intricacies of estate administration. Often, people choose a close family member because of their familiarity with the family dynamics. Still, it's also wise to consider their financial acumen and organizational skills. In some cases, appointing a professional, such as an attorney or a financial advisor, might be the best route to ensure your estate is managed according to your wishes.

The Probate Process

Probate is the legal process of reviewing a will to determine its authenticity and validity. It's often misunderstood and feared for its potential to be time-consuming and costly. However, understanding this process can demystify it and reveal strategies for simplification. For instance, assets held in a trust, designated as "payable on death" (POD) or "transfer on death" (TOD), and jointly held assets often bypass probate entirely. Many states offer an expedited probate process for smaller estates, reducing the time and paperwork required.

Common Mistakes to Avoid

In estate planning, even minor oversights can lead to significant issues. Some common pitfalls include:

- Failing to update your estate plan: Life changes such as marriage, divorce, and the birth of children should trigger a review and, if necessary, an update to your estate plan.
- Neglecting digital assets: In today's digital age, including digital assets like social media accounts and digital currencies in your estate plan is crucial.
- Overlooking the impact of taxes: Proper estate planning can help minimize the tax burden on your heirs, ensuring they receive the maximum benefit from their inheritance.

Visual Element: Estate Planning Checklist

A comprehensive checklist can visually guide readers through the estate planning process, ensuring no detail is overlooked. This checklist could cover everything from gathering important documents to considering tax implications, and it would serve as a handy reference for anyone embarking on estate planning.

Interactive Element: Executor/Trustee Decision Tool

An online tool could help individuals decide who might be the best fit to manage their estate or trust. Users could gain insights into the most suitable candidates by answering questions about their potential choices, such as financial savvy, organizational skills, and emotional resilience.

Estate planning is more than just a set of legal documents; it's a thoughtful process that ensures your legacy is preserved and your loved ones are cared for according to your wishes. With a clear understanding of the basics and a strategic approach to avoid common pitfalls, you can build a solid estate plan that stands the test of time.

9.1 Estate Planning Tools Everyone Should Consider

Estate planning encompasses a variety of tools beyond wills and trusts, each playing a unique role in ensuring your wishes are respected and your loved ones are protected. From designating someone to make decisions on your behalf to directing how specific assets should be distributed, these tools form the backbone of a solid estate plan.

Durable Powers of Attorney

A durable power of attorney is an indispensable instrument, granting someone you trust the authority to manage your financial affairs if you're unable to do so. This could be due to illness, injury, or any other incapacity. Unlike a standard power of attorney, which becomes invalid if you become incapacitated, the "durable" aspect remains in effect, ensuring continuity in managing your financial responsibilities. It's a preemptive measure, preventing potential legal battles or delays in decision-making that could adversely affect your estate and financial well-being.

When setting up a durable power of attorney, you'll select an agent, typically a trusted family member or friend, who will have the legal authority to handle tasks such as paying bills, managing investments, and even selling property on your behalf. It's a role that requires trust and responsibility, underscoring the importance of choosing someone who understands your preferences and can act in your best interests.

Advance Healthcare Directives

Advance healthcare directives, comprising living wills and healthcare powers of attorney, provide instructions on your healthcare preferences in situations where you're unable to communicate them yourself. A living will outlines the types of medical treatments and life-sustaining measures you do or do not want, such as mechanical ventilation or feeding tubes, in the event of a terminal illness or permanent unconsciousness.

A healthcare power of attorney, on the other hand, designates a representative to make healthcare decisions on your behalf, guided by the preferences you've outlined in your living will. This combination ensures that your healthcare wishes are known and respected. It provides peace of mind to you and your family by clarifying your desires in advance and designating a trusted person to advocate for them.

Beneficiary Designations and POD/TOD Accounts

Beneficiary designations on retirement accounts, life insurance policies, and other assets bypass the will and probate process, directly transferring the asset to the named beneficiary upon your death. This straightforward way ensures that specific assets are passed to the intended individuals without delay. Regularly reviewing and updating these designations is critical, especially after major life events like marriage, divorce, or the birth of a child, to ensure they reflect your current wishes.

Similarly, payable on death (POD) and transfer on death (TOD) accounts offer a simple mechanism to transfer assets like bank accounts and securities directly to a designated beneficiary without going through probate. Once you register an account as POD or TOD and name a beneficiary, the assets in the account will automatically transfer to the beneficiary upon your death, streamlining the distribution process and providing immediate access to funds that may be needed for expenses.

Life Insurance in Estate Planning

Life insurance is pivotal in estate planning, offering a versatile tool for meeting various estate planning goals. Beyond providing financial support to your beneficiaries, life insurance proceeds can be used to pay estate taxes, debts, and final expenses, ensuring your estate can be distributed as you intended without being diminished by outstanding obligations.

Strategically, life insurance can also be used to equalize inheritances among beneficiaries. If, for instance, you wish to leave a family business to one child, life insurance can provide equivalent value to your other children, maintaining balance and reducing potential conflicts.

For those with larger estates, life insurance can be structured to fund a trust, offering additional control over how the proceeds are used and distributed. This can be particularly useful in providing for minor children, dependents with special needs, or managing the distribution of assets over time according to the conditions you set.

Incorporating these estate planning tools into your overall plan provides a more straightforward path for managing your affairs. It offers reassurance that your wishes will be honored and your loved ones will be cared for. Each tool serves a specific purpose, from ensuring decisions can be made during times of incapacity to directing the distribution of your assets according to your wishes. Careful consideration and regular review of these instruments are vital to maintaining an estate plan that accurately reflects your desires and adapts to your changing life circumstances.

9.2 Beneficiary Designations: Avoiding Common Mistakes

The clarity of our intentions plays a pivotal role in crafting a secure future for our loved ones. Nowhere is this clearer than in the realm of beneficiary designations. These selections, often made in a moment and tucked away in the documents of various accounts, carry the weight of our wishes beyond our lifetime. Yet, the simplicity of making these designations belies the complexity of their impact, making it crucial to approach them with precision and foresight.

The Critical Role of Accurate Beneficiary Designations

The act of naming a beneficiary is, at its heart, an act of specifying the future stewards of our assets. Whether for a retirement account, life insurance policy, or investment portfolio, these designations direct the flow of our assets directly to the named individuals, bypassing the often lengthy and complex probate process. However, inaccuracies or oversights in these designations can lead to unintended consequences, diverting assets from those we intended to benefit, potentially sparking disputes among loved ones, or contributing to legal challenges. The accuracy of these designations is not merely a detail but a cornerstone of effective estate planning.

Regular Reviews and Updates: A Necessity

Life is a tapestry of change, with significant events weaving new patterns into the fabric of our experiences. Marriages, births, divorces, and deaths reshape our relationships and, by extension, our estate planning intentions. Therefore, it is essential to review our beneficiary designations periodically and, if necessary, update them to reflect our current wishes accurately. This process ensures that the individuals we intend to support are the ones who will ultimately benefit from our assets, aligning our estate planning documents with the evolving landscape of our lives.

Ensuring Alignment with Your Estate Plan

Beneficiary designations, while powerful, are only one piece of the broader estate planning puzzle. To ensure a harmonious picture, these designations must be meticulously coordinated with the other elements of your estate plan, including your will, trusts, and powers of attorney. This coordination ensures a seamless transition of assets, reflecting a unified vision rather than a fragmented array of disjointed instructions. For instance, if your will outlines a specific distribution of assets, but your beneficiary designations direct those assets elsewhere, the latter will prevail. Regular consultations with estate planning professionals can help navigate these complexities, ensuring that your beneficiary designations complement and reinforce your overall estate planning objectives.

Navigating Special Situations

Life's intricacies often present us with unique situations that require thoughtful consideration in our estate planning:

- Minors as Beneficiaries: Directly naming minors as beneficiaries can complicate the distribution of assets, as minors are legally unable to take control of the assets until they reach adulthood. Establishing a trust or using a custodial account under the Uniform Transfers to Minors Act (UTMA) or the Uniform Gifts to Minors Act (UGMA) allows for a more structured management and distribution of assets to minor beneficiaries.
- Complex Family Dynamics: In families with complicated relationships, clear and carefully considered beneficiary designations can help prevent conflicts and ensure that assets are distributed according to your wishes. In these cases, it is wise to be explicit about your intentions, including a letter of explanation with your estate planning documents to provide context for your decisions.

This section of our exploration underscores the nuanced nature of beneficiary designations within the broader scope of estate planning. By emphasizing accuracy, advocating for regular reviews, ensuring alignment with overall estate planning goals, and thoughtfully addressing special situations, we pave the way for our assets to support our loved ones according to our true intentions.

As we conclude this exploration of estate planning, it's evident that the decisions we make today, from the grand strategies to the minute details, shape the legacy we leave behind. Our journey through wills, trusts, powers of attorney, and beneficiary designations reveals a landscape where foresight, clarity, and regular review guide us toward our estate planning goals. With these principles in mind, we move forward, prepared to face the future with confidence, knowing that our plans are crafted not just for our peace of mind but for the benefit and well-being of those we cherish most.

10

Crafting a Fulfilling Retirement

Retirement opens the door to a new phase of life, one abundant with time previously spoken for by the demands of a career. It's a period ripe with potential, waiting to be shaped into whatever form you desire. However, without the structure work often provides, you might find yourself at a loss for what to do next. This chapter is dedicated to filling that canvas with vibrant purpose, engagement, and personal growth.

10.1 Finding Purpose After Retirement

Exploring New Interests

Imagine standing in front of a buffet filled with more dishes than you could possibly try in one sitting. Retirement is much the same, offering a plethora of activities and interests to explore. Now is the time to try your hand at painting, start that garden, or learn to play the piano—activities you might have put on the back burner. Local community centers and online platforms offer classes ranging from art to zoology. Pick something that piques your curiosity. Who knows? You might discover a passion you never knew you had.

Volunteering and Giving Back

Giving your time to causes you care about can be incredibly rewarding. It's a chance to give back to your community, connect with like-minded individuals, and make a tangible difference. Whether mentoring young students, working at a food bank, or participating in environmental clean-ups, volunteering offers a sense of purpose and fulfillment. Consider the causes close to your heart, and explore how you can contribute. Many non-profits and charities constantly need volunteers and would welcome your help.

Continued Learning Opportunities

The pursuit of knowledge doesn't have an expiration date. Retirement is an excellent opportunity to dive deeper into subjects that intrigue you or to explore entirely new fields. Many universities and colleges offer reduced or free tuition for seniors, and online courses provide flexibility to learn at your own pace from the comfort of your home. Whether it's taking a course in history, attending a workshop on digital photography, or joining a book club, continued learning keeps your mind sharp and engaged.

Setting New Goals

Retirement doesn't mean the end of achieving goals; rather, it marks the beginning of new ones. These goals might be personal, like improving your fitness level, or more outward-facing, like starting a blog to share your life experiences. Setting goals gives you something to work toward and can help structure your days.

Ensure these goals are specific, measurable, achievable, relevant, and time-bound (SMART) to keep you motivated and on track.

Visual Element: "Retirement Bucket List"

An infographic showcases various activities, hobbies, and goals one might pursue in retirement. Categories could include travel, education, hobbies, volunteering, and personal development, each with inspiring icons or images.

Interactive Element: "What's Your Retirement Passion?" Quiz

An online quiz designed to help retirees discover new interests or hobbies based on their preferences and personality. Questions could range from preferred ways to spend a day to how they like to interact with others, culminating in personalized suggestions for activities to explore.

Textual Element: Real-life Examples of Post-retirement Projects

A collection of brief stories highlighting retirees who found fulfilling post-retirement projects or hobbies. This could include someone who took up beekeeping, another who started a community garden, or someone else who wrote and published their first novel. These real-life examples serve as inspiration and a testament to the limitless possibilities retirement holds.

Retirement is not just about leaving the workforce; it's about entering a stage of life where you have the freedom to design your days as you see fit. It's a time for exploration, contribution, learning, and personal growth. By exploring new interests, volunteering, pursuing continued learning opportunities, and setting new goals, you can craft a fulfilling and enriching retirement in every aspect.

10.2 Staying Active and Connected in Retirement

A fulfilling retirement is not solely about managing your finances but also about maintaining your health, nurturing your social connections, and embracing life's adventures. This section delves into the importance of physical activity, the benefits of social engagement, the thrill of travel and adventure, and the joy of hobbies and clubs.

Physical Activity for Health

The significance of regular physical activity can't be overstated, especially as you transition into retirement. Regular exercise is crucial for sustaining your health, enhancing your mood, and increasing your energy levels. Activities like walking, cycling, swimming, or participating in group fitness classes keep your body in peak condition and provide opportunities for social interaction. Consider activities you enjoy and are likely to stick with, whether it's yoga, dance classes, or even joining a local hiking group. Remember, the goal is to find joy in movement, making it a part of your daily routine that you look forward to.

Social Engagement

Staying socially engaged as you transition into retirement is vital to your well-being. It's a time when you can nurture existing relationships and cultivate new ones. Here are a few strategies to ensure you remain connected:

- Reconnect with old friends: Retirement can provide you with the time needed to rekindle friendships that may have waned due to the busyness of career and family life.

- Family time: With more flexibility in your schedule, you can create deeper bonds with family members. Regular family gatherings can strengthen these ties, whether in person or via video calls.
- Community involvement: Engaging in community events or joining local clubs can expand your social circle and connect you with individuals who share similar interests.
- Social media and technology: Embracing social media platforms and communication technologies can help you stay in touch with friends and family members, regardless of distance.

Travel and Adventure

Retirement opens up a wealth of opportunities for travel and adventure, allowing you to explore new cultures, cuisines, and landscapes. Here are some tips for making the most of your travel experiences, even on a budget:

- Plan off-season trips: Traveling during off-peak times can significantly reduce costs and offer a more relaxed experience with fewer tourists.
- Home exchanges and rentals: Consider home exchange programs or renting apartments instead of staying in hotels. This can offer a more authentic and cost-effective experience.
- Group travel: Joining travel groups or clubs can provide companionship and often leads to discounts on trips planned for members.
- Local adventures: Don't overlook the adventures that await you closer to home. Exploring local parks, museums, and historical sites can satisfy your sense of adventure without the need for extensive travel.

Hobbies and Clubs

Diving into hobbies and joining clubs provide meaningful ways to spend time, learn new skills, and meet people. Here are some suggestions to get you started:

- Gardening clubs: If you have a green thumb, or even if you're a novice looking to learn, gardening clubs offer a great way to connect with nature and fellow gardening enthusiasts.
- Book clubs: For those who love reading, book clubs offer a structured way to explore different genres and provide a social setting to discuss ideas and opinions.
- Crafting and art classes: Local community centers often offer classes in various crafts and arts. These can be wonderful creative outlets and great places to form new friendships.
- Sports clubs: Joining a golf club, tennis club, or bowling league can keep you active while offering a competitive yet friendly social environment.

In embracing these activities and strategies for staying active and connected, retirement can be transformed into a period of life that's as enriching and fulfilling as any other. With physical health, social engagement, and the pursuit of interests at the forefront, the days ahead promise to be vibrant and purposeful.

10.3 Budgeting for Hobbies and Travel in Retirement

The golden years of retirement bring with them a wealth of time to explore, learn, and indulge in activities that bring joy and fulfillment. Yet, aligning these pursuits with a well-thought-out budget ensures that this period is rich in experiences and financially sustainable. Here's a roadmap to crafting a leisure budget that supports your dreams without compromising your financial health.

Creating a Leisure Budget

Initiating this process requires a clear view of your overall retirement finances. From the outset, delineate a portion of your budget dedicated solely to leisure—hobbies, travel, or other pursuits that enliven your days. This budget segment is your ticket to adventure, creativity, and discovery. Begin by listing your monthly or annual retirement income sources alongside your fixed and variable expenses. The residue, post the essentials, earmarks your potential leisure fund. Using tools like spreadsheets or budgeting apps can simplify tracking and adjusting this budget as you navigate through retirement.

Prioritizing Spending

With your leisure budget defined, the next step is prioritizing how these funds will be allocated. Not all hobbies or travel desires carry the same weight of importance or fulfillment. Sit down with a notepad or digital document and list your leisure interests in order of significance. Perhaps sailing the Mediterranean tops your list, followed by photography classes, then golf club memberships. This prioritization acts as a guide, ensuring funds flow first to what matters most, enhancing satisfaction from your leisure budget.

Cost-saving Tips

Stretching your leisure budget without sacrificing enjoyment is an art in itself. Here are some strategies to get the most out of every dollar:

- Leverage Discounts: Many organizations offer discounts for seniors. Museums, parks, educational institutions, and travel services often provide reduced rates that can make activities more accessible.
- Embrace Off-peak Travel: Airfare and accommodations often see a dip in prices during off-peak seasons. Planning trips during these times can save substantially, allowing for more or extended adventures.
- DIY Over Buying: Engaging in hobbies like gardening, crafting, or woodworking? Consider do-it-yourself projects over purchasing ready-made items. Not only does this save money, but it also adds a personal touch and a sense of achievement.
- Share Experiences: Group activities or travel can split costs among participants. Organize a painting group or a local exploration team, or travel with friends to share the financial load.

Investing in Experiences

The true value in allocating funds for hobbies and travel lies in the experiences and memories created rather than the material possessions acquired. Studies suggest that experiences contribute more significantly to long-term happiness than tangible items. When planning how to utilize your leisure budget, consider options that promise new learning, adventure, and the joy of discovery. Whether mastering a new skill, witnessing the aurora borealis, or immersing in a foreign culture, these experiences enrich your life tapestry in irreplaceable ways.

As this chapter on enriching your retirement through well-planned hobbies and travel concludes, remember that the essence of a fulfilling retirement lies in balancing financial wisdom with the pursuit of passions. This delicate equilibrium ensures that your retirement years are financially secure and brimming with joy, growth, and adventure. As we transition to the next chapter, we carry forward the principles of thoughtful planning and wise spending, applying them to the broader context of maintaining health and vitality in retirement.

11

Navigating New Waters: Identity and Finance in Retirement

The moment you step away from your work life, it's as if you've set sail from the familiar shores of your career into the vast, uncharted waters of retirement. For many, work provides more than just a paycheck; it offers a sense of purpose, a framework for daily life, and, importantly, a component of one's identity. The transition into retirement, therefore, isn't just about adjusting your financial sails; it's equally about steering through the emotional currents that come with redefining who you are beyond your profession.

11.1 Coping with the Identity Shift in Retirement

Adjusting to Life Without Work

Changing from a structured work life to the freedom of retirement can feel like switching from a fast-paced sprint to a leisurely stroll. Suddenly, the routines that governed your days are gone, and the professional title that may have formed a part of your identity is no longer applicable. Acknowledging this shift is the first step. Recognize that it's normal to feel a mix of relief and disorientation. Many find solace in gradually reducing work hours before fully retiring, offering a smoother transition.

Rediscovering Yourself

Retirement opens up a space for self-discovery. Think back to interests and passions you might have shelved due to work commitments. Was there a hobby you loved or perhaps an interest you never had the time to explore? Now's the chance to pursue these with vigor. Whether painting, gardening, or learning a new language, engaging in these activities can be immensely fulfilling and form part of your new identity.

Building a New Routine

Creating a new routine is vital for shaping your days. Without the external structure work provided, it might quickly feel untethered. Start by setting regular times for meals, exercise, and hobbies. Plan outings and social engagements in advance. This structure doesn't have to be rigid; the beauty of retirement is having the flexibility to adjust your schedule as you please. Yet, a semblance of routine can provide comfort and a sense of normalcy.

Seeking Support

Finding others who are navigating the same transition can be incredibly reassuring. Consider joining retirement groups or forums where you can share experiences and tips. Talking to a counselor can provide professional guidance if the identity shift feels particularly challenging. Remember, seeking support is a sign of strength, not weakness.

Visual Element: "The Retirement Identity Compass"

An infographic that visually represents the journey of rediscovering one's identity in retirement. It could feature four main directions: North for exploring new interests, South for building a new routine, East for seeking support, and West for adjusting to life without work. Each direction could offer tips and activities to guide retirees in navigating this transition.

Interactive Element: "Rediscover Your Passions" Quiz

An online quiz that prompts retirees to answer questions about their preferences, pastimes, and dreams. The outcome could suggest new hobbies or activities to explore, tailored to their interests. This interactive tool would be engaging and provide personalized suggestions to help retirees embark on a path of self-discovery.

Textual Element: Real-life Adjustments Checklist

A checklist includes practical steps for adjusting to retirement, covering how to phase out of work, ways to explore new interests, tips for building a new routine, and resources for finding support. This checklist could serve as a tangible guide for retirees, helping them to navigate the emotional aspects of this transition with confidence.

Adjusting to life without work involves more than just filling your days with activities; it's about redefining your sense of self outside of your career. Rediscovering your passions, establishing a new routine, and seeking support are all crucial steps in this journey. Remember, retirement isn't just an end to work; it's an opportunity to design a life that reflects your true self, unbound by job titles or workplace identities.

11.2 Protecting Your Retirement Savings from Inflation

The value of money doesn't remain static. Over time, inflation can subtly erode its purchasing power, turning today's comfortable nest egg into tomorrow's scanty sum. For retirees, understanding and mitigating the risks associated with inflation is crucial for safeguarding the longevity of their savings.

Understanding Inflation Risks

Inflation represents the rate at which the general level of prices for goods and services rises, subsequently eroding purchasing power. For those in retirement, the impact is twofold. While living expenses climb, the value of their savings may not keep pace, potentially diminishing their standard of living. Recognizing this risk is the first step. The next involves devising strategies to shield your savings from inflation's grasp, ensuring your financial well-being remains intact throughout your retirement.

Investment Strategies for Inflation

To fortify your retirement savings against inflation, incorporating investment strategies designed to counteract its effects can be highly effective.

- Treasury Inflation-Protected Securities (TIPS): TIPS are government bonds indexed to inflation and designed to increase in value along with the Consumer Price Index. The principal value of TIPS rises with inflation, offering a safeguard for your investment.

- Real Estate: Investing in real estate can also serve as a hedge against inflation. Property values and rental incomes typically rise with inflation, providing an appreciating asset and a source of increasing income.
- Dividend-Growing Stocks: Companies with a history of increasing dividends can offer a double advantage. Not only do they provide an income that potentially rises over time, but they also represent ownership in businesses that may be able to pass on inflationary costs to consumers, thereby preserving their profit margins and your investment's value.
- Commodities: Direct investment in commodities like gold or oil or through commodity-focused funds can provide a buffer against inflation. Since commodity prices often rise with inflation, they can offer a counterbalance to the depreciating purchasing power of cash holdings.

Budget Adjustments

An adaptable budget is your frontline defense in maintaining financial stability amid inflation. Regularly revisiting and tweaking your budget can ensure that your spending aligns with the current cost of living. Some steps include:

- Annual Review: Conduct an annual review of your expenses, comparing them to the previous year's, to identify significant changes and adjust your budget accordingly.
- Discretionary Spending: Evaluate your discretionary spending with an eye toward flexibility. Recognizing areas where you can cut back or redirect funds can free up resources for essential expenses that may have increased due to inflation.

- Fixed Income Adjustments: For those with fixed retirement incomes, exploring options to supplement your income can be beneficial. Part-time work, freelancing, or turning a hobby into a source of income can provide additional financial cushioning.

Staying Informed

Staying abreast of economic trends and forecasts enables you to anticipate and react to inflationary pressures. Financial news outlets, economic reports, and advisories from financial institutions can offer valuable insights into inflation trends and their potential impact on your retirement savings. Moreover, engaging with a financial advisor who can monitor these trends and suggest timely adjustments to your investment strategy can be invaluable. They can provide personalized advice tailored to your financial situation, helping you navigate inflation's challenges with informed, strategic decisions.

Inflation poses a subtle yet significant threat to the purchasing power of your retirement savings. Understanding the risks it presents, adopting investment strategies that offer protection, making thoughtful budget adjustments, and staying informed about economic trends can effectively shield your finances from inflation's erosive effects. This proactive approach ensures that your retirement savings endure and thrive, supporting the comfortable, fulfilling retirement you've worked so hard to achieve.

11.3 Adjusting Your Investment Strategy in Volatile Markets

In retirement planning, navigating the seas of market volatility requires a map and a compass to guide you through the ebbs and flows of economic tides. The strategies you employ to manage your investments are pivotal in ensuring financial stability, especially when the waters get rough. Here, we explore the nuances of crafting a resilient investment approach in the face of uncertainty.

Embracing a Long-term Perspective on Investments

Adopting a long-term viewpoint is one of the first steps to mitigate the stress of market fluctuations. Though often dramatic, short-term market movements tend to smooth out over the long haul. This perspective encourages patience and restraint from making hasty decisions based on temporary downturns. It's akin to watching the horizon while sailing: the immediate waves might be choppy, but your focus remains on the distant, steady line where the sky meets the sea. Keeping your eyes on the long-term goals makes it easier to ride out short-term volatility without veering off course.

Diversification as a Defense

Diversification acts as your portfolio's bulwark, a defensive strategy that spreads investments across various asset classes to reduce exposure to any single risk. It's the investment equivalent of not putting all your eggs in one basket. Suppose one sector or asset class takes a hit. In that case, the impact on your overall portfolio is cushioned by the performance of others. Effective diversification might include a mix of stocks, bonds, real estate, and cash, with further diversification within each category. This approach doesn't guarantee against loss but can significantly dampen the impact of market volatility.

Rebalancing Your Portfolio

Over time, the initial asset allocation in your portfolio can drift due to varying investments' performances. Rebalancing is the process of realigning the weightings of assets in your portfolio back to their target allocation. This might involve selling off investments that have grown beyond their desired proportion and purchasing more of those that have diminished. For instance, if your target allocation was 60% stocks and 40% bonds, and due to market gains, your stocks now represent 70% of your portfolio, you would sell some stocks and buy bonds to rebalance. This disciplined approach ensures that your portfolio maintains its intended risk profile, which is crucial for long-term investment success.

Seeking Professional Advice

In times of market uncertainty, the guidance of a seasoned financial advisor can be invaluable. They possess the expertise to analyze market conditions, suggest adjustments to your investment strategy, and offer reassurance when doubt creeps in. A professional can help you stay disciplined, reminding you of your financial goals and how your current strategy aligns with achieving them. They can also provide insights into new investment opportunities you might not have considered, further enhancing your portfolio's resilience against volatility.

Financial markets are inherently unpredictable, but you can confidently navigate their uncertainties with a well-thought-out investment strategy. Adopting a long-term perspective helps maintain focus on your retirement goals, diversification provides a buffer against market downturns, regular rebalancing ensures your portfolio stays aligned with your risk tolerance, and seeking professional advice can offer clarity and direction. These strategies together forge a path through volatile markets, securing your financial foundation for the years ahead.

As we wrap up this exploration of adjusting your investment strategy in volatile markets, it's clear that a thoughtful, disciplined approach is vital to maintaining financial equilibrium. The strategies discussed here shield your retirement savings from market fluctuations and position you to capitalize on growth opportunities. With these principles in mind, you're well-equipped to face the financial challenges and opportunities that lie ahead, ensuring your retirement years are as rewarding and secure as you've envisioned. Now, let's turn our attention to the next chapter, where we'll delve into the importance of staying healthy and active, ensuring that your retirement is financially sound and rich in well-being and vitality.

Embracing Technology for a Richer Retirement

In a world where technology evolves at breakneck speed, staying in tune with the latest tools and apps can significantly enhance the quality of your retirement life. Far from being just gadgets and gizmos, technology offers practical solutions that can simplify financial management, boost your health, foster continuous learning, and even enrich your travel experiences. This chapter highlights how retirees can leverage technology to keep up with the times and thrive in their golden years.

Financial Management Tools

In the age of smartphones and tablets, managing your finances has never been easier, thanks to a plethora of apps and online tools designed to keep your retirement savings on track. Here's how technology can serve as your financial ally:

- Budgeting Apps: Apps like Mint and You Need A Budget (YNAB) can simplify tracking your spending and savings. With features like automatic expense categorization and

personalized budget suggestions, these tools make it easy to see where your money goes and how to optimize your spending.
- Investment Tracking: Tools like Personal Capital offer a bird's-eye view of your assets for those with a portfolio of investments. You can monitor your investments' performance in real time, making it easier to adjust your strategy as needed.
- Bill Pay and Financial Alerts: Gone are the days of missed payments or overlooked due dates. Set up automatic bill payments and alerts for upcoming expenses to ensure your financial obligations are met without a hitch.

Incorporating these tools into your daily routine can save time and provide peace of mind, knowing that your finances are organized and under control.

Health and Fitness Apps

Maintaining a healthy lifestyle is crucial in retirement, and technology offers an array of apps to keep you on track:

- Exercise Apps: Whether you prefer yoga, strength training, or cardio, there's an app to guide your workout routine. Many offer customizable plans based on your fitness level and goals, complete with instructional videos.
- Diet and Nutrition Trackers: Apps like MyFitnessPal make it easy to log your daily food intake and monitor your nutritional goals. Tracking what you eat can help maintain a balanced diet and support your overall health.
- Meditation and Mindfulness: For mental well-being, meditation apps such as Headspace provide guided sessions to help reduce stress and improve sleep quality.

Making meditation a regular part of your routine can enhance mental clarity and emotional balance.

Adopting these apps can motivate you to stay active and mindful, contributing to a healthier and more vibrant retirement.

Lifelong Learning Platforms

Retirement is an excellent time to explore new interests or deepen your knowledge in a favorite subject. Here's where technology comes in:

- Online Courses: Platforms like Coursera and Udemy offer courses on virtually every topic imaginable, from photography to philosophy. Many universities also provide free or low-cost access to their courses, making higher education more accessible than ever.
- Language Learning Apps: Are you dreaming of learning Italian or brushing up on your Spanish? Apps like Duolingo and Babbel make language learning fun and interactive, preparing you for your next overseas adventure.
- Creative Skills: For those interested in exploring their creative side, sites like Skillshare feature courses in drawing, writing, music, and more taught by experts in the field.

With these platforms, the joy of learning is literally at your fingertips, offering endless opportunities to grow and engage your mind.

Travel and Leisure Apps

For retirees bitten by the travel bug, technology can vastly simplify the planning and execution of your adventures:

- Travel Planning Apps: Apps like TripIt can organize your travel itinerary in one place, from flight details to hotel reservations and activities.
- Deal Finders: To stretch your travel budget further, apps such as Hopper predict flight and hotel price trends and alert you when prices drop.
- Local Exploration: Once you're at your destination, apps like Google Maps and Yelp can help you discover local attractions, restaurants, and hidden gems, making your travels richer and more exciting.

Embracing these apps makes travel less stressful and more enjoyable, allowing you to focus on the experience rather than the logistics.

When wielded wisely, technology can significantly enhance the retirement experience. From managing your finances with ease to staying healthy, continuously learning, and traveling with confidence, the digital world offers tools and resources that cater to nearly every aspect of retired life. Integrating these technological solutions into your daily routine allows you to enjoy a simpler, more organized, richer, and more fulfilling retirement.

12.1 Automating Your Savings and Investments

In financial management during retirement, ensuring a steady growth of your savings and investments without the daily hassle is a significant advantage. Automation stands out as a beacon of efficiency, offering a streamlined approach to securing your financial future. This segment delves into the myriad benefits of automation in savings and investments, guides you through setting up automatic transfers, introduces the concept of robo-advisors, and underscores the importance of keeping a watchful eye on these automated systems.

Benefits of Automation

The decision to automate your savings and investment contributions is akin to planting a garden that flourishes almost independently, with minimal regular upkeep. Here's why automation is a smart choice:

- Consistency: By setting up automatic contributions, you're committing to a consistent investment plan. This consistency is crucial in building wealth over time, adhering to the 'pay yourself first' principle.
- Simplicity: Once established, automated contributions relieve you of the need to manually transfer funds each month. This simplicity translates to more time enjoying retirement and less time managing finances.
- Emotional Detachment: Market fluctuations can tempt even the savviest investors into making impulsive decisions. Automation helps maintain your investment strategy unaffected by market volatility or emotional biases.
- Compounding Benefits: Regular, automated investments allow you to capitalize on the power of compounding interest, significantly impacting your savings growth over time.

Setting up Automatic Transfers

The process of setting up automatic transfers to your savings and investment accounts is straightforward, yet it requires careful planning:

1. Assessment: First, assess your monthly budget to determine a realistic and sustainable amount you can commit to saving and investing after covering living expenses.
2. Instructions: Log into your bank's online platform or visit in person to set up automatic transfers. You'll specify the amount, the accounts from which and to which the money will be transferred, and the frequency of transfers.
3. Coordination: If you have multiple savings or investment accounts, consider how to distribute your contributions to align with your financial goals, such as retirement savings, emergency funds, or specific investment portfolios.

Automated Investment Services

Robo-advisors represent a fusion of technology and investment management, offering a hands-off approach to managing your portfolio:

- Tailored Portfolios: After you input information regarding your financial goals and risk tolerance, robo-advisors create a personalized investment portfolio typically composed of low-cost index funds or ETFs.
- Rebalancing: These services automatically adjust your portfolio to maintain your desired asset allocation, ensuring your investments stay aligned with your objectives and risk level.

- Accessibility: Robo-advisors are generally more accessible than traditional investment advisors. They often require lower minimum investments and charge lower fees, making them an attractive option for retirees looking to optimize their investment strategy.

Monitoring Automated Systems

While automation in savings and investments offers convenience and efficiency, it is not a 'set it and forget it' solution. Active monitoring ensures these automated strategies continue to serve your best interests:

- Regular Reviews: Schedule periodic reviews of your automated savings contributions and investment allocations. This is especially important in retirement when your financial situation or goals may evolve.
- Performance Checks: Keep an eye on the performance of your investments, especially those managed by robo-advisors. Ensure they are performing as expected, and adjust your strategy if necessary.
- Fee Analysis: Regularly assess the fees associated with automated investment services. Over time, even small fees can eat into your returns, so it pays to stay informed and consider alternatives if fees become too burdensome.

By embracing automation in your financial management strategy, you can enjoy a more streamlined and stress-free approach to growing your retirement savings. However, remember that automation does not replace the need for periodic personal oversight. Staying engaged with your financial strategy ensures that your automated systems remain aligned with your evolving retirement goals, allowing you to make the most of your golden years.

12.2 Staying Informed: Financial News and Resources for Retirees

In the golden years of retirement, staying abreast of the latest financial news and trends is not just about keeping busy; it's about safeguarding your financial future. This era of your life should be marked by wisdom, not just in how you spend your time but also in how you manage your resources. With the right approach to consuming financial news and leveraging online communities, you can ensure your retirement planning remains current and effective.

Curating a Personalized Financial News Feed

The digital age brings abundant information, but not all is beneficial or relevant to your needs. Creating a personalized financial news feed allows you to filter out the noise and focus on what truly matters for your retirement planning. Here's how to do it:

- Start by identifying your main interests and concerns. Are you keen on learning more about investment strategies, tax planning, or the latest in retirement living options? Pinpointing your focus areas will guide your selection of news sources.
- Use news aggregator apps such as Feedly or Flipboard. These apps let you subscribe to various publications and organize articles into categories or 'feeds' based on your interests.
- Remember to include local news sources. They often provide vital information on state-specific tax laws or retirement benefits that national news might overlook.
- Finally, adjust your subscriptions as your interests or financial goals evolve. Your news feed should grow and change with you.

Reliable Financial News Sources

Discerning which sources to trust is crucial with the vast selection of financial news available. Here are some recommendations for reliable financial news outlets known for their accurate reporting and insightful analysis:

- The Wall Street Journal and The Financial Times are renowned for their comprehensive coverage of financial markets, economic policy, and personal finance.
- Bloomberg offers up-to-the-minute market data, news, and analysis, making it invaluable for those keeping a close eye on their investments.
- Forbes and Kiplinger provide accessible articles on retirement planning, investment strategies, and financial advice tailored to a non-professional audience.
- Always cross-reference news from multiple sources to get a well-rounded view and verify the accuracy of the information.

When evaluating financial information, consider the source's reputation, the author's credentials, and whether the content is fact-based or opinion-driven. This critical approach ensures you base your financial decisions on reliable information.

Online Communities for Retirees

The wisdom of a community can be a powerful tool in navigating the complexities of retirement planning. Online forums and communities offer a platform for retirees to share experiences, advice, and support. Websites like Reddit have subreddits dedicated to retirement and personal finance, where members actively discuss and share insights. Similarly, the Bogleheads forum, inspired by the investment philosophy of John Bogle, founder of Vanguard, provides a wealth of knowledge on low-cost investing, a crucial aspect of retirement planning. Engaging in these communities allows you to learn from the experiences of others, ask questions, and even offer guidance based on your journey.

Continuing Financial Education

The pursuit of knowledge should never cease, especially in retirement. Thankfully, the digital era makes continuing your financial education more accessible than ever. Here are some ways to keep learning:

- Webinars and Virtual Conferences: Many financial institutions and educational platforms host webinars covering investment strategies and estate planning topics. These sessions often allow for live Q&A, giving you the chance to have your questions answered by experts.
- Podcasts: Financial podcasts can be a great way to absorb information while on the go. Look for podcasts that focus on retirement planning and personal finance. They can be a source of both education and inspiration.
- Online Courses: Platforms such as Coursera and edX offer courses taught by university professors on economics, personal finance, and more. Many of these courses are free or low-cost.

Consuming financial news, engaging with online communities, and seeking educational opportunities ensures you remain informed and proactive about retirement management. This approach helps protect your financial well-being and enriches your retirement life with continuous learning and growth.

With these strategies for staying informed, you're better equipped to navigate the ever-changing landscape of retirement planning. By curating a personalized news feed, relying on reputable sources, engaging in online communities, and pursuing ongoing education, you're taking active steps to ensure your retirement strategy remains robust and responsive to the world around you. As we move forward, let's carry this spirit of informed engagement into all aspects of our retirement journey, from managing our health to exploring new passions.

13

The Annual Retirement Plan Health Check

Imagine your retirement plan as a garden you've meticulously cared for over the years. Just as gardens require regular tending, fertilization, and sometimes a bit of pruning to flourish, so does your retirement plan to ensure it sustains and nourishes you through the years ahead. An annual review of your retirement plan is not unlike this careful gardening, where examination and adjustments ensure your financial well-being continues to bloom.

13.1 How to Conduct an Annual Retirement Plan Review

Setting a Review Schedule

Marking your calendar for a regular annual review of your retirement plan can be as habitual as changing batteries in smoke detectors or scheduling a yearly physical—necessary tasks that maintain the health and safety of your household and yourself. The end of the year, or the beginning, often serves as an ideal time for this review, providing a natural pause to reflect on the past year and plan for the next. However, aligning this review with significant personal milestones or tax deadlines can also offer practical benefits, ensuring your plan remains responsive to your current life stage and financial landscape.

Assessing Financial Performance

The first step in this annual review involves a close look at the performance of your investments versus your expectations and the market as a whole. It's like comparing this year's harvest to those of years past, understanding which crops (investments) thrived, which didn't, and why. This evaluation should cover:

- Returns on investments: How did your stocks, bonds, mutual funds, or other assets perform? Did they meet, exceed, or fall short of the market or the benchmarks you use for comparison?
- Fees and expenses: Have costs associated with managing your investments, such as account management fees or fund expense ratios, changed? High fees can eat into your returns over time.
- Asset allocation: Does the distribution of your investments across different asset classes still align with your risk tolerance and retirement timeline? Market movements can skew your original allocations, necessitating adjustments.

Tools like financial dashboards or consultations with a financial advisor can provide clarity and insight during this assessment, illuminating your portfolio's successes and areas for improvement.

Adjusting for Life Changes

Life is a river, constantly flowing and occasionally changing course. Significant life events—such as health changes, family dynamics shifting, or even relocating—necessitate a review and possible adjustment of your retirement plan. This part of the review ensures your plan remains tailored to your current circumstances. For example, a new health diagnosis may lead to increased medical expenses, requiring a reallocation of funds to cover these costs. Alternatively, a change in marital status might prompt a revision of your beneficiary designations or a re-evaluation of your long-term financial needs and goals.

Seeking Professional Advice

Sometimes, the best course of action involves seeking guidance from those who navigate these waters daily. A financial advisor can offer an objective perspective on your retirement plan, helping you make informed adjustments based on your financial performance review and any life changes. They can also provide insights into strategies you might not have considered, such as tax optimization techniques or new investment opportunities. It's like having a seasoned gardener advise you on how to rejuvenate your garden, offering tips on what to prune, plant anew, and protect against pests (or financial pitfalls).

Visual Element: Your Retirement Plan Review Checklist

An infographic checklist can visually guide you through the essential steps of conducting your annual retirement plan review. This checklist could include:

- Confirm the review date on your calendar.
- Gather necessary financial documents and statements.
- Assess the performance of your investments.
- Evaluate your current asset allocation.
- Reflect on any significant life changes in the past year.
- Decide if a consultation with a financial advisor is needed.
- Plan adjustments to your retirement strategy.

Interactive Element: Reflection on Changes

An interactive online questionnaire prompts you to reflect on any significant changes over the past year that could impact your retirement plan. Questions might cover health, family, housing, and hobbies, providing a structured way to consider how these changes intersect with your financial planning.

Textual Element: Real-Life Adjustments and Adaptations

A section is dedicated to sharing anonymized case studies of how individuals have successfully adjusted their retirement plans in response to life changes and financial performance. This segment can offer practical examples and inspiration for readers facing similar situations, showing how flexibility and proactive planning can keep retirement goals on track despite life's unpredictability.

By embracing the annual review of your retirement plan as a vital practice, you ensure that your financial well-being remains aligned with your evolving life circumstances and goals. This diligent attention to your financial garden helps secure the nourishment and growth of your retirement savings, allowing you to enjoy the fruits of your labor in the coming years.

13.2 When Life Changes: Adapting Your Retirement Plan

Life's only constant is change, and this truth doesn't pause during our retirement years. Significant transformations in our health status, family structure, living situations, or financial state can unexpectedly alter the landscape of our meticulously planned retirement. Recognizing and adapting to these shifts is not just prudent; it's necessary for maintaining the security and happiness we aspire to in our later years.

Navigating Health Changes

Health changes rank among the most impactful events in retirement, affecting not just quality of life but also financial stability. Adapting your retirement plan to accommodate these changes involves several key strategies:

- Re-evaluating healthcare coverage: As health needs evolve, so do your healthcare coverage requirements. Consider supplemental health insurance plans or long-term care insurance to mitigate new or increased health-related expenses.
- Adjusting your budget: Increased medical costs may require adjusting your monthly budget. This could mean allocating more funds to healthcare and reducing non-essential spending.
- Exploring healthcare savings accounts: For those eligible, health savings accounts (HSAs) offer a tax-advantaged way to save for future medical expenses. Contributions are tax-deductible, and funds can be withdrawn tax-free for qualifying medical expenses, making HSAs a valuable tool in managing health-related financial changes.

Dealing with Family Dynamics

Family transitions, be they joyous or challenging, necessitate thoughtful adjustments to your retirement plan:

- Marriage or divorce: These significant relationship changes can lead to adjustments in your financial planning, beneficiary designations, and estate planning documents.
- Supporting family members: The need to financially support aging parents or adult children can emerge unexpectedly, requiring a careful reassessment of your budget and savings strategy. Creating a separate fund can help manage these additional expenses without compromising your retirement savings.
- Inheritance considerations: Receiving or leaving an inheritance can significantly impact your financial landscape. Receiving an inheritance might offer new opportunities for investment or charitable giving. In planning to leave an inheritance, one might pursue detailed estate planning and discussions with financial advisors and family members.

Relocation Considerations

Relocating in retirement, whether for lifestyle preferences or cost of living adjustments, carries with it a host of considerations:

- Cost of living changes: Moving to a new area can either alleviate or increase financial strain depending on the cost of living differences. Researching and planning for these changes is crucial in ensuring your retirement savings can support your desired lifestyle in a new location.

- Tax implications: Different locales come with varying tax burdens. Some states offer tax benefits for retirees, such as no state income tax or exemptions on retirement income, which can influence your relocation decision.
- Social network impact: Moving can also affect your social connections and support network. Building new relationships and finding community in a new place are essential for maintaining emotional well-being in retirement.

Unexpected Financial Setbacks

Even the best-laid plans can be upended by unforeseen financial challenges. Here's how to handle unexpected setbacks without derailing your retirement:

- Emergency fund: Maintaining an emergency fund is a critical buffer against sudden financial needs. Ideally, this fund should cover several months of living expenses and be easily accessible.
- Revisiting investment strategies: A significant market downturn can impact your retirement savings. Consulting with a financial advisor to reassess your investment approach may help mitigate losses and reallocate assets more conservatively if nearing or in retirement.
- Reducing discretionary spending: Temporarily adjusting your lifestyle and spending habits can help you manage financial setbacks. Prioritizing essential expenses and finding cost-saving measures can make a significant difference.
- Income supplementation: In some cases, supplementing your income through part-time work, freelancing, or tapping into a hobby that can generate income may be

necessary. This provides a financial cushion and adds structure and social engagement to your days.

Life changes, both expected and unexpected, are a natural part of the retirement landscape. By staying attuned to these shifts and ready to adjust your plans, you can ensure that your retirement remains as fulfilling and secure as you envisioned, regardless of twists and turns.

13.3 Staying Flexible: The Key to a Successful Retirement

Flexibility in retirement planning is akin to navigating a ship through unpredictable seas. Conditions can change swiftly, and the ability to adjust your course is vital to reaching your destination safely. This section explores the essence of staying adaptable in life's inevitable shifts, ensuring your retirement remains rewarding and secure.

Embracing Change

Life's constant evolution demands we remain open to change, not just as an inevitability but as an opportunity for growth and enrichment. This mindset is particularly crucial in retirement, a period marked by significant transitions. Embracing change means viewing each new phase not with apprehension but as a chance to enhance your life's tapestry. It's about recognizing that the most well-thought-out plans may need revision as circumstances evolve. Therefore, remaining flexible allows you to easily navigate life's surprises, ensuring your retirement plan continues to serve your needs and aspirations.

Incorporating Flexibility in Financial Planning

A solid financial plan is the backbone of a secure retirement. However, true strength lies not in rigidity but in the capacity to adapt. Here are strategies to weave flexibility into your financial planning:

- Diversified Portfolio: An investment portfolio that spans various asset classes can better absorb market fluctuations, providing a steady course through economic storms. Consider a mix of stocks, bonds, real estate, and commodities to protect your financial well-being against different types of risk.
- Emergency Fund: Life has a way of presenting unexpected expenses, from home repairs to healthcare costs. An emergency fund is a financial cushion, ensuring you can cover these surprises without disrupting your retirement savings. Aim to have funds to cover several months of living expenses, and review this amount periodically to ensure it matches your current lifestyle needs.
- Adjustable Budget: An adaptable budget is vital. Regular reviews allow you to shift funds between categories as your priorities change, ensuring you allocate resources to what matters most at any given time. This might mean reallocating entertainment funds to healthcare costs or vice versa, depending on your current phase of life.

Psychological Adaptability

Adapting to change isn't just a financial strategy; it's a state of mind. How you perceive and react to change can significantly impact your happiness and well-being in retirement. Cultivating a positive outlook on life's transitions can transform challenges into adventures and uncertainty into opportunity. Here are ways to foster psychological adaptability:

- Stay Curious: Approach new experiences with curiosity rather than apprehension. This can lead to discovering new passions and joys in retirement.
- Build Resilience: Reflect on past challenges you've overcome. This reflection can strengthen your resilience, reminding you that you have the skills and resources to handle future changes.
- Seek Support: A strong social network can provide emotional support and advice when navigating life's changes. Don't hesitate to lean on friends, family, or professionals for guidance.

Learning from Experience

Every change, challenge, or success in your life offers valuable lessons. Reflecting on these experiences provides insights that can guide future decisions, making you more adept at navigating the twists and turns of retirement. Consider keeping a journal to document or share these reflections with loved ones. This practice not only aids in personal growth but can also offer guidance and encouragement to others on their retirement journey.

In closing, the path to a fulfilling and secure retirement is marked by adaptability. By embracing change, incorporating flexibility into your financial planning, maintaining a positive outlook, and learning from experience, you can confidently navigate whatever the future holds. This approach ensures your retirement is not just a final chapter but a continuing story of growth, discovery, and joy. As we move forward, let's carry these principles, ready to adapt, grow, and thrive no matter what lies ahead.

The Early Exit: Assessing Your Readiness for Early Retirement

In a world where the concept of retirement is often painted with broad strokes of leisurely days sans work-related stress, the allure of early retirement can be particularly strong. The dream of reclaiming one's time while still in the prime of life is a potent one. Yet, the shift from a structured work life to the freedom of early retirement is akin to stepping off a well-trodden path into uncharted territory. This chapter focuses on the multi-faceted assessment necessary to determine if early retirement is not just a desirable option but a viable one.

Financial Readiness

Determining financial readiness for early retirement is akin to planning an extended trip. Just as you would estimate costs, save money, and possibly consider income sources while traveling, early retirement planning follows a similar blueprint. Here's a breakdown of what to consider:

- Savings: Evaluate your current savings. Do they align with the 4% rule, which suggests you can comfortably withdraw 4% of your savings annually without depleting your nest egg prematurely? Though a helpful starting point, this rule may need adjustments based on your expected lifestyle and inflation.
- Investment Income: Assess your investments' ability to generate income. Stocks, bonds, and real estate can provide streams of income that supplement your savings. Consider whether these sources are reliable and can adjust for inflation over time.
- Healthcare Costs: With early retirement, employer-sponsored healthcare is often no longer an option. Calculating potential healthcare costs before Medicare eligibility at 65 is crucial. Marketplace insurance or health savings accounts (HSAs) can bridge the gap. Still, they come with their own costs and considerations.

Emotional Readiness

The emotional landscape of early retirement is vast and varied. It's not just about leaving a job; it's about entering a new phase of life. Here's what to reflect on:

- Leaving Your Career: Consider how your career influences your identity and social interactions. Stepping away from work means finding new ways to fulfill these aspects of your life.
- Finding Purpose and Fulfillment: Consider how you'll spend your days. Volunteering, hobbies, or part-time work provide structure and a sense of purpose. Reflect on what brings you joy and how you can integrate these activities into your daily life.

Lifestyle Considerations

Lifestyle changes that accompany early retirement are significant. They touch upon how you live, who you spend time with, and how you manage your day-to-day life. Key considerations include:

- Daily Structure: Without the work routine, your days might feel unmoored. Planning how you'll structure your time can help transition into early retirement smoothly. Will you adopt new hobbies? How will you ensure social interactions remain a part of your life?
- Living Arrangements: Early retirement might offer the chance to relocate. Whether downsizing or moving to a dream location, consider how your living situation fits into your retirement plan. Consider the cost of living, proximity to healthcare facilities, and opportunities for social engagement in your chosen location.

Risk Assessment

With early retirement comes a unique set of risks, primarily financial but also emotional and social. Here's how to evaluate and mitigate these risks:

- Longevity Risk: The possibility of outliving your savings is a real concern. Strategies like annuities or a more conservative withdrawal rate can help manage this risk.
- Market Volatility: Early retirement means your savings must last longer, making them more susceptible to market downturns. A well-diversified investment portfolio and a flexible withdrawal strategy can help navigate this volatility.

- Social and Emotional Risks: Losing social connections and a sense of purpose can impact well-being. Actively maintaining friendships and pursuing interests that provide fulfillment are vital.

Visual Element: Early Retirement Readiness Checklist

A checklist that helps you assess your readiness for early retirement, covering financial, emotional, and lifestyle considerations. This tool can be a practical guide in evaluating your current situation against the requirements of early retirement.

Interactive Element: Are You Ready for Early Retirement? Quiz

This online quiz asks you a series of questions about your financial situation, emotional state, and lifestyle preferences to help gauge your readiness for early retirement. The results can offer insights into areas where you may need to focus more on planning and preparation.

Textual Element: Case Studies on Early Retirement

Real-life examples of individuals who successfully transitioned into early retirement: These stories can highlight strategies to overcome challenges and provide a more nuanced understanding of early retirement.

Assessing your readiness for early retirement requires a comprehensive look at your financial health, emotional state, and lifestyle expectations. It's about making sure your savings can support you, you're prepared for the emotional shifts, and you have a clear vision of how you want to spend your early retirement years. Through careful planning and honest reflection, early retirement can be not just a dream but a rewarding and fulfilling chapter of your life.

14.1 Understanding the FIRE Movement

The Financial Independence Retire Early (FIRE) movement is more than just a trend; it's a shift in how we view work, life, and the concept of retirement itself. At its core, FIRE is about accumulating enough financial resources to allow you to retire much earlier than traditional retirement age. This doesn't necessarily mean leaving work altogether but having the financial security to choose work on your terms.

Variations of FIRE, such as "lean FIRE," where individuals live frugally to retire sooner, and "fat FIRE," which involves saving more for a more comfortable retirement lifestyle, reflect the diversity within the movement. Each path to FIRE is unique and tailored to individual ambitions, lifestyles, and definitions of financial independence.

Maximizing Savings Rates

Central to achieving FIRE is the ability to maximize your savings rate – the percentage of your income that you save and invest. Here are strategies to significantly increase this rate:

- Budget Optimization: Scrutinize your current spending to identify areas where you can cut back without sacrificing quality of life. This might involve swapping costly subscriptions for free alternatives or choosing more budget-friendly travel options.

- Increasing Income: Look for opportunities to boost your income, whether pursuing promotions, taking on freelance work, or starting a side business. Every additional dollar earned is another step closer to FIRE.
- Reducing Expenses: Examine your most significant expenses, such as housing, transportation, and food. Minor adjustments, like cooking at home more often or choosing a less expensive car, can significantly impact your savings rate over time.

Investment Strategies for FIRE

Investing wisely is just as critical as saving when it comes to achieving FIRE. It's about making your money work for you, generating passive income that grows over time. Here are key strategies:

- Low-Cost Index Funds: These funds mimic the performance of market indexes like the S&P 500 and come with lower fees than actively managed funds. They're a favorite in the FIRE community for their simplicity and effectiveness over the long term.
- Real Estate: For those inclined towards tangible assets, real estate investments can provide both rental income and appreciation. This requires more hands-on management but can be a lucrative component of a FIRE strategy.
- Diversification: Spreading investments across different asset classes reduces risk and provides more stable returns. This might mean holding a mix of stocks, bonds, real estate, and even alternative investments like peer-to-peer lending.

Life After FIRE

Achieving financial independence opens up a new world of possibilities. However, managing your investments and ensuring financial security in early retirement requires careful planning:

- Withdrawal Strategy: Establish a sustainable withdrawal rate that allows your portfolio to last. Given the longer retirement horizon, this rate may need to be lower than the traditional 4% rule.
- Healthcare Planning: With early retirement comes the responsibility of securing healthcare coverage independently. Research your options well in advance, considering health-sharing plans, part-time work that offers benefits, or the healthcare marketplace.
- Ongoing Investment Management: Your investment strategy may shift in early retirement. Moving towards more conservative investments or rebalancing your portfolio to match your changing risk tolerance will help protect your nest egg.
- Finding Fulfillment: Retirement isn't just about financial independence; it's also about personal fulfillment. Many find joy in pursuing passions, volunteering, or even starting a new career or business venture. The key is to find activities that bring purpose and joy to your days.

Achieving FIRE isn't simply about reaching a financial milestone but redefining what retirement means to you. It's a personal journey that requires dedication, planning, and a bit of creativity. Whether you're aiming for lean FIRE, fat FIRE, or somewhere in between, the principles of maximizing savings, investing wisely, and planning for life after reaching your goal will guide you toward a future where work is optional and financial freedom is a reality.

14.2 Healthcare and Insurance Before Medicare

Navigating the waters of healthcare before reaching Medicare eligibility presents a unique set of challenges for those considering early retirement. The safety net that comes with employment - employer-sponsored healthcare - disappears, leaving a gap that must be thoughtfully bridged to ensure uninterrupted and affordable healthcare coverage.

Healthcare Options

Several avenues exist for securing healthcare coverage prior to Medicare eligibility:

- Marketplace Insurance: The Affordable Care Act (ACA) marketplace offers a range of healthcare plans. These plans are categorized from bronze to platinum, reflecting their coverage levels and premium costs. Subsidies based on income can make these plans more affordable for early retirees.
- COBRA: The Consolidated Omnibus Budget Reconciliation Act allows you to extend your employer-provided health insurance for up to 18 months after leaving your job. While COBRA ensures continuity of coverage, it can be expensive since you'll be paying the full premium amount, including the portion previously covered by your employer.
- Health Sharing Plans: These are not insurance but rather cooperative healthcare plans where members share medical expenses. They often come with lower monthly costs but

may have limitations on coverage, such as pre-existing conditions or specific types of healthcare services.

Cost Considerations

Understanding and planning for healthcare costs before Medicare kicks in is crucial. Here's how to manage these expenses effectively:

- Premiums: These are your monthly payments for healthcare coverage. Premiums vary widely based on the type of plan, coverage level, and geographic location. Shop and compare plans to find one that meets your needs and budget.
- Out-of-pocket expenses include deductibles, copayments, and coinsurance. High-deductible plans often have lower premiums but require more out-of-pocket expenses before insurance covers them. Balancing premiums with out-of-pocket costs is vital to finding a cost-effective strategy.
- Minimizing Costs: Strategies to reduce healthcare costs include choosing a plan that covers your regular medications and doctors, using in-network providers, and taking advantage of preventative care covered under the ACA.

Health Savings Accounts (HSAs)

HSAs offer a tax-advantaged way to save for healthcare expenses. Still, you must be enrolled in a high-deductible health plan to qualify. Benefits include:

- Pre-tax Contributions: You can contribute to an HSA with pre-tax dollars, reducing your taxable income.

- Tax-Free Withdrawals: Funds withdrawn for qualified medical expenses are not taxed.
- Investment Growth: HSA funds can be invested, and any growth is tax-free, provided it's used for qualified medical expenses.
- No Expiry: Unlike Flexible Spending Accounts (FSAs), HSA funds roll over year to year and can be used in retirement.

HSAs can be a powerful tool for managing healthcare costs before Medicare, offering tax savings and flexibility.

Planning for Long-Term Care

Long-term care, not typically covered by Medicare, requires separate planning:

- Long-term care Insurance covers services like nursing home care, assisted living, or in-home care. Policies vary in coverage and cost, so shopping around and finding a policy that fits your needs and budget is essential.
- Hybrid Insurance Policies: Some life insurance policies include long-term care benefits, providing flexibility in how you use the policy.
- Savings and Investments: Setting aside a portion of your savings or investments specifically for potential long-term care expenses can also be a strategy, though it requires careful planning to ensure sufficient funds.

In closing, stepping into early retirement without the safety net of employer-sponsored healthcare demands careful planning and consideration. From exploring your options for coverage to understanding the nuances of HSAs and planning for long-term care, being well-informed will help you navigate this transition smoothly and ensure you're covered until Medicare begins. As we continue, we'll shift our focus to maintaining a healthy lifestyle, emphasizing the importance of physical well-being in enhancing the quality of retirement life.

15

Legacy Beyond Wealth: Making a Difference in Retirement

Retirement, often viewed through the lens of financial security and leisure, holds a more profound potential for impact—both in our lives and the wider community. This chapter shifts focus from the nuts and bolts of financial planning to the broader canvas of legacy. Here, legacy isn't just about assets; it's about influence, contribution, and the mark we leave on the world through philanthropy and charitable giving.

15.1 Philanthropy and Charitable Giving in Retirement

Identifying Causes and Organizations

At the heart of meaningful philanthropy lies a connection to the causes we care about. It's one thing to write a check; it's another to invest in a mission that resonates with our deepest values. Start by reflecting on the issues that stir you—whether it's education, environment, health, or social justice. Websites like GuideStar or Charity Navigator can help you vet organizations for their impact and financial health, ensuring your contributions go where they can do the most good.

Strategies for Charitable Giving

Philanthropy in retirement can take many forms, each with its own set of considerations:

- Direct Donations: The most straightforward way to support a cause. Scheduled giving, such as monthly donations, can consistently support your chosen organization.
- Donor-Advised Funds (DAFs): DAFs serve as philanthropic accounts, allowing you to make a charitable contribution, receive an immediate tax deduction, and then recommend grants from the fund over time. This can be an effective way to manage your charitable giving.
- Charitable Trusts: Setting up a charitable trust can offer tax benefits while supporting your philanthropic goals. A Charitable Remainder Trust (CRT), for example, can provide you with income during your lifetime, with the remainder going to your chosen charity upon your passing.
- Volunteering: Giving time can be as valuable as financial contributions. Many organizations rely on volunteers for day-to-day operations, offering a hands-on way to support a cause.

Tax Implications and Benefits

Charitable giving can offer tax advantages, potentially lowering your taxable income. For direct donations, keep detailed records of contributions for tax purposes. If you're considering a DAF or charitable trust, consult a financial advisor to understand the tax benefits and requirements. Remember, the goal is to make an impact while managing your financial health in retirement.

Volunteering and Non-Monetary Contributions

Beyond financial support, volunteering provides a direct way to contribute to the causes you care about. It also offers personal benefits, such as staying active, meeting new people, and learning new skills. Consider your skills and interests when seeking volunteer opportunities, and seek roles that offer personal fulfillment and community benefit.

Visual Element: Chart of Charitable Giving Strategies

An infographic outlines the different strategies for charitable giving in retirement, including direct donations, DAFs, charitable trusts, and volunteering. The chart highlights the benefits and considerations of each option, providing a visual guide to impactful giving.

Interactive Element: Philanthropy Values Exercise

A guided exercise to help you identify your philanthropic values and interests. This might include journaling prompts to explore what issues matter most to you and why, or a quiz that matches your interests with potential causes and organizations.

Textual Element: Real-Life Philanthropy Stories

This is a collection of stories from retirees who have found fulfillment and purpose through philanthropy and charitable giving. These narratives showcase the diverse ways individuals can make a difference, from local community projects to global initiatives, offering inspiration and practical ideas for your philanthropic journey.

Philanthropy and charitable giving in retirement open new avenues for leaving a lasting legacy. By aligning your charitable efforts with your values and utilizing strategic giving methods, you can ensure that your contributions have a lasting impact. Whether through financial donations, volunteering, or a combination of both, your retirement years offer a unique opportunity to give back and enrich both your life and the lives of others.

15.2 Teaching Financial Literacy to Future Generations

Financial literacy is a critical skill often overlooked in traditional education systems. As retirees, we hold a treasure trove of lived financial experiences that, when passed down, can empower our children and grandchildren to navigate their economic futures with confidence. This section explores how embedding financial education into our legacy can set the stage for future financially savvy generations.

The Importance of Financial Education

Financial literacy goes beyond understanding numbers on a spreadsheet; it's about making informed decisions that lead to a secure and fulfilling life. Teaching children and grandchildren the value of savings, the impact of investing, and the nuances of budgeting equips them with tools to achieve their dreams, be it higher education, homeownership, or entrepreneurial ventures. Moreover, it instills confidence to face financial challenges and opportunities head-on, ensuring they're prepared for economic ups and downs.

Effective Teaching Methods

Every age group absorbs information differently, demanding tailored approaches to financial education:

- For young children, storytelling can be a powerful tool. Use narratives around saving for a toy or planning a lemonade stand to introduce concepts of savings and cost.
- Teenagers often respond well to hands-on experiences. Consider setting up a mock stock portfolio or involving them in family budgeting exercises to teach investment and money management.
- Adult children might benefit from deeper discussions on retirement planning, estate planning, and the importance of insurance. Sharing your experiences, both successes and missteps can provide valuable real-life context.

Incorporating technology can also enhance learning, with apps and online games designed to teach financial concepts in an engaging way. Encourage them to set financial goals and track progress, fostering a sense of ownership and responsibility towards their financial future.

Incorporating Financial Education into Estate Planning

Estate planning isn't just about distributing assets; it's an opportunity to pass on values and knowledge. Consider these strategies:

- Educational Trusts: Setting up a trust with stipulations for financial education can ensure heirs inherit assets and have the wisdom to manage them. For instance, funds could be released as beneficiaries reach certain educational milestones, such as completing a personal finance course.

- Resource Provision: Include financial education resources in your will or as part of trust distributions. This could be a collection of books, subscriptions to financial magazines, or memberships to financial advisory services.
- Family Meetings: Use estate planning discussions to engage family members in conversations about financial values, the importance of philanthropy, and the responsibilities that come with wealth. These meetings can serve as informal financial education sessions, fostering a culture of transparency and learning.

Leading by Example

Perhaps the most potent method of teaching financial literacy is to lead by example. Demonstrating sound financial management, the importance of regular savings, strategic investing, and philanthropy can leave a lasting impression. Let them see you budgeting, hear you discussing financial decisions openly, and watch you navigating financial challenges with grace. Actions often speak louder than words; your financial behavior is a continuous lesson in prudence and planning.

By embedding financial education into our legacy, we do more than pass on wealth; we empower future generations with the knowledge and skills to grow that wealth responsibly. This ensures the longevity of our financial legacies and contributes to our families' financial well-being for generations to come.

15.3 Documenting Your Life and Values for Posterity

In the tapestry of life, each thread represents a story, lesson, or value that we've gathered along the way. As we consider the legacy we wish to leave behind, it becomes clear that our financial assets are only a part of the picture. Equally important, if not more so, are the stories, beliefs, and values that have shaped our journey. This section explores ways to ensure these intangible yet invaluable assets are passed on to future generations, enriching their lives and those beyond.

Creating a Personal Legacy Document

Imagine compiling a document that captures not just the milestones of your life but also the wisdom you've acquired, the values you hold dear, and the hopes you harbor for your loved ones. This is the essence of a personal legacy document. It's a way to share what you did, who you were, and what you believed in.

To create this document:

- Start with an outline that includes significant life events, lessons learned, values, and advice you wish to pass on.
- Include stories or anecdotes that illustrate these values in action. Perhaps a challenge you overcame that taught you resilience or a moment of failure that led to unexpected growth.
- Reflect on the advice you would have found useful at various stages of your life and share this with your future generations.

This document can evolve over time, growing richer as you continue to experience and reflect upon life.

Ethical Wills

Unlike a legal document, an ethical will is a heartfelt expression of what truly matters to you. It's an ancient practice, modernized to help you articulate your values, blessings, life's lessons, and hopes for the future.

To craft your ethical will:

- Consider the core values that have guided your life. What principles do you want to ensure live on after you're gone?
- Think about the hopes you have for your family's future. What wisdom can you share to help guide them on their path?
- Use simple, honest language. This is your voice speaking across generations, so let your true self shine through.

Ethical wills can be shared with your family while you're still alive, offering a profound opportunity for connection and understanding.

Oral Histories and Memoirs

Your life story is a unique narrative that holds lessons, joys, sorrows, and wisdom earned along the way. Capturing this story through oral histories or memoirs can be a precious gift to your family and future generations.

Consider these approaches:

- Audio recordings: Conversations about your life, captured digitally, offer a personal and intimate way for your descendants to know you. You might recount specific events, share stories of your ancestors, or discuss the values that have been important to you.

- Written memoirs: Writing your life story can be therapeutic, allowing you to reflect on your journey. Start with significant life events and expand by including the lessons learned and the values these experiences reinforced.

These narratives provide a personal connection that transcends time, allowing your essence and wisdom to be felt by generations to come.

Managing Your Digital Legacy

In today's digital age, our online presence is an extension of our lives, holding memories, conversations, and expressions of our interests and values. Managing this digital legacy is becoming increasingly important.

To ensure your digital legacy is handled according to your wishes:

- Make a list of your digital assets, including social media profiles, blogs, and digital photo libraries.
- Decide what should happen to these accounts and assets. Would you like them to be memorialized, passed on, or deleted?
- Use available tools provided by platforms (like Facebook's Legacy Contact) to ensure your wishes are carried out.
- Include instructions for your digital assets in your estate plan, providing access to accounts where necessary.

Your digital footprint is a part of your story. Managing it thoughtfully ensures that your online presence continues to reflect your wishes and values.

As we wrap up this chapter, it's clear that the legacy we leave encompasses far more than financial assets. The stories, values, and wisdom we impart can guide and inspire future generations, offering them a sense of connection and continuity. By documenting our life experiences, articulating our values through ethical wills, preserving our stories through oral histories and memoirs, and thoughtfully managing our digital legacy, we ensure that the essence of who we are lives on. As we move forward, let us embrace the opportunity to reflect on our lives, share our wisdom, and curate the legacy we leave behind, weaving a rich tapestry for those who follow in our footsteps.

Conclusion

As we draw the curtains on this comprehensive journey that unfolded from the pages of laying your financial foundation to the intricate dance of adapting and thriving in your golden years, I find myself reflecting with immense gratitude and a sense of shared anticipation. You've navigated through the pivotal areas of retirement planning, from the initial steps in understanding and leveraging financial instruments to mastering the nuances of healthcare, Social Security, and the digital realm, all the way to the profound realms of estate and legacy planning.

The key takeaways from our exploration are manifold. Early and informed planning stands as the bedrock of a secure future. The magic of compounding interest, the shield of healthcare readiness, the strategic maneuvers around Social Security, and the thoughtful curation of your legacy—each plays a critical role in sculpting a retirement that's not just financially sound but also rich in purpose and fulfillment. Moreover, the embrace of technology has emerged as an indispensable ally in this endeavor.

However, if there's one principle that threads through the fabric of successful retirement planning, it is adaptability. The landscape of life is ever-shifting, and with it, our plans must evolve. A static strategy is a vulnerable one. Thus, the importance of regular reviews, recalibrations, and the readiness to pivot when the winds of change blow cannot be overstated.

Now, I extend a call to action, not as a command but as an invitation. This is an invitation to step into the arena of proactive planning, regardless of where you stand today in life's timeline. The strategies and insights shared within these pages are your tools—wield them with confidence, seek counsel from seasoned professionals when you encounter crossroads, and remain an active participant in crafting your retirement narrative.

The journey of learning is perpetual. I encourage you to keep your curiosity kindled, your knowledge base expanding, and your eyes open to the evolving economic landscapes and opportunities they herald. This is not merely about financial security; it's about empowering you to navigate the complexities of retirement planning with agility and optimism.

I recognize that the path is strewn with challenges, but within you lies the capacity to surmount them. This book aims to be a compass, guiding you through the mazes and over the mountains, equipping you with the clarity and confidence to forge ahead.

Your stories, experiences, and insights are invaluable. I invite you to share them and contribute to a tapestry of collective wisdom and learning. We can continue this conversation through a dedicated platform—a website or social media—building a community of empowered individuals journeying toward a fulfilling retirement.

And while this book might seem like a destination, it's merely a checkpoint. The landscape of retirement planning is vast and ever-evolving. Stay tuned for further resources, updates, and guides that will continue to build upon the foundation we've laid together.

In closing, I express my deepest gratitude for your trust and companionship through this exploration. Your engagement and thirst for knowledge have enriched this journey and reinforced my commitment to assisting you in achieving the retirement you envision and deserve.

Let's look forward to the unwritten chapters, the plans yet crafted, and the dreams yet realized. Thank you for allowing me the privilege of being a part of your journey to a secure and enriched retirement.

Make a Difference!

In the end, thorough retirement boils down to this: Making sure you have everything aligned so that you can enjoy your time away from the working world with full peace of mind, able to fully enjoy all the good things it offers. We all deserve this, and this is your chance to help more people to find it.

Simply by sharing your honest opinion of this book and a little about your own experience, you'll help new readers find this essential information and make sure their retirement years are everything they dreamed they would be.

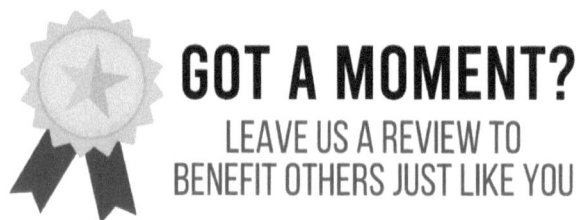

Thank you so much for your support. You're making an incredible difference.

>>> Click here to leave your review on Amazon.

References

Visualize Retirement: Retirement Planning Checklist https://www.troweprice.com/financial-intermediary/us/en/insights/articles/2021/q4/visualize-retirement-retirement-planning-checklist.html

Health Care Planning for Retirement https://www.wespath.org/health-well-being/health-well-being-resources/physical-well-being/healthcareplanningforretirement

What is financial flexibility and why is it so important? https://www.cnbc.com/select/what-is-financial-flexibility/

IRA vs. 401(k): How to Choose - NerdWallet https://www.nerdwallet.com/article/investing/ira-vs-401k-retirement-accounts#:

Roth IRA Contribution and Income Limits 2023-2024 https://www.nerdwallet.com/article/investing/roth-ira-contribution-limits#:

How to manage your retirement asset allocation https://www.fidelity.com/learning-center/personal-finance/retirement-asset-allocation

Taxation of Retirement Income | FINRA.org https://www.finra.org/investors/learn-to-invest/types-investments/retirement/managing-retirement-income/taxation-retirement-income#:

Why You Need To Do A Personal Financial Audit [+ How ... https://www.theconfusedmillennial.com/personal-financial-audit/

What's Your Net Worth Telling You? https://www.investopedia.com/articles/pf/08/ideal-net-worth.asp

6 Reasons You Need an Emergency Fund in Retirement https://getcarefull.com/articles/6-reasons-you-need-an-emergency-fund-in-retirement#:

Retirement Planning: A 5-Step Guide for 2024 https://www.nerdwallet.com/article/investing/retirement-planning-an-introduction

6 Reasons Why You Should Start Retirement Planning Early https://districtcapitalmanagement.com/start-retirement-planning-early/

Catch-Up Contribution: What It Is, How It Works, Rules, and ... https://www.investopedia.com/terms/c/catchupcontribution.asp

undefined undefined

How Much Will My Roth IRA Be Worth? Power of ... https://www.investopedia.com/one-day-your-roth-ira-will-fund-itself-4770849

Investment Diversification: What It Is and How To Do It https://www.nerdwallet.com/article/investing/diversification

How to Determine Your Risk Tolerance Level https://www.schwab.com/learn/story/how-to-determine-your-risk-tolerance-level

ETFs vs. Index Mutual Funds: What's the Difference? https://www.investopedia.com/articles/mutualfund/05/etfindexfund.asp

How to Rebalance Your Portfolio - Investopedia https://www.investopedia.com/how-to-rebalance-your-portfolio-7973806

Roth IRA vs. 401(k): What's the Difference? - Investopedia https://www.investopedia.com/ask/answers/100314/whats-difference-between-401k-and-roth-ira.asp

3 Strategies for Reducing Roth IRA Conversion Taxes https://www.schwab.com/learn/story/3-strategies-reducing-roth-ira-conversion-taxes

How Retirement Account Withdrawals Affect Your Tax ... https://www.investopedia.com/ask/answers/030316/do-retirement-account-withdrawals-affect-tax-brackets.asp

Tax Loss Harvesting: A Portfolio and Wealth Planning Perspective https://corporate.vanguard.com/content/dam/corp/research/pdf/Tax-Loss-Harvesting-A-Portfolio-and-Wealth-Planning-Perspective-US-ISGTLH_102020_online.pdf

How to Plan for Medical Expenses in Retirement https://www.investopedia.com/retirement/how-plan-medical-expenses-retirement/

How to Sign Up: A Guide to Medicare Enrollment https://www.aarp.org/health/medicare-insurance/info-2020/enrolling-in-medicare.html

Medicare Advantage vs. Medicare Supplement (Medigap) https://www.forbes.com/health/medicare/medicare-advantage-vs-medicare-supplement/

undefined undefined

How Social Security Benefits Are Calculated - Bankrate https://www.bankrate.com/retirement/how-social-security-benefits-are-calculated/

Determining The Best Age to Collect Social Security (for You) https://www.ml.com/articles/social-security-aiming-for-smarter-payments.html

Social Security Claiming Strategies for Couples https://www.aarp.org/retirement/social-security/info-2022/claiming-strategies-for-couples.html

Social Security Changes - COLA Fact Sheet https://www.ssa.gov/news/press/factsheets/colafacts2023.pdf

Estate Planning Basics https://www.fidelity.com/life-events/estate-planning/basics

How to choose an executor for your estate - TIAA https://www.tiaa.org/public/learn/life-milestones/how-to-choose-an-executor-for-your-estate

durable power of attorney | Wex - Law.Cornell.Edu https://www.law.cornell.edu/wex/durable_power_of_attorney

3 health benefits of volunteering https://www.mayoclinichealthsystem.org/hometown-health/speaking-of-health/3-health-benefits-of-volunteering

Lifelong Learning Opportunities for Older Adults and Retirees https://www.rightathome.net/blog/lifelong-learning-opportunities-for-older-adults-and-retirees

How to Plan for Travel in Retirement https://www.investopedia.com/retirement/how-plan-travel-retirement/

Participating in Activities You Enjoy As You Age https://www.nia.nih.gov/health/healthy-aging/participating-activities-you-enjoy-you-age

Adjusting to Retirement: Handling Depression and Stress https://www.helpguide.org/articles/aging-issues/adjusting-to-retirement.htm

How Retirees Can Protect Their Savings From High ... https://www.troweprice.com/personal-investing/resources/insights/how-retirees-can-protect-their-savings-from-rising-inflation.html

How to Rebalance Your Portfolio - Investopedia https://www.investopedia.com/how-to-rebalance-your-portfolio-7973806

How To Invest In Volatile Markets With A Financial Advisor https://www.forbes.com/advisor/investing/financial-advisor/how-to-invest-in-volatile-markets-with-a-financial-advisor/

Great Retirement Planning Tools and Software for 2023 https://money.usnews.com/money/retirement/401ks/articles/best-retirement-planning-tools-and-software

9 Ways To Automate Your Savings https://www.forbes.com/advisor/banking/savings/how-to-automate-your-savings/

Kiplinger | Personal Finance News, Investing Advice ... https://www.kiplinger.com/

30 Best Online Learning Platforms for 2024 https://www.learnworlds.com/online-learning-platforms/

8 Steps for Your Annual 401(k) Checkup https://www.kiplinger.com/slideshow/retirement/t001-s003-8-steps-for-your-annual-401-k-checkup/index.html

Managing Your Retirement Savings Through Life's Transitions https://www.alanet.org/legal-management/2018/february/departments/managing-your-retirement-savings-through-lifes-transitions

5 Retirement Planning Steps to Take https://www.investopedia.com/articles/retirement/11/5-steps-to-retirement-plan.asp

Facilitators and barriers for successful retirement https://www.ncbi.nlm.nih.gov/pmc/articles/PMC10237219/

Financial Independence, Retire Early (FIRE) Explained https://www.investopedia.com/terms/f/financial-independence-retire-early-fire.asp

Bridging the health care coverage gap https://www.fidelity.com/viewpoints/retirement/transition-to-medicare

How to Know When You're Financially Ready for Retirement https://www.accuplan.net/blog/financially-ready-for-retirement/

Financial Independence, Retire Early (FIRE) Explained https://www.investopedia.com/terms/f/financial-independence-retire-early-fire.asp

Charitable giving in retirement - Guardian Life https://www.guardianlife.com/charitable-giving

9 Tips for Teaching Kids About Money https://www.schwab.com/learn/story/9-tips-teaching-kids-about-money

How to Write a Legacy Statement - The Most Important Gift ... https://your-philanthropy.com/write-legacy-statement/

Managing Your Digital Legacy in 6 Steps | HealthNews https://healthnews.com/family-health/end-of-life-care/managing-your-digital-legacy-in-six-steps/

McGough, Nellah Bailey. "75 Retirement Quotes That Will Resonate With Any Retiree." Southern Living. April 25, 2024. https://www.southernliving.com/culture/retirement-quotes

Walsh, Angela. *31 Inspiring Retirement Quotes to Get You Excited About A New Chapter.* Sifton Properties. Last modified May 23, 2023. https://sifton.com/retirement-living/resident-resources/inspiring-retirement-quotes/

www.ingramcontent.com/pod-product-compliance
Lightning Source LLC
Chambersburg PA
CBHW030450100526
44580CB00002B/68